**A Step-by-Step Master Class
for People Who Want to Deliver Indie Games**

Six sets of questions to review and refine your
vision, skills and plans

Hundreds of tips and "lessons learned" from a 3-time
Inc. 500™ CEO and award-winning game designer

Based on Don Daglow's top-rated sessions at major games
conferences around the world

The only person who can define the path to creating your indie game is you. *Indie Games: from Dream to Delivery* helps you do just that, by leading you through a guided conversation with yourself.

Section by section, you'll record your answers to carefully chosen questions. Then we'll use your unique personal responses to build the customized roadmap you need to turn your indie game into reality.

Techniques to use, traps to avoid, terminology to understand. And how to fit it all into your life without damaging your relationships or your future.

Never started a business? We've got it covered. Skip what you already know, dig deeper on things you want to learn.

It's the one book you need to take your indie game from Dream to Delivery.

Also by Don Daglow

From Dream to Delivery:
How to Do Work You Love, Love What You Do
and Launch Your Dream Project

A parallel volume to this book, written for people in any craft or industry who want to create a dream project. Based on Don Daglow's work as an advisor with startups and growing companies in Silicon Valley and San Francisco.

Indie Games: From Dream to Delivery

INDIE GAMES: FROM DREAM TO DELIVERY

HOW TO DO WORK YOU LOVE, LOVE WHAT YOU DO, AND LAUNCH YOUR INDIE GAME

DON L. DAGLOW

Creator of the Emmy® Award Winning
Neverwinter Nights™ **and 3-time Inc. 500™ CEO**

Introduction by Rami Ismail

Sausalito Media, LLC
Sausalito, CA

ISBN 978-0-9967815-5-8 (Paperback)
978-0-9967815-6-5 (eBook)

Published by Sausalito Media LLC, PO Box 1035, Sausalito, CA 94966. Sausalito Media is a trademark of Sausalito Media, LLC. All Rights Reserved.

Cover design by D.V. Suresh. Cover illustration by Danielle Powers (artbydpowers.com).

This book is dedicated to our sons Michael and Christopher and their families.

As excited as I am about the future of games and interactive entertainment, I am most of all excited about the future that our children and our grandchildren will help to create.

Contents

PART VII. **NEXT STEPS**

Getting Started

"CHASE YOUR DREAMS TILL THEY GET TIRED OF
RUNNING AWAY.
JUST TAKE CARE OF YOURSELF AND YOUR FAMILY
ALONG THE WAY, BECAUSE ONCE THE FIRST DREAM IS
CAPTURED THERE WILL BE MORE TO FOLLOW."

— Don Daglow

It's All About the Questions

I started designing and programming games at age 19, and have now been a game designer, engineer and producer for over 40 years. I still go to work every morning loving the career and the art form that I've chosen.

I find game development today to be even more fascinating and fulfilling than it was when we worked on the original PlayStation over 20 years ago, or when our Intellivision team challenged Atari in the first great "Console War" almost 40 years ago.

Creating games is my passion. If it's your passion as well, then you have advantages and opportunities that we can work together to unlock.

This process is based on a series of over 90 questions that I developed working with indie developers and game publishers over the last several years. I've presented excerpts from this book as conference sessions at GDC San Francisco, GDC China (Shanghai), Devcom/Gamescom (Cologne), Quo Vadis (Berlin), DIG (London, Ontario) and at other events around the world.

I continue to refine these ideas based on my own game development experiences, and through lessons learned working with both new and long-term developer and publisher clients. If you'd like to explore working together I can be reached at ddaglow@gmail.com, and my personal website is at www.daglowslaws,com.

A Book About You

Most books tell a story about someone else. Their adventures, their hopes, their dreams.

When you and I finish this process, this book will be about you.

It will talk about what you want for your career and for your life. The obstacles you face and realistic, practical plans for how you'll overcome them.

This is not the Big Lie that says, "Imagine the road to a mega-hit video game to unlock fame and wealth!"

This is, "Let's find a realistic way for you to build and ship a game you love, and then let's refine those plans and strategies so you can make it happen."

So please think of this book as a private discussion between you and me.

Wait, check that. Think of this book as a private discussion between you and you. A chance for you to talk openly about your hopes, dreams and fears. No judgment, no criticism, no worrying about anyone else's feelings.

When you've finished answering each set of questions, I'll summarize how to turn your answers into productive next steps. We'll explore how to start writing your own script for your game and your career instead of accepting chapters that other people have written for you.

That's why I opened this book with my mantra to "Chase your dreams till they get tired of running away."

If you stick with the process and give yourself thoughtful and real answers, I think this story will have a happy ending.

Giving Ourselves Permission

Anyone who loves games and has learned how to make them can create an indie game. Your gender, ethnicity, religion, sexual orientation, background, education, personal characteristics and location are not an issue. Your game will speak for itself.

In fact, if you're not "the typical game developer" it may help you stand out in the crowd.

Your game won't be allowed to crash the user's smartphone, tablet or computer. You'll need to follow the community standards of the different app stores (e.g. no hate speech or personal attacks). Apart from these basic safeguards, on many platforms there are no gatekeepers you have to please, and there are no elites who can crowd in line ahead of you.

It's just a matter of whether you're willing to learn the necessary crafts and do the work to create your game. And then do still more work to find a way to get it into the hands of players.

There's a quote from Agatha Christie (although it's often credited wrongly to Mark Twain) that provides a central theme to this book:

"The secret of getting ahead is getting started."

To start this book, I had to give myself permission to spend a few hours over the course of one week. I plotted out the theme for each section and wrote down the first few questions in each category. For the next several months I used my free time to build out those first ideas, writing additional questions and creating the first sections on "What to do with your answers."

Each step I took encouraged me to take the next step, and after two years of part-time work the book is now written, published and in your hands.

We often talk ourselves out of starting things, for reasons I'll discuss. By doing so, we sabotage our chances to finish work that we would be proud to share with the world.

At some point in the process we may decide to drop an idea that isn't working. This often chain reacts into another, better idea.

But we still have to *start*. If a voice in the back of your head tries to talk you out of starting your indie game, ignore it. Your idea may or may not work out, but we have to give ourselves a chance.

The alternative is to accept failure, which I refuse to do.

What's the one thing you'd have to give yourself permission to do in order to start your indie game project? And I mean starting it now, not next month or next year.

Game designers start projects by sitting down to think, organizing their notes and writing down their ideas. Once you take that simple step, you'll have achieved more than the legions of people who never start at all.

This book will help you do it.

What You'll Need

How do you like to write down your ideas? A notebook or journal? An iPad or laptop? A yellow pad?

If you're comfortable and it's a quiet time and place where you can write down your thoughts as they come to you, the method doesn't matter.

I do, however, ask that you do two things:

Commit that you'll write down your answers, not just think about them. The process of writing things down forces us to clarify our thoughts, and is the enemy of wishy-washy indecision.

Since you're writing this ONLY for your own eyes, commit to yourself that you'll answer with complete honesty. Before you can discuss your plans with family and friends you need to decide how you *really* feel.

How to Use This Book

Each section of this book has three themes: "Questions," "My Story" and "What to Do with Your Answers."

The questions follow a logical sequence. We'll start by talking about your indie game and your vision for it. Then we'll discuss part-time and full-time work, and the issues of projects that involve teams ranging from small to large. We'll cover the different ways to organize your project and to make plans for the work to be done.

In the last three major sections of the book we'll gradually move into the issues of starting and running a business in the games industry, from tiny side projects to ambitious teams. Then we'll wrap things up with one final question.

There's one exception to this "start by discussing the game, the development process and the team, then move on to talking about business" structure. I raise the issue of marketing your game in the very first of the seven sections of this book.

That's because the issues of indie game marketing are so critical – and the environment so competitive – that I want to get you thinking about your marketing strategy as early in the process as possible. There are some preparatory steps you can start taking early in development of your indie game, and they can yield results many months later when you ship.

Please answer the questions in each section before moving on to that section's "What to Do with Your Answers." You'll always give yourself the best ideas if each question is fresh and new when you respond to it.

Not every question or discussion in this book will be relevant to you and your game, and the content is designed so you can skip the parts that don't fit into your plans.

For example, if you don't plan to hire anyone to work with you, just skip the questions about building a team. Use your best judgment as you proceed, and the story you create with your answers will bring your indie game to life.

Introduction by Rami Ismail

A decade ago, I was an aspiring developer showing Don Daglow around my university after he gave an opening keynote. We talked a little, although I was a little daunted by this industry veteran who was walking through the hallways of my school.

During our little walk-and-talk chat, he confirmed many things I believed about the games industry. And he dramatically exposed a number of myths about game development that I had believed were true until that point.

Nowadays, I find myself thinking of that conversation as I'm being shown around universities by aspiring developers. I dramatically expose a number of myths about the games industry as soon as possible for every aspiring developer I meet.

If I have your attention for a moment as you read through this introduction, there are three of these myths that I would love to discuss.

Myth I: Games are the Youngest Medium

Video games are young, but in this day of livestreaming and emojis we're not the youngest medium. Games are simply the latest iteration in the oldest medium of all – even older than spoken or written language.

When humanity was young, our survival depended on our curiosity and our playfulness. A human who practiced spear throwing on a tree was more likely to survive, just because they practiced through play.

Throughout the centuries, play has been a primal requirement for humans. The Roman poet Juvenal eternalized this in the phrase, "panem et circenses," or "bread and play."

Play took on various forms throughout history, as a way to entertain or teach. Some play took the form of pastimes and distractions, such as the mysterious Egyptian boardgame Senet from more than 5,000 years ago. Other play took on political forms, such as the Greek Olympic pankration fights, which could even end in death.

Play, more than anything, is an educator. Humanity has always learned through play, whether it's structured through games and rules, or unstructured experimentation or curiosity.

Today, play is ubiquitous – whether it's a blockbuster game played on a home console, an independent game played on your computer, a quick mobile game played on public transport, a sports event on television, or the achievements you unlock from your fitness tracker.

It is within this medium, a medium with centuries of history, that the games industry exists. We build upon thousands of years of play, and the history of language, video, drawing, music, physics, design, interaction, product design, technology, and programming.

Games in my eyes aren't exciting because they're young. Games are exciting because, despite their age, they continue to be at the forefront of innovation and the intersection between all the other mediums in life.

This is something worth remembering when you're stuck and wrestling with a problem in your game. Chances are that your answer can be found in one of the foundational sciences and mediums that games are built upon.

Myth II: The Games Industry Runs on Passion

It is absolutely true that our industry uses passion as a fuel – how could it not?

Games are created by highly trained specialists from competitive fields. We are programmers who could work at a major engineering company. We are artists who could work at an architecture or movie firm. We are sound designers who could work in live television or the music industry. We are designers who could work in product design and lucrative web projects.

Every person in any role in the industry could be safer, richer, and generally more respected by the world in any other field. Yet, despite the draw of stability and money, security and understanding from our families and friends, so many choose to remain in games.

That is passion.

Passion alone, though, is dangerous. The industry is also home to many stories of companies falling apart through stress, fights, drama, and burnout. The notion that anyone in games is older than 40 is worthy of a double-take, simply because so few can manage to stay around this exhausting, self-sacrificial industry for so long.

Few industries that require this high level of training have such a high turnover rate among people in their 30's. Passion will only carry you so far when you've got a family to feed, or a mortgage to pay. When people leave, it is often not driven by a lack of passion, but an exhaustion from the continual sacrifices demanded by that passion.

What balances our industry is pragmatism, discipline, and diligence. These might sound like boring concepts, but our medium can't be built on enthusiasm alone – it has to be built with care.

Any good game that is released consists of equal parts love and work, art and design, practicality and creativity. This medium cannot exist on exhausted creators, their passions extinguished by work beyond their ability to keep that flame alive.

So, each time someone advises you to be passionate, please remember my advice to be pragmatic. When you're reminded to work hard, remember also to work smart. Each time you're told to let your gut feeling guide you, remember to do due diligence. And each time you're inspired to make games for the art, remember the wise advice to figure out how to pay the rent doing what you love.

Myth III: Your Individual Skills are What Matter

Games are an incredibly complex medium – your ability to code, draw, model, engineer, design, and create are critical to your ability to work in this medium. They are not, however, the only key to thriving in games.

While it's easy to think of games as built from bits and bytes, the reality is that games are an extremely human medium:

As game designers, we try to inspire strong human emotions in our players. As coders, we try to translate human ideas into computer instructions. As artists, we trick human eyes into thinking geometric shapes and pixels represent characters and worlds. As sound designers, we use audio to create human tension, excitement, and drama.

We create games we can't control for people we will never know, in the hope that they will play until they've felt the emotions that we set out to inspire. Making a game is the most roundabout way of making a point, whether you're trying to make people feel great or small. Everything we do in games revolves around people.

That quest for connection applies not just to the game itself, but also to the creation of the game. Far more than your ability to create, the games industry calls for your ability to communicate and be compassionate and considerate.

We work across industries and mediums. Each has their own languages and specialties, their own workflows and pipelines. Somehow, we have to integrate all of it into one coherent product.

It's no wonder then that successful game studios don't just represent the skill of the individuals, but the ability of those individuals to work together. A great designer must be able to communicate their ideas. An amazing coder must be able to understand what is needed, and create code that can be worked on by others. A phenomenal artist must produce art that adheres to the specifications and fits the workflow.

Regardless of what you do in this industry, your ability to make the people around you feel safe and free to speak out to share their best ideas is what will define your success.

There is an abundant supply of great developers. But only a small percentage can get the best out of themselves and those around them while working in a team.

I was reminded that the industry consists of people when I was asked to write this introduction by Don. The first time we met, almost a decade ago, he had flown to the Netherlands, where I had recently founded my own games studio, to give a keynote at a local event.

I don't remember much of the day, beyond showing Don around my former university and chatting about game development – but one slide from his keynote speech will stay in my mind for as long as I live.

The slide said, "Decide, don't accept."

In many ways, our job as game creators – whether we are creatives, leadership, community management or public relations – is to make decisions. It is to take an incredible amount of information and possibilties and distill them into actionable choices, and then to evaluate and optimize the choices we pick.

Through our work, we then offer meaningful choices to our players and audiences. We give them worlds to exist in, characters to meet, experiences to live, and problems to solve.

It is incredibly easy to overlook how many decisions we're letting slip by us through assumptions. I do an exercise with students where I challenge them to make a game I'm thinking of in two days, and to figure out what I want them to make in twenty minutes of questioning.

They ask what the genre is, and I answer it's a platformer. They ask what the goal is, and I answer it's to get to the end of the level. They ask what powerups exist, and I answer there are things like mushrooms, fire flowers, and invincibility stars.

They all make Super Mario, and I fail all of them because what I wanted is Super Mario 64. Rarely do we confirm the little details that define whether there is real agreement.

The fallibility of words would be difficult enough if the industry weren't continuously re-inventing itself. New developments are revolutionizing the medium as you read this page.

Given how fast this industry evolves and how many skillsets go into a game, it's almost impossible to write a book that contains advice in the shape of answers. By the time anyone figures out an answer, writes it down and gets it distributed, the answer may very well be outdated.

So Why Write this Essay?

So why, you might wonder, am I writing the Introduction to a book filled with words of advice for game developers?

Because, when I was scouring through an early draft of this book, I realized I wasn't reading a book filled with answers to your questions. This is a book filled with questions for you to answer.

They're the questions of someone with the passion and diligence to work in this industry for decades, someone who has learned to hone their work skills and people skills evenly, and someone who recognizes that games are both a medium of their own and an extension of other creative efforts throughout history.

Your game is yours, and it grows from your vision, your passion, and your effort. Nobody can give you the shortcuts or answers to make it the best it can be.

But if you know what questions to ask, you can avoid letting choices slip by, and make decisions where and when they count. You bring the answers, as you and your team are the only people on this planet who can make your games.

I wish you all the passion, diligence, care, and pragmatism in the world to aid you in making your contribution to this millennium-old medium of ours.

Make games.

– Rami

Rami Ismail is the Business and Development Guy at Vlambeer, a Dutch independent game studio known best for *Nuclear Throne, LUFTRAUSERS, Ridiculous Fishing, GUN GODZ, Serious Sam: The Random Encounter & Super Crate Box.*

PART I

BIG DREAMS

CHAPTER 1

Big Dreams: The Questions

QUESTION 1.1

What is the game that you have you been thinking about creating that inspired you to read this book?

What objective would you like to meet by launching your indie game?

Please take your time, write down your responses, and answer fully from your deepest thoughts. Think only about your own opinions, not about what others may want you to think or do. Do not look ahead to other questions until you have finished this one.

QUESTION 1.2

What makes you passionate about this game?

In what game genre or category will reviewers classify it?

When did you first become interested in the play style, genre, category or theme that lies at the core of the game you want to create?

What was the first game you played in this genre that made you love the category?

Please take your time, write down your responses, and answer fully from your deepest thoughts. Think only about your own opinions, not about what others may want you to think or do. Do not look ahead to other questions until you have finished this one.

QUESTION 1.3

What is the first platform on which you plan to release your game?

What other platforms do you intend to support simultaneously, or soon after your initial launch?

Will your game require any additional hardware or peripherals for users to play, like VR headsets or alternate interface devices?

Please take your time, write down your responses, and answer fully from your deepest thoughts. Think only about your own opinions, not about what others may want you to think or do. Do not look ahead to other questions until you have finished this one.

QUESTION 1.4

In what programming language (or languages) will your game be coded?

Will you use a third party engine as the foundation for your game, or create it entirely from scratch?

If you're using an engine, will it be Unity 2D or 3D? The Unreal Engine? CryEngine? GameMaker? Something else?

Please take your time, write down your responses, and answer fully from your deepest thoughts. Think only about your own opinions, not about what others may want you to think or do. Do not look ahead to other questions until you have finished this one.

QUESTION 1.5

Is this your first game of this scale?

Have you pursued lots of indie games in your life?

Have you worked on other initiatives or startups that were similar in size to this project?

QUESTION 1.6

Dreams change as we live our lives. What is a game you once really hoped to create, but that is no longer as important to you?

Please take your time, write down your responses, and answer fully from your deepest thoughts. Think only about your own opinions, not about what others may want you to think or do. Do not look ahead to other questions until you have finished this one.

QUESTION 1.7

What game do you think you may want to build a few years from now that isn't as important to you today?

Why will you care more about it in a few years than you do now?

QUESTION 1.8

Do you have ideas for additional content or follow-up products that can be introduced if the first game is a success?

Please take your time, write down your responses, and answer fully from your deepest thoughts. Think only about your own opinions, not about what others may want you to think or do. Do not look ahead to other questions until you have finished this one.

QUESTION 1.9

Is it the technology involved in the making of the game that interests you?

Is it the genre or category of the game? The platform on which you'll create the original version? The style of interface?

Or do you take joy in the visuals of the game? The audio?

Some combination of the above choices?

QUESTION 1.10

What makes you believe that this game will draw players' attention in a crowded market?

Is this a completely new idea, or are you setting out to improve on a game that already exists?

Please take your time, write down your responses, and answer fully from your deepest thoughts. Think only about your own opinions, not about what others may want you to think or do. Do not look ahead to other questions until you have finished this one.

QUESTION 1.11

If you could describe your indie game to a stranger in just one sentence that would interest him or her, what would that sentence be?

What are the three most important features that will make someone want to play your game and spend money on the title?

QUESTION 1.12

What is the primary mood of your game? (e.g. happy, dark, frightening, goofy, stealthy, foreboding, curious, joyful etc.)

What is the pace of your game? (e.g. frenetic, thoughtful, alternating action and strategy, etc.)

How long will people play in a typical session, and where will they be playing? For two minutes waiting in line at the grocery store? Fifteen minutes on the bus? Three hours in the living room?

One of the first people to play your game has lunch with a friend. What do they say to the friend about how they were feeling as they played?

Please take your time, write down your responses, and answer fully from your deepest thoughts. Think only about your own opinions, not about what others may want you to think or do. Do not look ahead to other questions until you have finished this one.

QUESTION 1.13

What will the first two minutes of the player experience be like in your game?

Will you have a tutorial? How will users learn how to play?

Please take your time, write down your responses, and answer fully from your deepest thoughts. Think only about your own opinions, not about what others may want you to think or do. Do not look ahead to other questions until you have finished this one.

QUESTION 1.14

What will the first playable prototype of your game include?

Note: This is not a list of the features and scope of your planned game. I'm asking for an outline of what will be in the first bare-bones playable prototype where you'll first be able to watch people play your game.

QUESTION 1.15

What kinds of people will want to play your game?

What other games do those same people play? What websites do they visit?

Where would you find them on social media sites like Facebook, Twitter, Instagram etc.?

Please take your time, write down your responses, and answer fully from your deepest thoughts. Think only about your own opinions, not about what others may want you to think or do. Do not look ahead to other questions until you have finished this one.

QUESTION 1.16

What games are the most similar to your indie title?

How is yours different? What makes yours better?

Please take your time, write down your responses, and answer fully from your deepest thoughts. Think only about your own opinions, not about what others may want you to think or do. Do not look ahead to other questions until you have finished this one.

QUESTION 1.17

How would you feel if The New York Times, Wired magazine, Oprah Winfrey and your best friend's mother all said your game sucks?

QUESTION 1.18

You just won a mega-million-dollar jackpot in the lottery! You've cleared your to-do list and taken a 3-month vacation at a series of your favorite cities and resorts.

You return happy, rested and all caught up in every phase of your life. There's no to-do list for work, and nothing at home that needs to be cleaned, straightened, fixed, watered, painted, re-arranged or put away.

You no longer need to work, nor does your spouse or partner. If you have kids, however, they still attend the same grade of school and they still have to do their homework. Some things can't be changed by money!

From this moment on you can do whatever you want to do each day. In this "perfect world" how would you spend the first month when you got back?

Please take your time, write down your responses, and answer fully from your deepest thoughts. Think only about your own opinions, not about what others may want you to think or do. Do not look ahead to other questions until you have finished this one.

CHAPTER 2

My Story: The Big Company in Chicago

I've been part of several Silicon Valley startups, in roles ranging from engineer to manager to advisor to CEO. The most successful was Electronic Arts, where I was an early employee at a new company that ultimately went public.

When I was growing up in the San Francisco Bay Area, however, there were no careers in video game development. The games industry did not exist.

I was not one of "the popular kids," and I was shy. More accurately, I was shy until you wanted to discuss world history or theatre or science fiction. Those were passions where I would talk your ear off. And what I loved to talk about most of all was baseball.

I'm blind in one eye, so I could never play the game at an advanced level. Whenever my homework was all done — and sometimes when it wasn't — I would play a board game called *All Star Baseball*. Usually I played by myself, managing both teams.

I grew up in a loving family with inspiring parents, but recurrent medical problems cascaded into alcoholism. For years many evenings were full of anger and conflict as my parents argued. Things got better after I started my career, but many nights as I was growing up that board game was more than a distraction or a hobby – it was the safe place I could retreat to where I could shut out an angry world.

If it were baseball season and the San Francisco Giants were playing I'd listen to the real game on the radio as I played the board game. If there were no game I'd do the radio play-by-play for myself as I narrated the action in my own board game on the desk in my room.

So what does this have to do with big dreams?

All Star Baseball was a very simple game, because trial and error had taught the designers that a more complex version didn't sell.

The round game cards for different big league players were placed on a spinner that would point to a spot that determined the outcome of the play, accurately simulating the hitting of my heroes Willie McCovey, Willie Mays and Stan Musial.

But there were no pitching cards in the game, so Juan Marichal and Nolan Ryan were no more intimidating on the mound than a rookie pitcher.

This frustrated me until at age 15 I figured out how to fix it. Calculating the probability differences, I created a second set of pitcher cards to complement the hitter cards and get far more accurate results.

I remember thinking, "I should send this design to the big game company in Chicago that publishes *All Star Baseball* and see if they want to buy it. This modification keeps the game simple but solves its greatest flaw."

But, of course, my next thought was, "I'm just a 15-year-old kid. The big company in Chicago is never going to listen to me."

So I never wrote to them.

I never tried.

Four years later in 1971, I was one of the first college students to gain unrestricted access to a mainframe computer. I started using the mathematics I'd developed at age 15 for simulating baseball in a board game to program a far more accurate computer game.

The system worked, and although I didn't know it at the time I had written the first interactive computer baseball game in the history of what became the games industry. I went on to work with Hall of Famers Earl Weaver and Tony La Russa on baseball simulation titles that bore their names and won Game of the Year awards.

Ultimately I became CEO of a company that (among other titles) published computer baseball games, a smaller version of the big company in Chicago that published *All Star Baseball*.

But the lonely 15-year-old boy had no way of knowing that all this would happen. I thought that being part of professional baseball was just another impossible dream.

I've been very, very fortunate in my career, and I'm grateful for all of that good luck.

But what if that 15-year-old version of me had sent this new version of *All Star Baseball* to the big company in Chicago?

They'd probably have sent me a "no thanks, but you're a great kid" letter without even looking at the design. They might have ignored me. They might have loved the idea and sent me a check.

But we'll never know, because I didn't try.

Once I became a professional game designer I always remembered this story. I couldn't always take financial risks. I couldn't leave a job that paid the bills.

But I resolved that the adult Don would always remember what the 15-year-old Don did not yet know:

If you believe in something there will always be some reason-

able way to try to bring it to reality. There's always a way to pursue your indie game.

Sometimes individuals like you and me really can do better than the big companies in the big cities.

But we can't give up before we start. We have to try.

CHAPTER 3

What to Do with Your Answers

"EVERY GREAT DREAM BEGINS
WITH A DREAMER."

— Harriet Tubman, heroine of
The Underground Railroad

If you have not yet written down your answers, please go back and do so. Writing your thoughts down – even when you're the only one who'll ever read them – will produce far more insights than just answering silently to yourself in your head.

1.0.1 Business is a Game

It's easier than ever to publish indie games:

- Unity and other engines make it simpler than ever to develop a title
- Languages like Python, HTML5 and C# make it easier to code
- Submitting to the App Store, Google Play or Steam is straightforward
- Web-based games are even easier to share online
- Nintendo, PlayStation and Xbox include indie games in their online stores

The old barriers to entry have tumbled down. There are new obstacles, however, and we'll discuss them throughout this book.

If you plan to sell your game, offer in-app purchases etc., that means you're going to start a business. That may sound intimidating, but you have a big natural advantage.

Business is a game. As game developers and passionate players we understand games very, very well.

To leverage this advantage, you just have to take the time to learn the game's rules, develop your strategy, and then hone your tactics by playing.

1.0.2 The Recipe for Long Term Success

In my career as a game developer and entrepreneur I've tried to follow this recipe:

> 2 lbs. (900 grams) Personal Passion
> 1 lb. (450 grams) Creative Vision
> 1 lb. (450 grams) Industry Experience
> 1 lb. (450 grams) Healthy Skepticism
> 8 oz. (225 grams) Patience

> *Take Passion, Personal Experience, Common Sense and Skepticism and mix liberally. Season repeatedly with patience as needed.*

> *If nothing good is coming out of this recipe, search for more Passion to add to the mix, and keep practicing new variations on the recipe. Repeat as necessary.*

I'm having fun with the way I express this idea, but here's the principle behind it:

Personal Passion drives everything that's worth doing... including games. Getting up every morning to go work at a job you hate really sucks. Doing work that you're committed to doing and that you believe to be important feels like fun as well as work. And work you love is far more likely to be done well and to make you happier when you come home.

Creative Vision is what makes you believe that you're working on a good game, a title that's worth your time. It may be your own idea or something your team developed.

Industry experience reflects all the games you've worked on in your career. These are the platforms, genres, interfaces and styles of play where you have hard-won insider knowledge. A game that leverages that experience gives you real advantages in the marketplace.

Healthy Skepticism stops us from being victims. When you see an ad that says, "Make a Million a Month with My Secret Formula!" your skepticism stops you from sending the scam artists your money.

I see other books proclaim, "You can quit your job, tell off your boss and become independent!" They open with stories of people who successfully did all those things. It may not be as obvious as the million-a-month scam, but it's still a trick used to sell books.

Many authors never talk about people who told off their bosses and then boldly sailed into financial disaster. Your healthy skepticism reminds you to be careful with big changes in your life. My job in this book is to prepare you for the work required to plan any indie game, and to encourage you to do that research and preparation.

I'll also keep reminding you to retain your healthy skepticism as part of the overall process. That's what drives strong research and planning.

Patience is like salt. You need it for everything to taste right... but too much of it can spoil the meal. Being too impatient with the planning of your game can make you release your title too soon and sabotage your chances. Being too patient, waiting year after year to make your game absolutely perfect, can mean you never ship. Or maybe you never even start at all.

When I play a good game I expect to have conflicting priorities. I have to balance time and resources to get the best outcome. Balancing the "flavors" of Passion, Creative Vision, Experience, Healthy Skepticism and Patience is a similar exercise, and will produce a game and a business that are uniquely well-suited to you.

The Passion-Process-Product Method. In the pages that follow I'll give you a framework for this approach, which I call "The Passion-Process-Product Method."

You'll start with your passions and develop a practical way to do work that leverages your personal strengths and talents. When it feels like you've found the right recipe for success, you'll be ready to create a game that inspires passion in others.

1.0.3 The Difference Between a Hobby and a Profession

It is absolutely vital to think about – and listen to your feelings about – what activities you enjoy as hobbies and which you would enjoy as your profession.

Whenever a family member has a birthday I'm usually the one who makes their favorite kind of birthday cake. I really enjoy the process.

As much as I enjoy baking birthday cakes, however, I know that if I tried to do it even part-time I'd be miserable in two weeks. Starting with the fact that I don't like getting up at 3:00 or 4:00 AM every day, which is what real bakers have to do. Nobody wants day-old bread, cookies or cake.

I began my game development career designing and programming games as a hobby, then made the transition into the industry. I love what I do, and my choice of profession has never gotten old or boring.

As we go through this process together, please keep this thought in the back of your mind: what are the things I enjoy as hobbies, and what do I enjoy as my profession?

1.0.4 Assembling the Rocket

Most indie games fail to earn very much revenue – let alone a profit. It's a challenging environment, and it can be intimidating to look at all the obstacles.

As we consider building an indie game, however, we can learn a lot from the engineers in the space program. To launch a rocket a long series of decisions and commitments need to be made. They aren't done all at once, and if the engineers come up with a question they can't answer there will be delays.

As with a new rocket for the space program, there are multiple points in every project where you either discard the concept or re-commit to the idea and set about pushing ahead to the next stage.

In all of those early phases you're not "on the launch pad" and committed to doing anything. You're doing a series of self-assigned steps that may lead to the decision to launch your indie game.

Starting a project (or doing the whole thing) as a part-time activity makes it easier to consider all the possibilities. If it's a good idea, the moment will arrive when you realize that you are in fact "ready to launch."

As we start this journey together and discuss your ideas, remember that we can take our time and make sure you feel good about what you're doing before we proceed to the "launching" steps that we'll reach later in this book.

There's another lesson from satellite launches that applies to indie games: keeping it simple.

Almost every item on a space vehicle costs more to launch than it costs to build, because it takes so much fuel to get heavy objects into orbit. Nothing is added to each mission unless it is absolutely, irrefutably necessary (unless you're Elon Musk and you're sending a sports car into space to generate publicity).

What if you were to look at your indie game the same way?

- What if every feature in version 1.0 has to be super-valuable to avoid being labeled "do it later?"
- What if every job has to be super-critical to success, or you'll postpone filling the position?

- What if every item you buy with precious cash has to be a "can't do without" purchase?
- What if every major task on your to-do list has to be "mission critical?"

I'll be reminding you about this pattern of "simple as a core value" regularly throughout this book.

1.0.5 No "Hail Mary" Plays

In American football, the game is over when the time on the clock runs out. The team with the most points at that moment wins the game

If a team is losing and there's only time for one more play, they have to bet everything on that one opportunity. They run one last wild, long, almost-impossible play. It's almost certain to fail, but if it succeeds they will tie or win the game.

It's called a "Hail Mary" play, because you say a prayer and hope it works, even though it will probably just make the final score worse.

I read business articles all the time that seem to recommend that people try Hail Mary plays. Here's a fictional example:

Jane Hernandez started her multi-million dollar game company by using the last $200 in her savings account to buy a final, desperate round of near-perfect Facebook ads. Just six years later, she's used these five powerful rules of success to build a company valued at over $20 million!

I'm very happy for Ms. Hernandez, but in our story she got a great result from a terrible strategy. That's as rare as winning the lottery.

Her five powerful rules of business are probably great advice, but they won't let me turn $200 into $20 million. That's a copy-writing trick, an inferred promise of easy riches used to get people to buy training programs.

Launching a business is not about backing yourself into a corner and then desperately trying to achieve your goals with some dramatic (and usually foolish) exercise.

Launching your indie game is about figuring out what you deeply want to do, and then experimenting with ways that you could do it. Piece by piece, you learn enough from those trials to make the most of your chance to do work you love.

There may be a moment when you've saved up some money and decide to take a risk on a bigger experiment. But you do so when you feel you're well-prepared and ready to devote the time.

Here's a more practical summary of Jane's story that features common sense instead of desperation:

Jane Hernandez started her successful educational game company six years ago by saving up an "experimentation fund" of $1,200 to test and publish the educational game that she had prototyped in Unity for her touchscreen tablet.

During the week Jane worked as a teacher at a local school. Each Saturday morning she spent $65 to rent a small booth at the local Farmers Market. She borrowed tablets from family members so that she could watch kids play the prototype and then talk with their parents. Cash dropped in her donations jar offset some of the costs.

Each week more kids came to play. Each week she spent her evenings taking what she'd learned and revising the game.

Two months into this process kids were waiting at her booth as the Farmers Market opened. Both the bug list and her backlog had dwindled. Jane was having a great time doing what she loved.

She started planning her product launch, asking the parents at the

Farmers Market to share her website on their Facebook pages and Twitter feeds.

The local newspaper ran a story on "the educational game booth between the organic celery and the orchid stand." This brought more subscribers to her website.

Jane uploaded the first version of her game to the app store just as the school year ended, so she could devote the free weeks of summer vacation to her launch. She sent emails to everyone on her list, and distributed a press release to all the major game sites and local media.

This strategy did not instantly produce a million downloads, or any of the other unreasonable expectations that we dream of when we ship an indie game.

It did produce an initial burst of sales in her home town, which produced happy users and high ratings in the online store. There were more stories in the local media. Two game sites published positive reviews.

By the end of the summer Jane Hernandez had turned her $1,200 investment into $4,500 in revenue. She had beaten the odds: sales per month were still growing 90 days after launch.

Three years later and with three more games in her catalog Jane had saved enough that she took a leave of absence at her school and made the jump to making games full-time. She continues to love this new career.

There may not be a $20 million payoff to this Jane Hernandez tale, but it's the kind of story I've seen happen in real life, over and over again. The punchline is that the person is doing work they love and making a living at doing it.

If Jane's game had not been successful she would have lost time and money, but she had saved up for this experiment and could afford the loss if necessary.

There were no dramatic "Hail Mary" decisions where Jane had to risk losing her car or home in a made-for-Hollywood gesture of self-sacrifice. Just a smart, passionate individual executing on her plan.

What would you do with the money if you followed Jane's strategy and saved up your own "experimentation fund?"

CHAPTER 4

Your Indie Game (1.1-1.2)

DISCUSSING QUESTION 1.1

What is the game that you have you been thinking about creating that inspired you to read this book?

What objective would you like to meet by launching your indie game?

This topic is most relevant for: Everyone

1.1.1 Any Reason That Matters to You is a Good Reason

I love games, and I especially love creating games. I started writing games as a college student many years ago, just for the fun of it and to enjoy watching friends play.

When the video game industry was born and I had the chance to become a professional game designer the fun continued. But I also had to deal with issues like, "How do we make enough money with this game to be able to pay salaries long enough to build the next one?"

Whatever your reason is for building an indie game, it's probably a good justification for the work. If the project really matters to you, that alone is a great reason to build an indie game.

If you want to earn enough money to be a part-time or full-time game developer, that's great, too.

IMHO the only bad reason to build a game is, "To get rich." First of all, it's very unlikely that you'll meet that economic goal, for reasons we'll discuss. Secondly, trying to create games just to make money often produces bad games and miserable workplaces.

Here are some examples of good reasons for building an indie game, both personal motivations from my career and things I've heard from teams with whom I've worked:

• "I couldn't stop thinking about this game so I had to build it"
• "I needed to learn C# for my day job, and building a game with it seemed like a great way to learn"
• "We figured out a better way to teach basic math skills to middle grade kids, and fun games are what make kids learn the fastest"
• "We did this project for our Design 301 class, but it was so promising we decided to expand it into a full length game and try to sell it"
• "This is art, like painting or film. We'll share it for free to give people new insights into these issues"
• "We're building new tools and pipelines for our AAA game, and the sample game we used to test the system turned out to be a lot of fun"
• "I love physics, and fun little games are the best way to explain complicated ideas"
• "My sister and I realized that if we didn't do our dream project now life would pull us in different directions and we might never get to build it"
• "My friend and I realized we'd been talking about the same game idea for a year, and that's when we knew we had to build it"
• "I don't have professional experience and I didn't go to a famous school, so my path into the industry is to build great indie games and let them be my resume"

• "Six of us worked on games together in school, so when we graduated we thought, "Let's start a studio and give this a year and see
what happens"

1.1.2 Stay Out of the Shadows

Once we get in the middle of a project it's easy to lose track of the
original objective. Be sure to watch out for these traps that await
indie game teams:

- We keep adding features to a simple, fun game, so it becomes a
  complex game that isn't as much fun
- We lose track of what we think is fun and start copying the best-
  sellers in search of money
- We try to do something that's too big, get bogged down and
  never release the game
- We have lots of drawings and design documents and little
  demos, but we never actually start building the game

Finishing your game, launching it and seeing people play are the
three keys that open the door for the success of your indie game.
Be ruthless about getting back on track if the game is fun and you
drift from the path that leads to completing version 1.0.

1.1.3 The Many Kinds of Indie Game Projects

Some of the advice in this book is about creating any indie game,
whether it will be sold or given away for free. Other sections are
focused on the company-building and money-making part of the
project.

Some varieties of indie projects are:

The One-Person Initiative. Typically engineers are the ones who can execute this kind of project, or creatives from other disciplines who can also write code. They not only create the game, they're also the CEO, VP of Sales and QA Manager for their company.

The Small Team Indie Game. A small group of friends works on the project part-time, or enough money may be scraped together to make a go of it full-time and see if the business gets off the ground.

The Game Studio "Side Project." Work-for-hire game development studios, which do assignments for game publishers or other software companies, are accustomed to executing the product vision defined by their clients. When team members have free time, however, they may work on their own original game.

The Large-Scale Game Development Startup. This kind of new business is very rare, although when one is founded it gets lots of publicity. This option is normally only available to the leaders of teams that have produced major hits.

I have advised or been part of companies that fit all of the categories above. All of them have the same core goal: to build a great game that people will love to play.

1.1.4 Focus on the Journey, Not Just the Destination

Answering the questions in this book may deepen your commitment to your game idea.

It's also possible that your plans will change as you discuss your indie project with yourself.

The key is to let your thinking take you where your passions and your common sense want you to go. You may rearrange your priorities and change your focus several times.

I've always liked the advice of poet Ralph Waldo Emerson, who coined the phrase, "Focus on the journey, not just the destination."

Let's say that your game is a PC-centric RPG where players seek approval from the Greek gods by demonstrating the requisite qualities in the early missions in the game. At some point one or more gods will invite the player to join their forces.

If you refuse to consider any alternatives to this design you can miss lots of opportunities:

Alternative Platforms: There are lots of Greek Mythology games, especially on PC and console platforms. If Greek mythology fascinates you, could you alter course to develop for a less Greek-god-crowded platform like Nintendo Switch or mobile? To do so, you'd have to accept modifying your game idea.

Alternative Content: What if more movies based on the comic book character Thor are released? You might sell far more games based on the Norse gods than you could for those of Greece. But only if you're willing to change your initial focus.

Alternative Market: One of your friends grew up in China, and when she plays your game she says it could be very popular there. With changes in costumes and narrative to support traditional Chinese historical stories you might sign a deal with a Chinese publisher and retain the North American rights. But you'd have to be open to changing the initial target market.

This "adapt to seize opportunities" philosophy doesn't mean, "stop doing work you love and just do whatever makes the most money."

Your passion — not just your financial projections — has to drive your decisions. Just chasing today's hot trends means you're always behind the times tomorrow. Your games are likely to feel sterile and commercial.

By making the journey our focus, not the destination, we can experiment and decide, "Is this a great opportunity, or a distraction from doing the work that will lead to long-term success?"

DISCUSSING QUESTION 1.2

What makes you passionate about this game?

In what game genre or category will reviewers classify it?

When did you first become interested in the play style, genre, category or theme that lies at the core of the game you want to create?

What was the first game you played in this genre that made you love the category?

This topic is most relevant for: Everyone

1.2.1 What Matters Most to You?

Many people have a deep love for books. Some love great writing and devour every word.

Others gravitate to "coffee table" books with striking photos and illustrations.

I have friends who can feel the pages of a book and tell you all about the paper, the rag content of the stock, how it absorbs and reflects light, and how all of those factors affect the mood and attitude of the reader.

Committed gamers have the same kinds of qualities.

Some are drawn by the physical challenge of a game, and the way that a responsive and intuitive interface translates their hard-earned skills into results on screen.

Some players crave the strategic challenge, the need to think deeply and cleverly to be a winner.

Others look for great graphics and art styles that will transport them into the mood and setting of the game. Or music and sound that carry them forward through the story.

Still others crave the social interaction of multiplayer games, with the emergent gameplay and the new online relationships it spawns.

Which aspects of your game drive your passion for the work? What parts of the game do you and your team crave building?

It's important to understand these passions, because they may also reflect your greatest strengths.

1.2.2 Which Version of Me is Really Me?

Our lives have different phases. Our interests change. Old friend-ships fade away and new friendships are made.

Our skills grow, and with them our perspectives. We learn from our mistakes, and from our successes.

Why is it valuable to think back to when this indie game first excited you? To ask yourself the question, "Are the things that excited me back then still exciting to me now?"

Is the market opportunity for this game as great as when you first came up with the idea? Or have lots of games already filled this niche?

Is there a twist on the old idea that would make it more relevant to an audience now?

Is this really your passion, or is it someone else's dream that you've adopted?

Give yourself time to consider these questions over the next few days while you're in the shower, driving to work or walking the dog.

1.2.3 Heroic Hybrids

One classic "formula" for creating new game categories is to cross-breed existing genres. For example:

World of Tanks: "A multi-player shooter with tanks instead of soldiers, monsters or zombies, featuring fanatically well-researched historical vehicles from multiple nations and eras."

Rocket League: "Soccer played with rocket-powered vehicles, with huge crashes, wide goals, an oversized ball and non-stop action."

The lesson here is that you can build a hit if you:

- Take a popular game style and keep enough of the proven game play so it remains familiar, then...
- Add something wildly different that changes play dramatically, and...
- Tune the resulting hybrid game until it's really, really fun

1.2.4 Knowing You Can Finish What You Start

Completing any big project is hard work.

When the early excitement wears off and the finish line still looks far away, even the most dream-worthy of games can become a grind. If you're testing an early version of your title and improvements come in sets of "two steps forward, one step back," it can be exhausting.

Author and marketer Seth Godin refers to this discouraging middle zone as "the dip," and that's exactly what it feels like. Everyone who creates and then sells games for a living can recognize the feeling. His book, also called *The Dip*, is well worth reading.

What keeps people going until the goal is finally in sight and the positive momentum starts to build?

Passion.

What makes people continue to do quality work when they're tired and distracted?

Passion.

If you're unsure about your level of passion for this game, go back and add more details about why you want to pursue it. Make sure your answers are coming from a passionate fire inside you, not from a commercial idea that you think will earn money.

If all you see is interest in your mind, not passion in your heart, what would you have to change about your game to make you excited about doing the work?

Would you need to jump to a completely different game?

CHAPTER 5

How It's Built & Played (1.3-1.4)

DISCUSSING QUESTION 1.3

What is the first platform on which you plan to release your game?

What other platforms do you intend to support simultaneously, or soon after your initial launch?

Will your game require any additional hardware or peripherals for users to play, like VR headsets or alternate interface devices?

This topic is most relevant for: Everyone

1.3.1 Publishers, Self-Publishers, Distributors and Retailers

We'll be referring to these terms often in these pages, so it's good to start out by defining them.

Many indie teams are self-publishers. We start out as game developers, create our games and then offer them through the app stores, Steam and similar online systems. As publishers, we pay all the people on the team and all the other expenses as we create the game. We own the copyright and all other intellectual property (IP) rights to the game.

GameStop, Best Buy and Walmart are retailers. They don't create games, they just sell them.

The app stores, Steam and similar services are distributors and retailers. They have lots of users who are interested in games and are ready to spend money on them. They aggregate lots of products to sell from many different publishers, as is done by distributors. They then sell those products directly to users, which makes them retailers. They do not own any rights to the games, except that they agree to pay the publishers – both major and indie — a set royalty percentage (usually 70%, less a small connection charge) of the money they receive from selling them.

Being both distributors and retailers is called being "vertically integrated" in the marketplace, because they control what often would be two different steps in the chain that connects game publishers to our players.

A limited number of large companies act as publishers, and control much of the global games market. Some indie game teams work through these publishers. Activision-Blizzard, Bandai Namco, DeNA, Electronic Arts, GREE, Nexon, Riot Games, Rovio, Sega, Square Enix, Supercell, Take Two, Tencent, Ubisoft and Wargaming are all examples of game publishers.

International game publishers tend to be large, since the big budgets involved in high-end games make these categories impractical for smaller companies. Some large publishers are owned by still larger publishers: Supercell runs as an independent division of Tencent.

Publishers have multiple potential sources for new products:

• Create original games internally

- Acquire the right to movies, comics etc. and then create games featuring the licensed worlds and characters
- Buy smaller competitors and then continue publishing their games
- Acquire the rights to competitors' games when rivals encounter financial troubles
- Fund the creation of new games invented by "third party" developers, and in recent years this includes indies

Publishers almost always seek to control the IP for any game they publish, either directly or by negotiating contracts which give them significant rights to future versions and revenues.

In addition to being game console makers, Microsoft, Nintendo and Sony are also game publishers, and have separate divisions for each part of their operation. They are called "first party" publishers because they create games for their own systems.

So if 'first party" describes console manufacturers who develop games for their systems and "third party" refers to developers and publishers who are not console makers, what the heck are "second party" game publishers?

The answer is that the term has been used to mean different things in the US and the UK at different times in games history, most often to describe a studio that is partially or fully owned by a console maker. The term has almost completely dropped out of use.

Big game publishers are usually also distributors. Smaller game publishers may work with larger publishers to distribute their games to different areas of the world. Tencent has brought many major games to the Chinese market on behalf of other publishers, adapting both the languages and the cultural content of the games. Riot initially had their games distributed and supported by a distributor in Europe, then took over that role themselves once they grew into a large corporation.

Big publishers are even more vertically integrated than the app stores and Steam. They seek to control every step of the process, from game design to product distribution and direct sales to consumers, without involving any other company.

I'll discuss the business of games in detail later in this book, including key issues that come up when indie studios work with game publishers.

1.3.2 Choosing the Right Platform(s)

Choosing the initial platform(s) for our games may seem straightforward, but there are traps, risks and misconceptions waiting to sabotage the unwary. There are also opportunities for those who are prepared to explore and find them.

Here are some issues to keep in mind:

Exclusivity. On consoles, tablets and mobile platforms the hardware manufacturers will often give preferential treatment and enhanced promotion to games that are exclusive to their platform. Those exclusives can last from a few months to forever, based on terms that may be negotiated between the parties.

Over the last few years both Sony and Microsoft have had periods when they prioritized working with indies and offering exclusive indie games in their online stores. Each company has also gone through periods when indies were a much less important part of their mix. Nintendo has also had waves of interest in indie games for the Nintendo Switch.

If your game would play well on consoles, don't just assume that an exclusive (or non-exclusive) console version won't be of interest to one of the big hardware manufacturers.

We once pitched a game to a major publisher after the window of opportunity for a new hardware system was officially closed. To our surprise, the company loved the game and made a deal with us, despite the fact that they'd announced they had completed all such deals. You never know unless you ask.

To explore potential exclusives once you have some kind of demo to show, you can reach out to each company's Developer Relations groups. Their current contact information will be available on their websites. Be sure to do so well in advance of when you're ready to ship your game.

In some cases you may also be able to form alliances with chip makers like Intel, AMD, NVIDIA etc. and gain benefits by exclusively supporting their chipsets. These windows of opportunity open and close based on when new product lines are introduced and the shifting market positions of the competitors at any given time.

Support New Hardware. Some new phones, tablets and consoles from powerful manufacturers are almost certain to find a large audience – although it can take longer than expected on some cycles, as with the PS3 and Xbox 360.

Hardware introductions are unpredictable. That's why supporting a new platform early in its lifetime can earn extra promotion and other benefits from manufacturers.

One option that is "high risk, high reward" is shipping a "launch title," a game that is available at the same time as the first units of the hardware itself. I've led teams on such projects for a number of platforms.

If the system proves popular there will be many buyers and very few games, which I (with apologies to Jacques Cousteau) call a "feeding frenzy." The titles that are already available can rack up big numbers as users work to grow their game collections.

Of course, if the new hardware is not successful, less happy results await the allied game developers.

It's also worth noting that the hardware manufacturers remember the teams and publishers who support their platforms with launch titles. Building these relationships over a period of years can be very beneficial.

The most recent example of this kind of opportunity is the Nintendo Switch, where Nintendo for the first time aggressively courted indie game developers. The platform exceeded most pundits' sales projections, and the teams that supported the Switch early in its history were rewarded with higher levels of sales than the same games earned on other systems.

Support New Technology. Sometimes the opportunity doesn't come from a platform manufacturer, but from the companies that create new technology that works with multiple platforms.

The biggest current example of this is VR, which has been implemented as add-on headsets for PS4, PC and other platforms as well as in dedicated hardware systems.

Avoid Unproven Peripherals. Add-on devices that work with only a single system or with only one kind of game are more risky systems to support if they take much developer time, require many resources or come with restrictions of exclusivity.

I once heard an exec for a non-standard game controller brag that they had 20% penetration on the platform that held 20% of the video game market.

I looked around me in the meeting and could see everyone else at the table doing the same math. 20% of 20% is 4%. If we did a game that was dedicated to their peripheral the best result we could hope for would be selling a copy to every single owner of their device and gaining 4% market share.

But why spend time chasing a 4% share when making cross-platform games with standard interfaces allowed us to seek 100% of the market?

The exception to this rule: If, for example, you make high-precision car racing games, then supporting the top steering wheel peripherals is part of your branding as a quality product. The most avid players in that category own wheel controllers and expect that the premium quality titles will support them.

Shooters and flight simulators are examples of other categories that also have spawned this kind of premium peripheral marketplace.

If you discuss exclusivity with a hardware manufacturer or other partner, know what kind of a deal you want before you start. The most common arrangement is that the game developer receives a payment from the hardware maker, often broken up into a series of milestones that are paid gradually after the team has demonstrated each step of its progress on the target machine.

In return for this money, the team agrees to publish the game only on that one platform for a set period of time, which can range from a few weeks to two years or even more. This holds true both for new technology and for mature systems where the companies continue to aggressively support their platform or unique tech.

In this kind of deal the hardware company (usually) is not acquiring any rights to your game, and your IP remains yours. If you work with a publisher instead of a manufacturer, however, their contract will probably be very different. They are likely to want to control all the publishing decisions for your title and gain at least some level of control over the IP.

In either situation it's important to have a good attorney helping you with any such deals. I'll discuss many related issues later in this book.

1.3.3 Beware of Assumptions

Although we often see our platform choices as obvious and clear-cut, there are also potholes on the runway as we plan our indie titles. Here are some that I've seen:

"I've seen two new generations of game hardware come on the market and I know how to predict which devices and genres and play styles will succeed on each cycle." If you've worked through two major hardware transitions in the games industry you absolutely have a lot of valuable experience. You'll be able to leverage those perspectives in the next transition.

I've worked in the video games industry through every console generation and every era. I can tell you that some transitions surprise the hell out of everyone:

- The transition after the original generation of game consoles never happened when the games market collapsed in the early 1980's
- Nintendo's NES was a big hit in the late 1980's when everyone believed that "console video games are dead"
- Sega pushed Nintendo aside as the top console in the early 1990's
- Sony pushed Sega aside as the top console in the mid-1990's
- Cellular phones became a major gaming platform in the late 2000's, when they'd previously been a tiny niche
- The Wii outsold both the PS3 and the Xbox 360 in the late 2000's
- The Nintendo Switch was a surprise hit in the mid-2010's, after their previous system, the Wii U, had failed to gain any momentum
- PC games were declared a dead market due to piracy 20 years ago, but have returned to health today

That's a lot of surprises. As a long-time executive and producer in games, that history has taught me to "never assume," apart from assuming that there will be surprises to which my team will have to adapt.

"That platform doesn't have any super-deep RPG's! Let's build one (or port ours to run there)!" This may in fact represent a great opportunity, but before we seize it we need to ask, "Um, why is it that this platform has no super-deep RPG's?"

If it's a small-screen mobile device where 15 minutes is considered to be a long play session, there are no deep RPG's because any such prior games couldn't survive. We don't want to be the next skeleton in that desert.

Sometimes one game successfully blazes a new path, but all of the games that follow fail to match its numbers, as happened with 3D mobile racing games. *CSR Racing* was a major hit, but the big market category that everyone inferred from that success never materialized on a large and repeatable scale.

1.3.4 Quantity, Quality and Exclusivity

In a perfect world we would ship our game simultaneously on the eleven most popular systems in the world. All of the time and money we spent on marketing and PR would be super effective, since everyone who heard about the game would own at least one system where they could buy and play it.

In the worst possible world we would release our game only on one very unpopular system. Most of our marketing and PR budget and effort would be wasted, because almost no one whom we reached would own the hardware that could play our game.

In the real world we have to balance these two extremes. Two potential choices are:

Ship one version of the game, tune it to maximize stability and retention, then expand the game audience by porting to additional appropriate platforms one at a time. This is commonly done with mobile titles covering iOS and Android (where it's easier to update and test on Android but games often earn more money on iOS), or by console games targeting Microsoft and Sony platforms and perhaps PC.

Starting with just one SKU (Stock Keeping Unit, the way that retailers refer to each unique product) has many benefits:

• You never fork the code until the game is debugged and stable, reducing both programmer time and team insanity

• You're paying attention to initial bugs and customer issues in a single context

• Your marketing budget can be targeted at a single, well-defined group of users

• Your game can get extra promotion from the platform owner, support given only to exclusive titles

This disadvantage of this strategy, of course, is that if you succeed in creating buzz and excitement about your game "it's only news once," and the media's first and greatest wave of attention will benefit only one version.

Teams often try to address this weakness by shipping "almost simultaneously," where the second version is shipped immediately after the first wave of fixes based on user reports are completed.

Massive Parallel Ports, where several versions of the game are finished, but none is released until the complete set has been fully tested and certified as ready. This is more common with major AAA console games, since their publishers can budget the salaries and overhead for the extra time and lower efficiency of the process.

Just as this is a higher-cost strategy, it also is higher reward. Publishers can spend more on marketing and PR to back the introduction of the game, since there are multiple platform audiences who will hear the message and potentially buy the title.

There are other kinds of costs involved in smaller teams shipping multiple SKU's in a relatively short period of time:

A small team's customer support may be overwhelmed by user volume, damaging the game's momentum (as happened when *Pokemon Go* exploded in popularity).

With multiple SKU's ending and others starting it can be a uniquely stressful time:

- Post-ship vacations that families have been counting on get postponed when one SKU or another delays the whole juggernaut

- People working simultaneously on three different SKU's can make it feel like nothing runs efficiently

- The smooth start you may have pictured for your next game may be punctuated by constant interruptions for team members who are not yet free of trailing SKU's

If there are platforms of secondary value, look at the revenue from their projected sales compared to the work involved. Then decide if you want to release that port sooner or after some delay... if you decide you want to port to that platform at all.

Whatever your team size, track how long you'll have to wait to receive money from your initial sales. Depending on whether you work with a publisher, Steam, an app store or other distributor, cash does not arrive immediately once you launch your game. In my career I've had to wait from 60 days to almost six months to receive money from sales. If we were working through a publisher and had received "advances against royalties" we might never receive any additional cash from sales at all.

One of the problems many teams face is paying salaries and other costs after one project finishes and before the next project starts earning money, and it's critical to conserve cash to prepare for these transitions. I'll discuss these issues in depth later in this book.

1.3.5 Don't Confuse eSports with Platforms

I've encountered several dev teams recently who are trying to custom-build games for the eSports market. This is a misguided and backwards strategy.

The relatively new term "eSports" refers to professional leagues where the world's best gamers compete in super-popular video games. Fans will fill big arenas all over the world to watch the best players in the world compete on games that the fans themselves play at home. Millions more will watch online via Twitch or other services.

The only games that are chosen by eSports leagues are those that are already huge hits, because only games that are super-popular will draw audiences in arenas and on streaming services.

That's the key fact that game development teams need to remember. You can't custom-build a game for eSports because there's no way to predict you'll have a big hit. Cloning established games is even more useless, since fans don't want to pay money to watch people play a clone of their favorite game.

So what can you do to make it more likely that your game will be selected for eSports competitions?

- Make sure you have a great 1:1 two-player game
- If appropriate, include a team vs. team online play mode, and tune it till it's great
- Hone your game's speed and responsiveness so the controls can respond to the actions of to really good players
- You can't control the latency of the network, but you can maximize the efficiency of your own network code, which will further enhance speed
- If your game does become a big hit, do updates or a new version to add features that facilitate eSports play

1.3.6 What von Moltke Understood About Business

Helmuth von Moltke was a German general and military strategist who entered military service about 200 years ago, just after the fall of Napoleon.

He is the source of a famous quote that applies to business as well as it applies to armies: *"No plan survives contact with the enemy."*

Modern pundits have twisted this line into *"No business plan survives contact with customers."*

What can you do about this problem? Take advantage of it.

From the very start of every project, I assume that some of my most treasured design ideas will have to change once we start tests with real players.

I assume that those first playtest experiences will not go very well, and that we'll have to change and tune the game to reach the point where people are having fun and want to buy it on the spot.

I assume that lots of other things we've been thinking will change and that we'll have to adapt.

Sometimes I'll go home after work and have a drink and complain to my wife that what should be working with our players isn't working.

But even as I complain I know that this is part of what makes our careers and our art form great. It's hard to get bored doing work that's unpredictable.

DISCUSSING QUESTION 1.4

In what programming language (or languages) will your game be coded?

Will you use a third party engine as the foundation for your game, or create it entirely from scratch?

If you're using an engine, will it be Unity 2D or 3D? The Unreal Engine? CryEngine? GameMaker? Something else?

This topic is most relevant for: Everyone

1.4.1 Revving Up the Engine

Until about ten years ago most game engines were proprietary tools carefully guarded and managed by game publishers and large AAA developers. Their nature as cross-platform systems made them critical to fast, efficient ports. The need to "avoid re-inventing the wheel" literally saved months – and therefore millions of dollars – on major games.

Our team built, extended and protected one of those major cross-platform engines. Although we recognized that we could make money by licensing it to other teams, we felt that the competitive advantage it gave us as an exclusive tool was of even greater value to our company.

Fast forward to today, and the world has changed dramatically. Almost all 3D action titles, whether they're from giant publishers or tiny studios, are created on one of a handful of sophisticated com-mercially-available engines.

The growth of Unity, Unreal, CryEngine and other modern engines is one of the critical sparks that ignited the explosion in the number and variety of indie game titles, and their dramatic effect on the industry. A web search highlights press reports that Unity alone is being used for almost half of all games, and represents an even higher percentage on some platforms.

Not all games need an engine, but all game teams should give serious consideration to using one. If an engine supports multiple platforms where you intend to sell your game, the benefits from dramatically faster and simpler ports justify the use of an engine even without considering the many additional benefits.

1.4.2 Building on the Right Foundation

What comes first: choosing a programming language for your title or choosing a game engine? It's a "chicken or the egg" question.

Some programmers will look for an engine that is based on their favorite language or elect to forego an engine and create the game from scratch. Others will commit to using or learning the language that works best with the engine they want to use.

Choosing a game engine – or choosing not to use one – is one of the most important decisions you'll make for your game and your company. It's a central, pivotal choice at the start of development on any game, and one which both empowers and places limitations on the project.

It's also a decision that can be extremely difficult to reverse.

What's the best game engine? There is no one right answer. If you have no prior experience with engines I recommend starting your search with Unity. It's the most widely used and has been the engine for the most diverse set of games, which means it also has the most online documentation, support groups, YouTube instruction videos, etc. But do take the time to consider all your options, because for some games other systems will be better choices.

I named four different engines in this question, but there are several others that are widely used as well, including some specifically targeted at MMO's and online games.

Unlike the environment of just a few years ago, almost any game category is easier to enter with the head start that one of the major engines will give you.

Here are some factors to consider in your engine search:

Target Platforms. The most popular engines cover all of the major game platforms, while others may have a smaller reach.

Dev Platforms. All of the major choices support development on either PC or Mac systems, and on multiple operating systems.

Cost. Engines have very different pricing plans that are based on each company's unique criteria, and different platforms of the same engine will come with different prices and business terms. You'll need to check the options for your engine or engines of choice, since prices change frequently and they all have periodic sales.

Some services charge a monthly fee per seat (i.e. per person on the team who uses the engine), with basic elements offered for free and more advanced features costing more. Others charge no fee at all for using the engine for development, but take a royalty share from the game after it's published and earns revenue.

The major services that charge by the seat all have entry-level pricing tiers aimed at indie game developers.

2D or 3D. Unity supports both 2D and 3D, Unreal and CryEngine are specialized 3D engines, though they can also be used to build 2D games. Other systems offer their own tradeoffs.

Speed requirements. For games like console shooters and driving sims that require high-speed high-resolution graphics, Unreal is the market leader and CryEngine is their top specialized rival.

Feel. Sometimes in software it isn't about pricing or features. You use one leading program and it feels right, try another popular package and it doesn't seem to respond as you'd expect.

It's important to take the time to give each potentially relevant system a test run in order to discover whether any of them feel like they were custom-built just for you.

Language Support. Unity most broadly supports C# and JavaScript, while the powerful 3D engines start with C++, though there are additional scripting language options in each case. Other systems have their own sets of choices and requirements.

Time and Learning Curve. None of the powerful engines can be called "easy to learn." If you're learning a new language and a new engine at the same time it is a significantly larger challenge. These factors also affect how soon you'll be able to complete and ship version 1.0 of your game, since you have to factor for learning time.

If you are not a programmer the simplest games in the GameMaker Studio engine are made with no coding at all, with just a drag and drop interface that moves objects on the screen. But to go very far in their system you have to learn their own proprietary scripting language.

Unity, Unreal and CryEngine have also implemented visual programming menus to give non-programmers a chance to create less complex games in their systems.

Professional Development. Learning how to use a popular engine, especially one where you're coding, is a very valuable skill that also advances your career. Be sure to factor for this in your thinking.

CHAPTER 6

What Came Before (1.5)

DISCUSSING QUESTION 1.5

Is this your first game of this scale?

Have you pursued lots of indie games in your life?

Have you worked on other initiatives or startups that were similar in size to this project?

This topic is most relevant for: Everyone.

1.5.1 What Kinds of Dreams are Driving Me?

Some of the game teams I advise are made up of industry veterans who work inside large publishers. Others are launching their first indie company after gaining years of experience. I've advised teams of recent graduates whose school project spontaneously turned into a company.

People from any of these backgrounds can succeed, but they each face very different challenges. It's good to ask yourself what it is that's motivating you to start on this project, and if that motivation will sustain you to completion of version 1.0.

If you're a startup veteran, are you excited about being part of a new venture again? Is this unique concept truly compelling to you?

If you're leading your first company, is it the project itself that drives your passion, or is it the opportunity to captain your own ship for the first time?

If you're a recent grad, is it this game that motivates and drives you? Or is it the excitement of finally getting out of school and getting to work on real projects for (we hope) real paychecks?

If you're an individual setting out to make extra money doing part-time work that you love to do, are you ready to do the necessary paperwork and spend the required fees to go into business? Or do you just want to spend more time at a favorite activity?

1.5.2 A+, not AAA

AAA titles like *FIFA* or *Call of Duty* have hundreds of developers on their teams. *PlayerUnknown's Battlegrounds* already had 70 team members as the project started to take shape.

It's easy to think, "We want to build a game that looks as good, plays as well, and feels as deep as that one! We'll just make it smaller since we're a three-person team."

AAA games are called that because they require big teams and big budgets. If we try to build "smaller big games" as indies it's like trying to hike across Antarctica without a big support team. It's not going to turn out well.

I've designed and programmed one-person games, led small game dev teams and directed many AAA console titles. These are all very different challenges, and it's vital that we always choose the mission that's the right size for us.

What kinds of projects can we be doing two years or five years from now? That's fun to talk about, but we have to keep focusing on today.

AAA is about scale and size and quality. With tens of millions of dollars at risk any game that isn't really fun will be canceled early in development.

An "A" title is a really good game, and it doesn't have to be big. But even "A" games can get lost in a world with hundreds of thousands of competitors. Setting out to build an "A" game is setting the bar dangerously low.

"A+" is a very difficult goal to reach. How do you know when you've done it?

- "I have to tell all my friends about this."
- "I wanted to go to bed two hours ago but I just couldn't stop playing."
- "The first thing I did when I got up was check my game."

An "A+" is a game that attracts and retains passionate players. To build a truly successful indie game we need to inspire those feelings in our users.

1.5.3 The Post-Disruption Economy

If you've grown up with indie games, browser titles and touch-screen platforms, you're already a citizen of what I call the "Post-Disruption Economy."

There are lots of articles about "the Disruption Economy," the new patterns and methods in business since online apps starting gobbling market share in every segment. We've lived through:

"The traditional way of doing things," which for many years was a market dominated by boxed games, three console makers and a handful of large publishers.

"The coming of Disruption," when smartphones, browsers, Facebook and other platforms created many new genres, business models and audiences.

The number of indie game makers exploded. Many of the big publishers said to themselves, "We've seen all this before. It's a fad, it'll start to fade away. We're the ones, not Apple or Google or Valve, who will define what happens next."

"The Post-Disruption Economy," where it's now clear that the new audiences and platforms aren't small and are not going away.

The console market has already been reinvigorated in recent years as the hardware makers and game publishers embraced the same new digital channels and business models they once dismissed.

But consoles are now just one major component of a much larger and more vibrant games market.

I use the term "Post-Disruption Economy" to say that the battle is over. The genii aren't going back in their bottles. The old world is not returning.

If you consciously decide to operate as a citizen of that new, forever-changed world, you'll have an advantage in every phase of your indie game business over those who think that "disruption will settle down and the world will feel more comfortable and familiar again."

1.5.4 Smaller Budgets Can Build Bigger Games

Our financial resources for building indie games aren't just finite, they're often tiny. By being clever about how we leverage reusable assets, however, we can make our indie titles look bigger than their budgets.

Most of the costs for building games are tied to payroll and other people expenses, so anything that saves a lot of time can also save a lot of money. (And remember that living off your savings while you build your game is just another form of payroll!)

Here are some ideas to start you thinking about how to re-use assets in your indie game:

Stylized characters and environments. When we build realistic characters and environments we're always tuning, fixing, trying to improve our graphics and our animations. That's because players – including a game's creators – notice every little difference when you're trying to perfectly reproduce nature. Our eyes notice every tiny flaw.

Make a list of your favorite Pixar and Disney characters, TV characters like those in *The Simpsons* and *Family Guy*, or old cartoon characters like Bugs Bunny or Wile E. Coyote. You'll notice that most of them are not realistic. They're stylized, often with unique, recognizable silhouettes.

Because they don't look realistic, our eyes are not always finding fault with how these characters look or move. And game developers don't have to spend anywhere near as much time creating or tuning their models, rigging and animations.

Look at the backgrounds and environments that go with those favorite characters. You'll see they have simplified palettes, along with stylized landscapes, buildings and props. The colors, resolution, line style, proportions and everything else fit the designs used for the characters and objects.

Note: In the characters discussion below I focus on 3D games, but many of the same issues apply to 2D.

How could a stylized look and reusable assets make your game feel both fun and unique? Here are some initial ideas:

Make identical characters a feature, not a liability. We're used to playing games where there are many identical orcs, aliens, robots or monsters to defeat in battle. It's also routine to have characters with similar body types, so different skins differentiate their look and their rigs and animations can be re-used. But there are other kinds of identical characters who can be fun and interesting for the player.

In the *Toy Story* movies the Little Green Men with three eyes all look identical, but many of them appear together in scenes and we accept that they're individuals. The minions in *Despicable Me* all have some unique identifying characteristic, but those differences are skins or props. The characters as a group have very few different body types, and since their arms and legs are re-used across those body types their rigs and animations can also be re-used across many different characters.

Does your game idea allow for any identical or almost identical characters? Can roles for which you would have had to model, rig and animate a separate, unique figure be combined into one body type in this way? If you were planning to have eight distinct character models, is there a way to use these ideas to reduce the total to four or five?

Make environments do double duty. If RAM usage and file size are not an issue on any of your indie game's target platforms, engines like Unity, Unreal and CryEngine support the creation of procedurally generated terrain, so large scale, detailed maps become efficient to implement.

On platforms that require smaller footprints, however, levels and regions can serve double duty, just as the game's character models may do. Take a look at your game's level layouts or region maps and consider:

Reversing entrance and exit. In games where a player has to play from point A to point B, look for an opportunity to later have them play from Point B to Point A. This can be done explicitly by creating missions like "Fight your way back to the besieged fort at Clovyr Crossing to bring the energy shield to its brave defenders!"

In exterior locations, starship corridors, caves or monotonous cityscapes it may also be possible to reverse the direction of travel and disguise what you're doing from the player. Terrain can look very different when viewed from the opposite angle, and you may have played these reversed levels in other games without even realizing it. Level designers can heighten the effect by changing the lighting, skybox or elements like trees, boulders etc.

If your game has combat, enemies can use the terrain to fight in different styles the second time you use the level. You could have melee action in one direction, ranged combat in the other. Or wave attacks the first time through and snipers the second, etc. This further disguises the repeated environment.

Using mirror images. Think about mirroring and rotating maps, layouts or environments in different ways, in different scales, and on the x, y and z axes:

A 2D side-scroller where you fly through terrain could generate a second level by being mirrored in either the x-axis (so entrance and exit are reversed), or in the y-axis (so the stalactites become the stalagmites, or the floor becomes the ceiling).

A wilderness setting could have the altitude of its terrain mirrored, so the valleys turn into mountains and mountains become basins, canyons, fjords or sea floor. If you created natural paths in the original level they'll still be there in the non-submerged reversed terrain, and most trees, vegetation and props are likely to feel appropriate in the identical spots.

You can turn a seaside area into a new block of inland terrain by changing the elevation of each point into an absolute value , so the beach becomes a tectonic fault with mountains on either side. The new mountains are simply the reversed altitude of the sea bottom for the same terrain used elsewhere in the game.

Using different sizes of tiles. On many games the environments are tiled in a way so that the user sees clearly how the environment is structured. The visible tile system makes it clear to the player where they can move, where they can't, and how the terrain will affect movement.

Sets of 16×16, 32×32, 64×64 tiles etc. can each then be viewed as tiles themselves, reused and rotated at different angles to build much larger maps with connecting pathways wandering through them. This can produce maps that compress especially well on platforms where RAM is a scarce commodity, and which also can decompress rapidly.

Stamps. These larger tiles can also be rotated and overlaid as stamps to disguise the repetitive geometry, even in urban environments. These can be simple 90-degree rotations or more complex diagonal angles.

1.5.5 K.I.S.S.

The old saying, "Keep it simple, stupid!" (usually abbreviated as KISS) applies intensely to the process of game design. This issue comes in five flavors, all of which are themes that reappear throughout this book:

Start with a small game that fits the size and strengths of your indie team, as we discussed above.

Keep the play mechanics simple. Chess has been a successful game for centuries because it is easy to learn but challenging to master. Try to design your first game to emulate those qualities, which can apply to any platform and genre.

Avoid complexity creep. I'm always thinking of great new "small features" I can add to my game. But if I interrupt the truly important work for small distractions the game may never be completed at all.

Start playtests with outside players as soon as you can, and keep testing until the game is shipped and stable. The only way to know you have a great game is to see impartial new players learn and love it.

Keep doing your best work. A critical skill for people in the arts is the discipline to do your very best work every time you sit at the computer, the tablet or the drawing board. "I have to be proud of any piece that bears my name" is a powerful credo.

My mother was a professional illustrator and painter, and she learned about these issues of focus and distraction through her work. She told me the following fable that relates to how we challenge ourselves in our careers.

1.5.6 The Juggler and the Fifth Ball

Once upon a time, my mother told me, there was a young man who learned how to juggle. His father taught him to keep three balls in the air at once and he amazed everyone in his little village.

The boy moved to the big city and a local street performer taught him how to juggle four balls. It was difficult, but the young man made steady progress.

One day the young man asked his mentor to teach him how to juggle five balls.

The grizzled old man shook his head. "You are not yet ready," he told him. "You must master four balls before you juggle five. Do not stop when you achieve success. Seek mastery."

The boy protested, "I'm getting better every week! I know I can do it!"

Against his better judgment, the mentor relented. He taught the boy the techniques for keeping five balls in the air. The young man practiced hour after hour, and after just a few days he kept all five going while the old man counted to ten.

The wrinkled juggler nodded his approval.

That weekend, the mentor and the student performed together in the town square. The young man juggled four balls in the air, earning applause from the crowd.

Although the old man had forbidden him to do so, the boy suddenly pulled a fifth ball from his pocket and kept all five balls flying with his graceful movements. The crowd started to cheer, but then something went wrong.

A ball tipped off the boy's fingertips and fell towards the cobblestones. He lunged for it and two more balls eluded him. Soon all five balls had rolled away in all directions.

The crowd sighed. There were no boos, no jeers. They just wandered away. Soon the old performer and the boy stood all alone in the empty plaza.

"I'm sorry, sir," the boy told his mentor. "I should have waited to try to juggle five balls at a time in public."

The old man smiled. "It's all right, son. I knew that this would happen. But I wanted you to learn the most important lesson I could ever teach you."

"What's that, sir?" the boy asked.

The old juggler pointed to the balls scattered around the town square. "That's the lesson," he said. "When you reach for one too many of anything, you don't just drop that one. You drop everything else you were juggling before you went too far."

CHAPTER 7

Generations of Dreams (1.6–1.9)

DISCUSSING QUESTION 1.6

Dreams change as we live our lives. What is a game you once really hoped to create, but that is no longer as important to you?

This topic is most relevant for: Everyone

1.6.1 Learning from Our Past

I'm asking this question for several reasons:

Could the past idea, once you think about it, still be interesting to you? Could it be more interesting than what you wrote down as your current game?

Why did you lose interest in this older idea? Could you lose interest in your current idea in the same way? Or is your current game fundamentally different?

Did you abandon the prior idea because of some change in your life or in the games industry? Could you come back to it now?

Here's an exercise I like to do, which works for many kinds of projects in addition to games:

I'll start by writing down the one-sentence summary of the old idea, and the year in which I first came up with it.

Then I write the current year on the paper or screen.

Then I ask myself, "For this 'old' concept to be fascinating and a potential hit now, what would I have to change?"

The two dates on the page focus my thoughts on what has changed in hardware, the software marketplace, our business models. and in game audiences since I loved that old idea. For example:

- Could the game concept work even better on a new platform (e.g. Nintendo Switch)?

- Are there new interfaces (e.g. VR) that would make the game even more fun to play?

- Does the growth in the power of Unity, Unreal and CryEngine make the dev budget more realistic? Do the modern features in these top game engines suggest new kinds of visuals or gameplay?

- If I re-invent the story and characters but keep the gameplay (or vice versa) does the game suddenly sound vibrant and modern?

- If the genre has become crowded since then, could the gameplay migrate to a newer category? Could my endless runner become a retro RPG, where all that hand-crafted terrain would get a lot more use?

- Does the easy availability of 1:1 and team-based online play add something that makes the idea great again?

- Can an old packaged-game idea find new audiences in a world increasingly dominated by digital downloads of games, freed from the huge costs of manufacturing?

- There are lots of new audiences who've labeled themselves as gamers in the last few years – could this idea be adapted to appeal to them?

- What happens if the settlers become robots... or the terrifying aliens become cute bunny rabbits?
- Would something completely outrageous make the old idea brand new? Could the vampires seeking blood become time travelers looking for gluten-free sushi restaurants on the Left Bank in Paris in the 1920's?

Get together with your teammates or friends, indulge in your favorite beverage and brainstorm!

One last secret: All the approaches I just described for your old project will also work to make your new idea more unique and innovative as well!

DISCUSSING QUESTION 1.7

What game do you think you may want to build a few years from now that isn't as important to you today?

Why will you care more about it in a few years than you do now?

This topic is most relevant for: Everyone

1.7.1 Trapped in Our Own Web

We often temper our dreams with the need to be practical.

An engineer might say to herself, "It pays really well, but I'm bored with this non-games job. I'd love to build a Japanese-style PC platformer, but Steam is full of indie platformer games and all my games industry experience is in mobile. I'll go indie by creating mobile puzzle games since I play a lot of them and I know them well. I'm a lot more likely to be able to pay the bills with that strategy."

So the Japanese-style platformer gets filed in the "many years from now" department, even though it's the passion project. The mobile puzzle games are interesting, but not compelling.

The title of this book is, "Indie Games: From Dream to Delivery." It's not, "Plan your way to the next thing you think you ought to do, or that other people tell you that you should do."

We choose what we do each day, each week, each month. But our dreams tend to choose us instead of the other way around. They make themselves known via our hearts, and then our heads have to listen.

Of course, sometimes the real world makes these issues more complex. Our fictional engineer may have a family to help support with that good paycheck, and may even be helping an elderly parent as well. Just walking away from a well-paying job to try something new that may not earn any money isn't always a realistic option.

But if this engineer's passion lies with creating a Japanese-style platformer and she dreads going to the office each day to work on credit card systems, there might be other choices that don't involve risking her family finances.

She could reserve a few hours each week at night, early in the morning or on weekends to start work on the platformer part-time, using Unity or a different engine to simplify the project.

If she enjoys free-lance work and knows where to find a steady stream of assignments, she could leave the job she hates and go indie by contracting out as an engineer. But she might save one day a week or one week between each smaller project to work on the platformer.

None of this may apply to you, and your current indie game may be one that you're pursuing passionately.

But if your 20-years-from-now indie game is more exciting than the one we've been discussing, is there a way to pursue it now instead of later?

1.7.2 Changing Lanes

I've just advised you to stick to your passions in creating the indie game you really want to build, even if you don't feel your previous experience is relevant. But I can think of an exception, a case where more care is required.

I go to lots of evening meetups in San Francisco. In fact, I scan the events each week for a wide range of groups, looking for sessions where I can learn something new or get updated in areas that are changing rapidly.

At one recent games meetup I met an interesting man in his mid-30's. He had been working in theatre and film for almost fifteen years, but he loved games. He was resolved that he wanted to switch industries and start up his own indie games business.

He told me he knew that he was setting out to climb a steep, tall mountain, but that he felt his passion would help bring him to the top.

Here's what I told him:

I majored in playwriting in college, and had some professional success in theatre shortly after I graduated. I won a "New Voices" playwriting award from a major foundation.

It wasn't long, however, before the video games industry began. I became one of the original five programmers at what would grow into one of the largest development teams in the world. Two years later I was Design Director for a major video game console.

That was over 35 years ago, and the games industry has been my career – and my only major source of income – ever since.

"I was professionally trained in theatre and made money there 40 years ago," I told my new friend. "What advice would you give me if I told you I want to change careers and go to work in the theatre again? And I have to earn enough money doing it to support my family?"

He looked down, ran his fingers back through his hair, then looked up at the ceiling for a moment. "It's a tough business," he finally said. "A lot of it depends on... You have to have skills to make a living. And a network. You have to have something you're really good at, and you have to have worked with different groups of people so they'll call you whenever they start a project and they ask you to come work with them."

"That's great advice," I told him. "I had great training long ago, but I've spent my whole life building games. I don't have any of the in-demand skills – let alone a network of allies – to just go back to the theatre and make a living."

He thought about this for a moment. "So you're telling me to give up?" he asked.

"No," I told him. "I'm suggesting that the safer course is to go find a job in the games industry, a place where you can learn those skills and grow your network. Then start thinking about founding your indie game company a few years down the line."

"That's... I really care about this. Games are what I love to do."

"Then don't give up," I told him. "Just take a realistic path instead of a dangerous one."

I hope I see him again at another games meetup. I'm very curious about what he chose to do.

DISCUSSING QUESTION 1.8

Do you have ideas for additional content or follow-up products that can be introduced if the first game is a success?

This topic is most relevant for: Everyone planning to create a company that produces more than one game

1.8.1 Is It a Game or a Company?

If you plan to build your indie game but not build a second game after it's completed, you're not trying to create an enduring company. That's a perfectly reasonable goal, and the rest of this question's discussion won't be relevant.

If you are planning to keep going on a second game, that project may turn out to be even harder to launch than your first.

Very few first games make enough money to fully fund the creation of a second game. Most first games don't even break even on their own costs.

Very few games grow into franchises that remain popular and profitable for more than a few years. That's why even highly successful companies like EA, Microsoft, Sony, Nexon, Tencent and Wargaming are continually trying out new ideas.

Investors often tell CEO's after a pitch, "You have a product, not a company."

If the CEO is from our industry, what they're saying is, "You have one good idea. Even if we assume it becomes a hit, when that strong game eventually fades, there's no plan for what happens next."

Like all other products, games have life cycles. They are born, they grow, they start to age and eventually they die. For some games it takes a few days and for others it may take many years, but eventually any game will see declining revenues.

Even small publishers that are well-established have to sell multiple existing games and develop new ones, so that the revenue for the early stages of new products offsets the inevitable decline of older ones.

Put serious thought into how you could extend your product line, starting with DLC (DownLoadable Content) and moving on to sequels, extensions and successor products.

DISCUSSING QUESTION 1.9

Is it the technology involved in the making of the game that interests you?

Is it the genre or category of the game? The platform on which you'll create the original version? The style of interface?

Or do you take joy in the visuals of the game? The audio?

Some combination of the above choices?

This topic is most relevant for: Everyone

1.9.1 Passions Squared

Your passions are your greatest source of personal strength. When they are combined with strong professional skills you become a beacon that will attract other quality-focused people.

As you set out to create your indie game, are there ways to polish or grow the professional skills that magnify the value of your passions?

Is there a class you could take to update important skills, or to fill a gap in your training or experience? I've taken two evening tech classes this year and got a lot out of them.

Are there Meetup.com events you could attend to hear speakers who'll bring you up to date on best practices? I usually attend one or two such sessions a week, and they play a key role in my ability to adapt to changing markets and methods.

Keep looking for ways to enhance your knowledge, expertise and skills, so you can magnify your passions most effectively.

1.9.2 Passions Crossed

Our passions for one part of the process of making games can also create problems.

I once worked with a team that that had hired a talented new artist to create environments for an exploration-focused action game. But there was a problem.

"I've told him three times that the plaza scenes need a wider play-field area," the frustrated team leader complained to me. "And the side streets are designed for melee combat, but players keep dying because they can't see the enemies because it's too dark."

"Sounds like an easy fix," I told him.

"I wish," he groaned. "Our wonderful new artist won't change any-thing because he likes the mood of the space and he's decided that mood is more important than gameplay."

This tale (where I have changed many details to protect those involved) is a case where someone was passionate about one part of the project, not passionate about the whole game.

That doesn't work in game development. Our passions for the pieces have to be part of a greater passion for the game that peo-ple will love to play.

It isn't just one discipline that does this:

An engineer on a story-based game might build user menus that look like a printer interface. He staunchly defends them, saying "it's a consistent, rule-based system."

A designer might keep producing intricate hyper-advanced challenges for a puzzle game when the project is behind schedule and missing half of its early levels, arguing that "without depth we have no game."

I've fallen into the trap of adding extra small features that benefitted one aspect of the game at the expense of the greater experience. Not good.

As leaders it's our job to keep every individual on the team – including ourselves – focused on our passion for building great games.

In the worst cases a team member who can't take direction must be removed from the team quickly, as painful as such decisions may be. Leaders have to be willing to take such steps when the quality of the game is threatened by under-performing or uncooperative people.

CHAPTER 8

The Indie Game as a Product (1.10-1.11)

DISCUSSING QUESTION 1.10

What makes you believe that this game will draw players' attention in a crowded market?

Is this a completely new idea, or are you setting out to improve on a game that already exists?

This topic is most relevant for: Everyone

1.10.1 Your Best Friend Who Lives Next Door

As I've noted, most discussions of the business side of game publishing will be found in the second half of this book.

But there's one business topic I want to bring up early on. It's so central to the success of your game that you'll want to start thinking about it in the earliest stages of development.

Some really lucky kids live next door to their best friend. They go to school together, go to soccer practice on the same team and double date to the junior prom.

No matter how fascinating your answer to the question "What will draw players' attention?" may sound, you need to recognize that you need "a best friend next door," too.

Hint: It will be the person who leads the marketing for your game. Marketing is the element of the games publishing business that has to work hand-in-hand with game development through every step of the process.

If I just published this book and did nothing else to promote it, I know what would happen. Even the mighty power of Amazon, Barnes & Noble and Ingram would produce almost no sales at all, because this book would be lost in a sea of other books.

It's easy for us as game developers who've worked inside large publishers to think of marketing as "something somebody else does at the end of a project after we've done our part."

But as indies we are often responsible for our own marketing. We are faced with two choices:

- Spend long hours doing online research to learn what other successful indie teams have done to get games noticed. Go to Meetups, conferences, indie game festivals etc. to meet others and learn from them. Or...

- Find and work with one or more people who have experience in successfully promoting indie games without risking a lot of money.

As we discuss the next few questions in this section I'll raise a number of the key steps and issues involved in indie game marketing to help you plan for both "sides" of the publishing process.

1.10.2 What the Marketers Know

First of all, they know that in order to have great marketing you have to start with a great game. I was taught an invaluable lesson early in my career:

Great marketing cannot rescue weak game design. It just helps a bad game fail faster.

Whether it's dishwashers or indie games, marketers are trained that you have to connect to users through a four-step process in order to sell to them. This is an extension of "the buyer's journey," a traditional concept taught in business schools. The four steps are:

Step 1: Awareness: Appear in the user's research. As they research games they may want to buy, they have to be able to find you. In games we call this "player discovery."

Step 2: Consideration: Hit the right emotional notes. I'll discuss this issue in more detail below, but we buy things because we get an emotional desire for them. Your teaser video, your screen shots, the words you use to describe your game, the game's web page and all your other marketing and publicity materials have to inspire that spontaneous interest and emotion.

Step 3: Decision: Sell the game in the form that they want to buy. How do people who love your kind of play experience like to buy games? What platforms do they buy on? You have to sell through the online stores they're used to using, at a price point that feels routine, and support the target platforms where they concentrate their play.

Step 4: Retention: Keep them playing. Players who get bored quickly and quit are going to tell all their friends that your game is lame. Those who keep playing are likely to recommend it. Monitor your forums closely and interact with your players, so the company feels human and not like some distant corporation. Implement suggestions from your players, so they can see you listen and respect their opinions.

Marketers know that you have to get people through these steps of the buyer's journey in order to make them committed customers. Which brings us to The Elephant in the Room.

1.10.3 The Elephant in the Room: Player Discovery

There are over 3 million active apps in the iOS App Store alone as of this writing. Over 750,000 of them are games. Google Play's store has 2.75 million apps, and over 100 new games are submitted every day.

But there's an "Elephant in the Room," a problem so big that it cannot be ignored but that many people don't want to talk about.

These exciting statistics, with their story of millions of apps and games competing for attention, tell us that this new wave of opportunity and innovation brings with it major new problems – big problems. They all fit under the heading of player discovery.

Yes, that's the same player discovery we just listed as the first of the four steps in selling your game. And that's where I said that if you don't solve the problem of player discovery, your game is going nowhere.

We may work for months or even years to reach the point where we're ready to share our new game, this unique piece of ourselves that we want the world to love.

All too often, however, when we launch those games into the world something very frustrating happens.

No one has heard about the game. Because no one has heard of it, no one has tried the game. Because no one has tried it, no one can tell their friends about the game.

It just sits there in the online store. You check it every half hour and nothing changes. No sales. Day after day. No sales.

It's a terrible feeling.

Many new indie games never find a significant audience and never generate much money, if any at all.

Most new indie games today are created without a real marketing plan, which is one (but not the only) reason why they never make much revenue.

The big publishers, who may count their annual revenue in the billions of dollars, already have the email addresses of millions of players. They can send targeted emails to the users whose play patterns predict that they'll like a new game. The publishers control the ad banners that accompany their current games, and can use them to promote new titles.

When they ship a new game they have a sophisticated marketing plan. They send detailed information to a wide range of game journalists to build buzz before its release. They have the money to pay popular influencers to promote their games to their large online audiences.

With all these tools at their disposal the big publishers can create a wave of initial interest. If the game is fun to play that wave of PR, free ads, paid ads on other media and emails can generate enough word-of-mouth promotion to make it a success.

For small indie publishers there is no ready-made legion of existing players to whom we can promote our new titles. Our press releases don't automatically generate stories on the big websites or in the pages of major magazines.

Using limited funds to buy online ads or hire major influencers to promote a game that has not yet proven itself is almost certain financial suicide.

When a team ships its first game it's like moving to a new town and starting classes mid-semester at a huge new school. You're surrounded by a sea of faces but no one knows or notices you.

There is no easy recipe for solving this problem of Player Discovery. I share a lot of experiences and suggestions in the pages that follow, but I can't tell you how to guarantee success.

So why do we even try? When the odds are so tough, why do so many people still build and sell indie games?

Because it's work we love to do. We know that *some* great games from indie teams will find ways to get noticed and make money. Some of them will make a lot of money.

I'm working on a new indie game in parallel to writing this book. I don't share the statistics above to discourage you.

I share them so you go into the project with your eyes open and you're ready to manage the risks as well as the rewards. So you're ready to embrace strong marketing and strong marketers. So you're willing to learn new ways of building, testing and shipping games in order to earn the title of Indie.

If you're building indie games because you've been told it's a relatively easy way to make good money, whoever told you this was lying.

If you're building indie games because it's what you love to do and you're out to create a great game, I'm here to help.

If you're with me, let's keep going.

1.10.4 The Advantages of Small Indie Teams

Big companies have many advantages, but there are key advantages for small startups, too.

Short Approval Chains. I once worked with a publisher where it took 23 different signoffs to approve the box art for a game. You can imagine how long it took to get approvals on each title!

Small teams can accomplish as much going out to lunch and discussing a decision as a big company can accomplish in a month with fourteen meetings.

Deeper Commitment. Small teams that start new companies have a lot more freedom of action, a lot more individual impact on the game and many more potential rewards than the people at the big publishers. They're not just doing a job and picking up a paycheck, they're doing work in which they deeply believe. Some people working at the big companies are this motivated, but they're not what drive big corporate cultures.

Sharp Focus. Managing one game makes everyone focus on the details. A big company that has a catalog of 36 active games lacks that same across-the-board attention to the little things that add up to great games.

Freedom to Do Something New. Big publishers have to make big profits every quarter and every year in order to maintain and grow their stock price. They can't do projects that feel risky because stock analysts value companies with predictable revenue and profits. Small teams operate under none of these restrictions, which is why so much of our technical and creative innovation comes from smaller teams.

Lower Costs. Big publishers have to spend money on long term leases for large office complexes. Small teams can work in less expensive settings without long term leases.

Fast Reaction Times. If all five people in a company work together in one room and a game is losing its audience after level five, they'll keep attacking the problem until they find a way to fix it.

If someone in a large company notices the problem, however, questions arise:

- "Will my manager be angry if I share this, since he was the one who told us to crank up level five?"
- "Will I waste a lot of time on this without anyone following up and implementing a fix?"
- "I'm in operations and this is a design problem. Will anyone even listen to me?"
- "Is there a senior exec who signed off on the build who'll be embarrassed and angry if I report this?"

Researcher and analyst Dr. Chris Argyris of Harvard Business School wrote a landmark article about this issue, *Double Loop Learning in Organizations* (which you can find online via Google).

He pointed out that large organizations have layers of resistance to sharing bad news. The initial report of "40% of players quit after level five!" is diluted at each layer. By the time it gets to a high level it says, "Need to refine marketing message to set clear expectations."

If you don't hear about problems you can't try to fix them, and small teams working closely together out-perform their big rivals at this important skill.

1.10.5 The Two Acceptable Market Positions

Years ago I worked at Electronic Arts when it was still a small startup. Even in its infancy EA had an all-star marketing team. Our CEO, Trip Hawkins, had been Director of Marketing for Apple, starting there shortly after Steve Jobs and Steve Wozniak launched the flagship Apple II personal computer.

Marketing VP Bing Gordon (now a partner at VC firm Kleiner Perkins) and his early teammates David Grady and Stan Roach all joined with us in Product Development to operate informally as a single team, debating issues in a climate remarkably free of politics and ego.

All of these guys are brilliant, and they taught me many important business lessons. One of them is especially critical:

There are only two acceptable market positions for a product: First and Best.

If you're the first game in a category, you're unique. If your game is really fun to play, that's a very good combination.

If you're the best game in a category, you stand out. New and recurring sales come to you the same way that water flows down-hill.

But what if there's already a First and already a Best in your game category?

Hooked: How to Build Habit-Forming Products, by Nir Eyal, talks about how being "just a little bit better" won't move people to change their habits or to spend their money. Eyal is also an outstanding speaker and you can find videos of his talks online.

He shares how researchers have found that the process of deciding to buy a certain product moves from the decision-making part of the brain to the repeating-habits-without-thinking part of the brain.

Once someone becomes a regular player in our game they're likely to stay. That's good when we're the ones building that loyalty, but tough when it's extra hard to get our competitors' players to come play our titles. This is a key reason why First and Best are the only truly strong starting positions.

I've seen a long list of beautiful copycat MOBA's looking to compete with *League of Legends*, *DOTA 2*, *Heroes of the Storm* and other mar-ket leaders.

Each has some unique take on the MOBA experience. But would you stop watching the Super Bowl if someone came up with a football variant that was a little more exciting? Even if you enjoyed this new style of play, you'd stick with the NFL because it's a habit that you share with all your friends.

Since First and Best are the most rewarding goals, is there a way to make your game the first title in a new genre instead of just another entry in an old category?

What would it take to build the best title in your genre?

If your category is crowded with big-budget competitors, is there a similar category or another platform where it will be easier to be first or best?

1.10.6 The Blue Ocean and the Green Swamp

Every few years a new best-selling book comes along that tells us how we should dramatically change the way that startups innovate.

These books often have real value, and in fact I refer to several of them in this volume. But their simple terminology can hide traps, even as it teaches us new ways to find treasure.

One such book is *Blue Ocean Strategy* by W. Chan Kim and Renee Mauborgne. The authors point out ways in which companies didn't take an existing product category and produce a better item or service in that category. Instead, they produced products that created entirely new categories, where they had no competitors.

You'll hear me use the word "unique" a lot in this book, and producing unique products that many people love is a great and appropriate goal.

One of the most famous "Blue Ocean" examples actually comes from the games business. In the mid-2000's Sony and Microsoft were locked in an ongoing battle to produce the most sophisticated video game console to serve the most demanding players.

Nintendo realized that their rivals were so focused on the high-end core audience that an even larger audience was not being served. There are many people who like playing games but don't have the time or interest to master challenging AAA titles. As the emergence of casual games has shown, this audience was looking for games that were simpler to learn and play, and which required shorter time commitments.

So Nintendo produced the Wii. Instead of using controllers covered with buttons, the Wii let you move a smaller, lighter remote in the air, so to play golf you swung the controller like a golf club. It had simpler graphics, games that were easy to learn, and cost far less than its rivals.

And for over two years the Wii confounded Sony and Microsoft by outselling the PS3 and the Xbox 360, forcing them to add the same functionality to their machines. The Wii was a huge surprise hit.

This is an example of a brilliant Blue Ocean strategy succeeding. So why did I mention a Green Swamp?

Let's say that I'm going to open a new restaurant. I'm all excited as I tell you about my brilliant Blue Ocean idea. My restaurant will have:

- No salads on the menu. Everyone has salads.
- No burgers. Fast food places have burgers.
- No sandwiches or pizza, default lunches for many people. Same for seafood, noodles and soups.
- No fatty foods like bacon or sausages or deli meats, no eggs, no sweet breakfast dishes or desserts.
- Nothing Italian, Thai, French, Indian, Japanese, etc. because those niches are saturated.

This is a Blue Ocean Strategy, because my restaurant is not like any other restaurant. But this approach forgets a key fact:

Making a small audience very happy with any product or ser-

vice doesn't work if you don't earn enough money to keep the business operating.

My hypothetical restaurant probably won't draw enough customers to make money. Once I exhaust my savings I'd have to close the business.

Blue Ocean products serve large groups of users that were being ignored or forgotten by existing companies. Green Swamp products serve small groups that will generate relatively little revenue, and they are usually fatal to the startups that produce them.

DISCUSSING QUESTION 1.11

If you could describe your indie game to a stranger in just one sentence that would interest him or her, what would that sentence be?

What are the three most important features that will make someone want to play your game and spend money on the title?

This topic is most relevant for: Everyone

1.11.1 The Great One-Liner

This kind of statement is called a "high concept" or "the x-factor" in some media businesses, or a "positioning statement" in other segments. It may also just be called "the one-line pitch."

The value of the one-liner (and the feature list we discuss next) isn't limited to promoting your game and your team. The thinking that goes into these top-level descriptions also benefits you by laying the foundation for the core of your game design.

Whatever you decide to write as your one line summary, it has to accurately describe the heart of your game.

Here are some examples to inspire you (written in my words, not those of the publishers):

- *League of Legends*: Multiplayer online battles where you and your friends team up in a Warcraft III-inspired world

- *Grand Theft Auto*: A cinematic story-driven open-world action game where players can do almost anything, good or evil

- *MLB: The Show*: A baseball game that's so realistic you can recognize the faces of real major league players

1.11.2 The Loud Party

Here's an exercise I use to teach the process of writing a great one-line summary:

Imagine you're at a party, and that you're single. The music is loud, so you have to raise your voice and you don't hear every word of what people are saying.

Out of nowhere, a friend introduces you to one of the most attractive people you've ever met. You control the urge to stammer awkwardly when you say hello. The new person says, "I hear you're working on a really interesting new game! What is it?"

At that moment someone across the room calls out to your new friend. They wave back and call out "Be there in a moment!" Then they turn back to hear your answer to their question.

You have just one sentence in which to describe your game in a way that will impress this gorgeous person and make them want to circle back to talk with you. The room is loud, and their friend is waiting impatiently.

What do you say in just a few very clear words to make your project – and you – sound fascinating?

1.11.3 After the One-Liner

The one-line description is designed to make your game appeal to people in two important ways: logically and emotionally.

In the words of Bill Reichert of Garage Ventures, we're going for the "Wow!" factor. The one-line description tries to capture all that "Wow!" in just a few words.

After the drama of a "Wow!" statement, the best way to keep their interest is with facts.

Look back at the three features you listed for your indie game. Are they the three things that are most likely to make someone want to download or buy it?

Do they make your game sound unique, so it stands out in a sea of "slightly different" titles?

Ask friends or associates who are familiar with your game to tell you what they think are the three most important features you should present on your Steam, app store or website listing.

You may give them a list of ten or more potential features to start the discussion, but don't tell them in advance which ones you think you should emphasize.

If you're like me, you'll often get very different answers from the ones you chose all by yourself. On one project an advisor was thrilled about a feature that I thought was secondary and took for granted.

It turns out that the game's audience agreed with the advisor, and it was lucky that I'd sought out that advice.

1.11.4 The Power of Characters and Stories

A game that has interesting characters and stories is easier to describe, it's a more interesting pitch to hear, and often it's a more entertaining game to play.

Angry Birds was a clone of prior games like *Crush the Castle*, and far outsold its predecessors. The designers added a story, fun cartoon characters and a simpler game mechanic to the earlier games' designs.

In *Crush the Castle* I always felt bad about toppling buildings on the heads of medieval men and women whom I knew nothing about. What had they done wrong?

In *Angry Birds* the pigs steal unhatched eggs from the birds' nests so they can eat then. They snort, taunting the little birds. No wonder the birds are so angry! I want to knock down those buildings and punish those pigs!

This strategy only works for the first title that uses it. *Angry Birds* has itself been cloned many times by competitors, with little success.

1.11.5 Don't Confuse Features with Styles

We've all heard the advice, "Your game has to have exciting features and its own unique style."

I think that's good input. If your game looks like hundreds of other games, it's hard to get noticed. If your game could have come from any one of hundreds of developers, it's hard to get players to care about the name of the studio that created the title.

In that context, be careful not to confuse features with styles. All too often I've heard teams say, "Our game is like [big hit title], but...

- "We have an anime art style!" (Or Steampunk, or Blade Runner, or whatever)
- "The mood is gothic!"
- "The game is set in Prohibition era America!"
- "We only support the keyboard interface, so the experience is totally PC and not console!"

Having a unique, readily-identifiable style is valuable and something I always try to achieve. But if the game's features aren't compelling, a clever style is usually not enough to make it a hit.

Mismatched visual styles and play styles can also dilute your audience. I worry when I see a tag line like, "For anime fans who love RTS games, medieval settings stealth-based gameplay and old-school keyboard interfaces!"

CHAPTER 9

How It Feels to Play Your Game (1.12–1.13)

DISCUSSING QUESTION 1.12

What is the primary mood of your game? (e.g. happy, dark, frightening, goofy, stealthy, foreboding, curious, joyful etc.)

What is the pace of your game? (e.g. frenetic, thoughtful, alternating action and strategy, etc.)

How long will people play in a typical session, and where will they be playing? For two minutes waiting in line at the grocery store? Fifteen minutes on the bus? Three hours in the living room?

One of the first people to play your game has lunch with a friend. What do they say to the friend about how they were feeling as they played?

This topic is most relevant for: Everyone

1.12.1 Mood and Personality in Games

If I look at all the game proposals and pitches that I see over the course of a year, I see two patterns that make games look "just like a hundred other games."

No mood. Simple is a very good ingredient in game design. It makes games easy to learn, and simple games can have fascinating strategy. In chess you see the full 64-location playfield and know all about the six character classes before you ever start a game. Yet it's one of the most popular games in the world.

The problem: For arcade games, puzzles and other "simple" apps, in many indie games the title screen appears and the mood is, "Here's a game." When you're competing against games with catchy music, interesting fonts and bright graphics, players will move on in search of something more exciting.

It's easy to over-do adding personality to simple titles, which can make games cheesy instead of charming. But doing nothing and having a blah title is even more dangerous.

I discussed above how adding characters and story can make a game feel more fun. If you have a simple game that lacks personality, here are some examples to get your ideas flowing:

- A theme ("A hidden object game as it would have been painted by Vincent Van Gogh")
- A character ("Bobby the bat has dropped his glasses and he can't see anything without them. Can you help find his glasses in this scene?")
- A twist ("Play as Shania Holmes, Sherlock Holmes' smarter sister!")
- A mascot ("I'm Al the Alien and I challenge you to get the high score on my asteroids game!")
- A time period ("A noir mystery puzzle game, with music and style from the era of Sam Spade")

- Good and evil (As in *Angry Birds*' cute birds and really annoying pigs)

The Same Old Mood. A lot of the titles I see proposed all try to evoke the same mood: dark.

Dark and foreboding. Dark and suspenseful. Dark and depressed. Dark, ironic comedy. Dark and blood-spattered. Dark noir mystery. Dark and stormy. Dark exploration and adventure. Dark because the main character is a mushroom farmer who works in a cave.

Those are all very different games, but players take a quick look at your trailer on YouTube or a playthrough on Twitch or the images on your website. That's all you get, a quick look. If all of the different dark games I listed above look very similar, that quick look may be the last look your game ever gets.

The fix: Watch three or four episodes of your favorite dramas. How many different moods do you see across several episodes of the same series? What kinds of emotions do they evoke?

How do the lighting and the color palette of the show reflect those moods in each of those situations?

Your favorite show has a primary mood, which for dramas may very well be dark, frightening, foreboding, even paranoid. But there will be contrasting moments as well, with other strong emotions and feelings.

Whatever the mood of your game, remember that to make it effective you have to have contrasting moments as well. This is how we create experiences that strike the player (both the primary mood and the exceptions) and avoid monotony.

The same is true of pacing. A game that is always frenetic or always runs at the same slow-n-steady pace usually won't hold players' attention as well as games where the speed and intensity of play varies.

One of the strengths of tower defense games, for example, is the ebb and flow of waves of increasing pressure on the player. Action games with boss fights have this varied rhythm in their pacing, as does *Candy Crush*'s mix of harder and easier levels.

If your game is dark in tone, you've made a choice that groups your title in with lots of other games. What can you do so that the first images, the first video, the first words a user ever sees about your project also present contrasts? How can that first look communicate how your game is unique?

Could dark and foreboding be a mood that you save for special sequences, so it's a striking contrast instead of the prevailing mood? Does the action ever burst into blinding sunlight that offers a new challenge?

If your game has many scenes with low levels of lighting, remember that on portable devices users often play in daylight or in well-lit spaces. Even with the screens' auto-adjustment of contrast and brightness on these systems, players won't see the action in the way that you intend.

Finally, if you have a simple game that is consistently happy in tone, consider what other feelings you could introduce to add texture without changing the focus.

1.12.2 To Every Platform There is a Session

If you play extensively on each platform on which you plan to ship your game, you know that you'll have to adapt game play on different devices, sometimes dramatically.

Smartphone games are often played waiting in line at the store, waiting for the bus or the train, or in the waiting room at the dentist or doctor's office.

Smartphones use touchscreens, game sessions are short, players may enter and leave the game several times each day, and it (usu-ally) has to be transparent that when you return you'll be in the same position you were when you left. Users may be watching other media on other screens at the same time.

Console games, we all know, are very different. They're played on big TV's on controllers that players can use from across the room. Play sessions are much longer, and challenges are presented in much larger chunks. You may have to reach a save point before you can lock in your progress and stop playing. Many times the game will demand your attention, making multi-screen environ-ments less likely.

Teams trip and fall on these issues when they support platforms where they don't usually play games. In fact, it may be a platform that they don't even like.

It isn't just indie teams that struggle with these more-than-just-a-port versions. A number of strong AAA console publishers have seen their teams fail when executives commissioned mobile ver-sions of their best-selling console games.

If you're going to support a platform that's very different from your initial target system, make sure that whoever leads the redesign plays and loves games that use the native interface and the native play style on the new machine.

1.12.3 Changing It Up

As game designers we often build games we personally love to play, so the choice of target device, interface, play style and pacing naturally match.

It's worthwhile, though, to take your thinking one step deeper. Are there contrasting styles you can offer that still work for users playing on that device? Could your endless runner have a bonus side quest where something other than speed drives the action?

There's a long tradition of big AAA console titles changing the pace with mini-games, and there are ways to do this in almost any title.

1.12.4 It's Not Just What People Think

As innovators we are anxious to hear what people think about our game.

What's actually most important, however, is how people *feel* after they play it.

I mentioned above Nir Eyal's excellent book, *Hooked: How to Build Habit-Forming Products*. One of its themes is that our brains do not start with logic. We do not think, "This is an excellent breakfast cereal. I've decided I like it a lot."

What researchers have found is that we have an emotional reaction to the smell, appearance, taste and texture of the cereal. We spontaneously harvest the feedback from all of our senses and mix all those sensations into an emotion.

Then, with the emotion already defined, our brains step in and start trying to explain the emotional decision that has already been made. "I really like this cereal," the brain says. "It smells like cinnamon and it has a crunchy texture. And the box says it has 5 grams of fiber and it still tastes good with only 8 grams of sugar."

In other words, our brains try to make us feel like we're being logical, but in reality it's the emotions that control much of what we do.

Our brain can also contradict feelings when it comes to products. I taste the cereal and love it, but then see that one bowl in the morning will cost me 900 calories. As much as I love the flavor, I now hate the cereal.

But wait! "Hate the cereal" is also an emotion! And hating our game is one of the emotions we most want to avoid in our players.

After you make a list ranking the key features for your game, do the same for your key competitors. Then take the process one step farther and look at how people *feel* after they play your title, and how they feel after they play the rival games.

Are there ways you could change things up to get more of the emotional reactions you want than your rivals are able to inspire?

1.12.5 Ask the Right Questions First

Nir Eyal advises us to always start feedback sessions by asking the "how do you feel" questions. Don't move on to "What do you think?" until all the questions about emotions have been answered.

Researchers found that discussing opinions can "erase" our memories of feelings as we make that transition from "Mmmm, I love this" (emotion) to "Delightful taste and texture, and less calories than you'd think" (logic explaining emotion).

We want to record all the feelings the players remember before we switch gears to the opinions. If we wait too long or ask other questions first, it's normal for people to forget the emotions behind their first impressions. After that all you'll get is the second hand explanation of logic.

DISCUSSING QUESTION 1.13

What will the first two minutes of the player experience be like in your game?

Will you have a tutorial? How will users learn how to play?

This topic is most relevant for: Everyone

1.13.1 The Vehicle Keeps Accelerating

Smartphones, tablets and multi-screen lives have impacted many aspects of our culture. In the entertainment business we have far less time to capture the attention of our audience. If your game is not interesting very quickly, you'll be swiped, tapped, clicked, shaken or stirred into oblivion.

Hence my question about the first two minutes of your game. Ten years ago we'd talk about 20 minutes or a half hour.

Now two minutes is all we get, and that's being optimistic.

George Lucas and Steven Spielberg are famous for starting films with several minutes of intense and exciting action that begin during the opening credits. *Star Wars* and *Raiders of the Lost Ark* are great examples of "not waiting to capture the user's attention," and worth re-watching for that reason.

In any modern game, the first few minutes of user experience (including anything that precedes play) has to be tested and re-tested with "cold" users playing for the first time to find the right balance for your title.

Mobile game designers know that having the right tutorial is essential for any game that isn't "pick up and play on the first try." That tutorial is tuned and re-tuned to retain more players. Games with multiple mechanics offer additional short tutorials when a new style is introduced, ones that are just barely long enough to help you "open the next box of fun."

Explicit tutorials are not right for every game. In some categories players expect games to immediately challenge experienced users. This requires opt-in (rather than default) tutorials, and introductory missions that are exciting while still being instructional.

Consider the first two minutes of your game. Are there ways to emulate Spielberg and start the excitement almost immediately?

Is there a way to create that excitement without making the first few minutes of play so difficult, confusing or challenging that many players give up and abandon your game?

CHAPTER 10

Your Product Marketing (1.14–1.15)

DISCUSSING QUESTION 1.14

What will the first playable prototype of your game include?

This topic is most relevant for: Everyone

1.14.1 How Many Parts Does it Take to Build a Car?

Let me think about this. The car has to be drivable, though only on a very short trip. I'm building this prototype to evaluate its basic functions before I start adding more parts.

Aluminum pipe and threaded joints to build an inexpensive frame. Seat, steering wheel, motor, accelerator, brake pedal and brakes, fuel tank or battery, differential, two axles, four wheels with tires. And the necessary bolts, screws and brackets to attach them all together.

After driving this car on a short (and probably frightening) trip, I'd have a great list of what I needed to add next.

I like to share this exercise with dev teams because I know that (as I confessed above) I can easily get distracted by new ideas in the early stages of a game.

If I actually implemented them, soon my code would look like a sketchbook instead of a structured program. I'd have completed segments of the game scattered amid drafts of ideas I played with and roughed in.

Writing down new ideas as they come to you is important, because otherwise you'll forget.

But doing more than that is a big mistake. Every item that distracts us from building the game slows us down, which may cross something far more vital off the feature list.

Our prototype car has no radio, no fuzzy dice, just a laser focus on a primitive version that will teach us what's needed to take the next steps.

Later in this book we'll discuss creating a "Minimum Viable Product" (MVP) to gather feedback from players who are spending real world money. The kind of primitive prototype we're discussing here comes long before any MVP.

If you used this kind of laser focus on your game, what would your first primitive prototype contain?

DISCUSSING QUESTION 1.15

What kinds of people will want to play your game?

What other games do those same people play? What websites do they visit?

Where would you find them on social media sites like Face-book, Twitter, Instagram etc.?

This topic is most relevant for: Everyone

1.15.1 Looking Past the Mirror

Teams often have multiple objectives when they build games, but leaders have to choose one key priority that drives the project. I typically see three kinds of primary team motivations when I work with startups:

The team driven by a product vision. They're building a game they'd love to play themselves, and they think that lots of other people will want to play it, too.

The team driven by an opportunity vision. They're building a game in a hot new category where there aren't a lot of competitors. They may not be fans of the genre, but they think that millions of people will rush to buy this game.

The team driven by an artistic vision. They're trying to make a unique game that they're proud to work on and play. They hope and hypothesize that other people will love the game, but they're driven primarily by an internal artistic compass.

Each of these styles of product vision is valid and has its advantages. But each also has its pitfalls:

- The team building a game they'd love to play may focus on their
  own tastes and miss the mark with a larger audience
- The team trying to please an unfamiliar audience can never
  understand the user experience as well as someone who's passionate about the category
- Artistic visions are by definition driven by values other than revenue. They are the least likely to earn money for their creators

Have you researched what kinds of people buy games in this
genre? Have you investigated how many hit games have found success with this kind of audience?

Are there other target audiences that might be interested in your
game? What changes would you have to make to reach them?

1.15.2 Lessons from Great Marketers

Whenever I think about these issues I remember two secrets of
great game marketing that I was taught many years ago:

Pick a Person. When we try to picture a million people who might
like out game, there aren't any faces in the image. Many game categories have at least a million active players, but we wouldn't recognize any of them on the street.

I was taught that what you do instead is picture just one person. If
your friend Jennifer loves shooters and that's what you're building,
then picture Jennifer when you're thinking about your audience. Go
so far as to put her picture on the side of your computer, to remind
yourself of who your audience is.

It's a lot easier to discuss, "Would Jennifer like this feature?" than it is to discuss, "Would millions of people all over the world like this feature?"

This approach gives you a concrete goal instead of a fuzzy one.

Practice the Most Critical Skill. I was taught that the number one skill in marketing isn't being a great communicator or a great strategist.

The most valuable skill in marketing is being a great listener.

Great marketers won't just play the competition's games. They'll go onto social media sites to read what people are saying. They'll read all of the competitors' forums and their Amazon review pages. They'll do deep searches on IGN, GameSpot and other sites.

Great marketers will sit silently and watch the first groups of outside consumers play the game. They'll watch people play competitors' games the same way.

If consumers discuss the game the marketers won't respond or comment. They'll just sit and listen to what people say about their experience and their feelings.

I always want to explain, to clarify, to help those first consumers.

But I know from working with great marketers that the most valuable skill is to keep my mouth shut and be a great listener.

1.15.3 Conferences, Events and Meetups

How do you find those players so you can listen to them? A lot of us who are game developers are introverts, but we have to overcome any reticence and get out there and interact with people.

Conferences, conventions and trade shows. I talk a lot in these pages about spending wisely and conserving cash. One expense that may be justified for an indie game budget is attendance at top events where you can meet potential partners, show and get feedback on the current version of your game, and learn from experienced speakers.

You'll want to be very selective on spending money and not go on lots of trips without understanding in advance the benefits of each. Do research on events that are within driving distance of you rather than assuming you need to go to an expensive event like GDC.

Applying to speak at conferences where your experiences will be interesting to audiences will get you a free pass into the event if you're accepted. This is also a great way to build interest in your game, even though you can't directly promote products in your presentation.

Even when you believe the value of a trip is clear, be wary of expensive flights and hotels:

- Look for ways to stay with friends, room up with allies, or use Airbnb and VRBO when hotel prices spike for events
- Use travel sites to search for the best flight and hotel prices, but be watchful for hotels that require you to travel in dangerous areas of major cities
- Research the least expensive way to get from the airport to your hotel, ideally via mass transit
- Factor for the cost of Uber/Lyft if your hotel is not close to the site of the event and there is no public transit option

IGDA Chapters. The International Game Developers Association has chapters around the world, especially in areas with major universities. Chapter meetings will give you the chance to learn from speakers and meet other game developers, journalists and industry professionals.

You may be able to show your game, get valuable feedback and build buzz for your title.

If your game has not yet been announced publicly, these events may draw competitors, so use discretion in what you say and show. But it's rare that a game fails because competitors learned about it in advance.

Meetup Groups. Go to Meetup.com and search for groups within driving distance of you that are focused on game developers, game marketers, game players or some other relevant audience.

As a game designer and developer I especially value game marketing talks, since it's a vital skill for indies to learn.

It's free to "join" as many Meetup.com groups as you want, which means you'll be notified the next time each group has a meeting. These events may draw a different audience than those hosted by the IGDA, with varied kinds of potential allies. Some meetups have especially strong and well-respected speakers.

Demo Tables. In some IGDA and Meetup groups you can pay relatively small fees for a "demo table," where you can show your game demo and spread the word about it. The questions users ask in these settings will also give you useful feedback.

1.15.4 "Influencers"

The emergence of popular Twitch and YouTube video streamers as "influencers" has changed the face of game marketing. Many such streamers have 10,000 or more followers who regularly watch their live or recorded streams, and a number of leading voices have over a million followers.

I've read some articles online that say that you can't create a hit indie game without the help of streamers and other influencers. That's not true, but they can certainly be a big help if you can find the right allies at the right price. And sometimes the right price will be free.

If one of those streamer influencers plays your game online and tells their audience it's great, thousands of people – or hundreds of thousands of people – may see it. That's a big boost for your title. If the streamer's audience agrees that the game looks like fun, it can be some of the most powerful game marketing in the industry.

Other media influencers are reality, film or television stars who may have millions of Facebook, Instagram, Twitter or YouTube followers. They are less likely, however, to use their fame to promote games.

Of course, marketing power like this does not come for free. Top influencers are making hundreds of thousands, even millions of dollars a year in fees for their reviews and endorsements. These fees are paid by game and comic publishers and other businesses.

You may be asked to pay an influencer's fee before you know exactly how they'll play and promote your game, and before you know whether that play session will inspire users to buy your title. It's important to ask questions and to get key points written down and signed off on paper by both parties before any money changes hands. If in doubt, don't commit and don't spend the money.

For years it has been easy to blow your entire marketing budget on online ads and achieve very few sales as a result. The same can be said for influencers, and "betting the farm" on a single high-profile endorser can sink a company just as easily as it can launch a hit.

Some approaches for successfully working with influencers are:

If you're a small team, look for free support instead of paying an influencer. There are a good number of streamers with small to mid-sized loyal audiences, and good games are often played and streamed for free. Why? Because the game is fun, the streamer loves it and they enjoy building their audience by sharing games they love.

Look for streamers who have played games that appeal to the

same audience as your title, and pitch them to showcase "a great new game from an indie team living off ramen and pizza."

Don't just look for people. Look for channels. Not all influencers are a single individual. Some are built around topics, interests or themes. The new *Madden* or *NASCAR* might be featured by sports game streamers, but so might your indie game of baseball strategy. A cooking game might get attention on recipe and food streams (and there are a lot of them). If your game fits their needs for programming the fee you pay may be small, or they might feature content from your game for free.

Consider how the system fits the game. Games for core gamers are especially popular on Twitch. Simple casual games might do best with influencers who've built a following on Instagram, where a single image can tell the story well at far lower costs. YouTube supports huge diverse audiences with a wide range of interests, and the YouTube based influencers are likewise diverse.

If you have a budget for influencer sponsors, start with a small number of influencers who each have a few thousand followers. Their fees will typically be far lower than the big guys, and they may be easier to communicate with. You're looking for collaborative people who want to produce the best show for them and the best sales results for you.

Try working with these smaller influencers one at a time, so you can measure the sales increase from each event and learn what works and what doesn't work with your audience. The data may show that subtle differences in influencers produce dramatic differences in your sales.

Take the time to research influencers and their audiences carefully. Do they play games that appeal to your potential audience? What impact have they had on prior titles in your category? Have they engaged in weird online behavior (such as openly racist comments) that could offend your users?

Once you learn the fee structure for a potential influencer, run spreadsheet projections on how many additional copies of your game you'd have to sell in order to make a profit on the deal.

Does that increased sales volume feel realistic and possible? Often the answer will be, "No." That's when it's better to go for a smaller audience or stay with streamers who will share your game for free. It makes no sense to spend marketing dollars on initiatives that lose money, because every business school in the world teaches managers that the whole point of marketing is to take actions that make you money.

Be transparent, not tricky about your promotional activities. Ethical influencers will label paid content they create on your behalf as sponsored. Openly state that you're paying for these activities and endorsements. Consumers will recognize the patterns and figure it out anyway, and they'll respect your transparency. In some jurisdictions laws may formally require that you make and document these disclosures.

Get help. If you're working with a publisher they may be able to get coverage for your game that you couldn't have gotten on your own.

Consider the hardware. Does your game show off the great new features of a top graphics card or a major console? If a hardware maker like NVIDIA, Intel or AMD loves your game they may also facilitate influencer coverage of your project, and do so at no expense to you.

1.15.5 Your Game's Web Page or Website

Every indie game needs to have a web page (or a complete website) dedicated to the title. You'll use this home base to reach out to potential users and to communicate with existing players.

Buying the domain name for your game (and. If different, for

your company name) is an important step to take once the official product or brand name is identified. For example, if your came is called *Suicide Scrollers*, your domain name might be "suicidescrollers.com" and the URL for your game would be "http://www. suicidescrollers.com" – the address you type into your browser to display the page.

Avoid game titles where the domain name is already owned by someone else and they are offering to sell it. Sellers will often over-charge (as in "attempt to blackmail the buyer") when they think someone is locked in to having to use a particular word or words.

Unclaimed domain names are inexpensive, so if the game name changes before it's released you can usually get a revised domain name.

Domain names that have already been sold may also be subject to trademark protection, which effectively makes them off-limits. You'll need to work with an attorney to confirm that you can or cannot proceed.

People don't need to own a trademark to buy a domain name, how-ever, and many "domainers" have bought up terms so they can re-sell them at a profit. If the domain name suicidescrollers.com is already taken you might still successfully trademark the name for your game. In that case, you don't get rights to the exact domain name but you can choose something like "suicidescrollers-game.com" and still have a strong connection between the game and the URL

Domain names are paid for by the year, so you can sign up for one year at a time, or longer. The companies that offer these services are called domain registrars, the largest of which is GoDaddy. Any registrar can secure your domain name for you.

If your domain has a common suffix like ".com" (which is by far the most effective for ranking highly in Google searches) it should cost less than $15 per year to register. If it costs more than that, then exit the page and find another registrar. GoDaddy often has sales that make domain names especially inexpensive. (Note: I have no business relationship with any of the companies mentioned in this section aside from being a GoDaddy customer.)

If you're not already experienced in building websites, there are some easy ways to get going. My favorite approach is to create a WordPress site, an open standard that produces websites that are easy to use and that search engines love. WordPress is technically a blog system, but it's so powerful that it will work for any kind of website.

With WordPress you choose a "theme" (which can also be free or purchased for a fee), and that theme defines the standard layout, colors etc. for pages on your site. "Plug-ins" are code modules (some free, some sold at relatively low prices) that can be dropped almost seamlessly into a WordPress site, and there are many highly useful plug-ins.

If you Google "WordPress hosting" you'll see a list of companies that will host such a site for you on the cloud, including Google Cloud's own offerings. Costs are based on storage and bandwidth used per month, and you don't need to buy larger plans until your visitor traffic requires them.

For most teams cloud hosting is far better than hosting a WordPress or other site on your own computer or server and dealing with all the security, bandwidth and storage hassles. Basic-featured WordPress hosting sites will offer free hosting, but more sophisticated options will charge a fee each month.

An alternative to using WordPress is to use Squarespace, Wix or Weebly, online services that allow you to choose options from menus and then assemble the selected style, format and font choices into a website. They will then host the website for you in the cloud in return for a monthly fee, which is how they make their money. The downside here is that you're locked in with the service and don't have the freedom to choose your hosting company as you do with the open standard of WordPress. If you change suppliers you'll have to rebuild many aspects of your website elsewhere.

Services like Feedblitz. MailChimp and others (which each operate in different ways) allow you to invite site visitors to opt in for email updates, which lets you create an immediate and highly valuable link with users.

The web presence for your game can be anchored by:

A product page on your company website, which helps build web traffic for your company since busy sites rank higher on Google searches. This is best if you plan to publish multiple games, and people are more likely to know your company name (e.g. Supercell, Wargaming, EA).

A separate game-specific website, which allows you to use the name of the game as the site domain name and URL (e.g. www.mygreatgame.com). This works best if you have just one game, so people are more likely to search for the game's title than to search for your company name. You can also add a separate company website with general information, but don't duplicate the same content on both sites – this will lower the search rankings for each site.

If you host the games page on your company website you'll still want to buy the domain name that goes with the game (at a minimum the .com version). This prevents someone else from buying it and creating confusion for search engines and users.

There are two skills you'll need to learn in order to maximize the effectiveness of your website. Both represent rapidly-changing, dynamic topics where best practices can and do mutate every few months. In each case you'll want to do online searches for recent articles to keep abreast of these changes. The two categories are:

SEO (Search Engine Optimization) – We're all familiar with how Google searches give us prioritized links to valuable information. The algorithms they use in this process are updated continually, so if we want our website to rank on the first page of any search (and most users never go farther than that first page) we have to study the current wisdom on best practices for Search Engine Optimization. Then we modify the text, layout, etc. of our site to give ourselves the best chance to rank highly.

"Mobile First" is a key principle of current SEO, because more online searches now come from smartphones than from desktop computers. The term means, "If you have to choose, make sure the mobile version of your website is prioritized in your SEO."

A WordPress plug-in called "AMP" (among others) will facilitate optimizing your website for mobile users.

Keyword Analysis. Every page on a website can have a keyword attached to it, and Google uses these keywords as part of how they pick the best pages to show to users. Using WordPress to create and maintain your site makes assigning keywords especially easy.

The process of choosing the right keywords for each page is highly dependent on what keywords similar pages are already using. You'll never outrank Apple or hundreds of other big companies if you want to use the keyword "iPhone" to draw people to your page. But you'll find fewer big competitors for a term like, "mobile cooking game," which could put you high on the front page of a search for that term or a similar one.

Whether it's a free-standing website or a page on your company site, you'll want to do consistent updates. You can then post links to the new content on Facebook, Twitter, etc. (discussed below). When users click on those social media links they'll be brought to the appropriate page on your website. This makes your page the center of information for the product, while using the same content (text, link, photo, video, etc.) to do updates on all of your social media platforms.

Elements you should consider adding to your game's web page include:

Text. Whatever you write about your game on your website has the potential to help market your title. It may be a description of the game, quotes from early reviews from influential journalists, or any other interesting content. It needs to be concise and easy to read. We want text that appeals to people's imagination, so they start thinking about how much fun it will be to play your game. Text will also be the largest component of how you tune the SEO strategy for your site.

Links to app stores and online sites where users can buy your game. Where possible, link to the game's page, not just to the store landing page, to make it easier for players to buy your title.

Screenshots make great updates for the game, and can be used to build connections (and ultimately relationships) with players. For example, instead of just showing off your new prodigal barbarian character, you could ask users, "What should we call this new character class of highly intelligent barbarians?"

Just remember that the resolution in your screenshots has to match the resolution in the final game. If you have high-res preview images for a lower-res game, users can later believe that you misled them.

Videos can be used to show off great animation, short "cut scenes" etc., but only after they're completed at a high quality level. Make sure that resolution and frame rate match the final game, as you would with other assets. (See also the paragraph about Twitch streaming below).

A trailer can be an effective promotional tool as you near completion of the game and have lots of polished assets from a variety of different levels or scenes.

Use caution with video and trailers, however. It's easy to use video editing software to produce two minutes of game highlights with great music and sound. If you make changes to the game after you've released a high quality trailer you may anger players by "not delivering what you promised."

I've seen teams develop beautiful trailers when the game is over a year away from shipping, and when many environments, characters and other assets have yet to be completed. Assembling "the pieces we've already done" to make the game look more complete makes the dev team feel great. But it wastes a lot of precious time that would be better spent on creating in-game assets.

You never want to hear the comment, "Wasn't your game 'almost done' 14 months ago?"

I've also attended game pitch events where teams showed a well-edited trailer for their game, sometimes even integrating original live action footage. When you looked at the game itself, however, the graphics were substandard and the animation was clunky – a suicidal strategy in today's competitive market. The team had executed a high quality trailer but the game itself looked amateurish.

It's the game, not the trailer, that will earn you money. And there are many games like *Fable Legends*, which had beautiful trailers… but never shipped.

Links to great reviews or stories in the press, which can be highly effective marketing tools.

Dev Diaries can be very effective ways of building a sense of community with users who love your game, and doing a Google search on the term will give many excellent examples. These work better on more complex games than they do on simple ones, and you can rotate between comments by designers, engineers, artists, audio and music professionals etc.

FAQ pages, hints, tips, etc. These features are interesting to players, and may also dramatically reduce the number of emails coming in to your support email address.

Contest and event announcements, which inspire users to play the game immediately in return for unique opportunities, prizes, sales, special recognition etc.

Leaderboards and other score-publishing activities that encourage players to play and to compete with each other.

1.15.6 Almost-Free Marketing on Social Media

We've talked about various ways to market games, and how some of those methods can be very expensive.

Social Media is a proven category of marketing for drawing attention and potential players to your game. If you already have a large number of Facebook friends, Twitter followers etc. it can cost relatively little money to publicize your game through these channels to start the ball rolling. This won't make a game get noticed by millions of people all by itself, but it's a great start.

What if you don't have lots of social media friends or followers? Use the time while you're developing the game to start creating your "presence" on social media. Reach out to friends, write interesting posts, tweets etc. about games you like and respect, and comment on quality posts and messages you see from others. The only way to create good neighbors in the community is to act like a good neighbor yourself.

These methods do take time, and to be effective they require that you update your chosen channels consistently. Many indie game developers start out with good intentions but then postpone updates, giving users the feeling that the project may have been abandoned. This can undermine the power of your social media efforts.

Most successful indie game marketing programs will involve multiple channels, although picking the most effective media is important. A game with stunning graphics and audio needs to be promoted with video, regardless of the outlet, and many social media platforms now support video. A simple online word game that challenges players' vocabulary might benefit most from quiz-based promos on Facebook, Instagram or Twitter.

Facebook can also be a platform for publishing social games that leverage collaboration as well as competition.

One downside of social media platforms: they all keep changing the rules on us. The algorithms for what gets shown at the top of the page, what gets shown at the bottom and what doesn't get shown at all keep changing. The only thing worse than having to deal with all these changes is giving up on social media, which is almost always a terrible decision for game marketers.

Before you start revealing your game via any method on any channel, consider when to start this kind of publicity.

You want to start early enough to give yourself time – usually several months before the game is released – to build interest in the title and have a significant number of people who want to download or buy the game the same day it becomes available.

You don't want to start too early, and give competitors time to speed-develop a similar game that can ship before you do.

You don't want to start the unveiling process until you have something compelling to show that is unlikely to change before the game ships. It may be a trailer, initial screen shots or some other kind of asset, but it has to have the "Wow!" factor that will draw players' attention. It also has to be sufficiently complete that it won't change materially before the game ships.

If you aren't already a member, join each of the popular social media sites, find friends, and play with the various systems. As you watch the people around you and the content that appears each day, you'll start to understand which services are best-suited to promote your game.

Social media sites to consider include (in alphabetical order):

Facebook – The largest outlet and the one with the most diverse demographics, Facebook has the power to share a wide variety of assets and links, including high quality screenshots and video.

In recent years, however, Facebook has forced accounts belonging to businesses to become "pages" instead of having all the same features of individual accounts. Content posted in these business pages has a much lower priority on friends' pages than your cousin Irving's cat pictures, which means that until your game has a lot of followers you have to buy Facebook ads to publicize your title. Those ads are highly targetable and effective, but can also be expensive.

If you're posting from your personal Facebook account these limitations don't matter, but personal accounts are capped at 5,000 friends. Business pages can have millions of followers.

Instagram – Instagram excels at reaching a younger, millennial audience, and its image-driven content is ideal for games where screen shots or videos will interest teen and young adult players. Instagram is owned by Facebook, and is following in the footsteps of its parent in requiring businesses to advertise in order to grow their following.

Unlike the other systems discussed here, with Instagram users can't click through to other websites via links you post. You can create an awareness for the game, but users have to do a separate online search to actually find your website.

LinkedIn – LinkedIn is a professional network rather than a social one, although a lot of friendly messaging goes through their system. The LinkedIn news feed mimics the Facebook format. It can be a useful place to post if you have a network of friends on the service, especially those in the games industry, super-especially games journalists. If not, you can replicate Facebook posts here but it's unlikely to sell a lot of games.

Pinterest – The audience here is dominated by women, so it's prime territory for games aimed at female audiences. Pinterest works best if your game has striking screenshots, since its users create and copy from boards of favorite images. You'll want to update your images frequently for maximum attention, and Pinterest is likewise making it harder to build large audiences without buying paid advertising.

Twitch – For traditional genres of video games, streaming on Twitch is the #1 channel for getting a title noticed, and #2 trails far behind. If you're not familiar with the service, you need to sign up and start studying game streams and how they work as part of your critical planning.

Studying popular Twitch streams that cover your category and platform of game can help you plan how to build followers and do your own streams to publicize your game. This is a marketing imperative in many game categories, which explains the growth of paid online "influencers" (discussed above) who can help promote your game.

If you're not confident with video, you or someone on your team needs to get comfortable with it. (Yes, Twitch streaming is that important for your game.) Your stream can focus on the screen with voice-over (VO) narration on top of it, or you can tile two or more video sources to have both a human face and the screen represent your game.

Twitter – Like Facebook, Twitter can feature text, screenshots and videos. Unlike other channels, however, your tweets can quickly be buried by the high volume of traffic seen by active users. Twitter is experimenting with how to solve this problem, but the traditional remedy is to repeat tweets every few hours for a short period of time to maximize exposure without angering or boring your audience.

Remember that Twitter is also a two-way system for interacting with your users. By tweeting messages with a @yourgamename tag players can send you public messages as well as direct private direct tweets about your game.

Unity — Unity is an engine, not a social network, but they do a great job of creating opportunities for indie teams to publicize their Unity-based games. This is not a small audience outlet, since Unity plays such a central role in indie game development around the world and has so many active users.

Unreal — I'm starting to see Epic do more of this kind of promotion as well.

YouTube – For non-game marketing YouTube is the king of video social media, despite the efforts of Facebook and Twitch to lure its audience. There are many companies and influencers streaming games on YouTube, but the number remains smaller than the corresponding activity on Twitch.

1.15.7 Writing a Press Release

There are many excellent online articles about how to write a good press release, including some devoted solely to games. I will not cover that ground here since guidance is readily available via a Google search.

I do have three guidelines for your press releases that you may not read somewhere else:

Remember that your game announcement is only news once. If you want the games press to publicize the game, you'll get one shot to convince them to do so. If you send a press release before the game looks and feels interesting, no one will write about it. Not now, and not later.

If you send out a release and then send along more information later, your indie game is no longer "news" when that second mailing arrives. It will be much harder – though not impossible — to get journalists' attention.

Don't do mass mailings. Treat every outreach to a journalist as a unique personal communication. If you build a list of fifty game journalists, bloggers and streamers it's tempting to do a mass mailing. You could send the same cover note, documents and links to everyone on the list, since it will save a lot of time.

We've all tried it. Once. Because it almost never works.

Game journalists are like you and me: they want to be treated with respect as individuals, as real people. Take the time to research what each person has written, or what their podcasts or streams cover. Then write an individual personal note that discusses the games they've been covering and why your game would fit well with their other content.

This strategy won't always get a response, but it will get far more responses, and higher quality stories, than the best mass mailing.

Beware of Swag. Many game publishers have sent journalists press kits packed in what looks like Indiana Jones' suitcase. They've sent collectible Darth Vader helmets, autographed NBA basketballs. They've included 18-inch-tall game character action figures with articulated limbs. All of these items can be referred to as "swag."

If you're a billion dollar company this might be worth doing once in a while. But leading journalists get so much swag that a lot of it gets tossed in the trash, left in the lunch room for people to take home to their kids, or passes through multiple hands and then gets sold for cash on eBay.

Leading journalists are looking for great games to review, not swag.

This doesn't mean your product introduction or marketing have to be boring. I've seen beautifully-written material packaged in illustrated envelopes and folders that just screamed, "This is really cool!

Open and read me now!" These kinds of initiatives cost far less to pull off, and can have an even more dramatic impact on your visibility in the press.

CHAPTER 11

Passion and Personality (1.16–1.17)

DISCUSSING QUESTION 1.16

What games are the most similar to your indie title?

How is yours different? What makes yours better?

This topic is most relevant for: Everyone

1.16.1 The Power and Perils of Niche Games

As game designers we choose to create games in the same genres and styles as the titles we love to play.

When designers know every nuance of the user experience players can feel that personal connection. It deepens their enjoyment of and their commitment to the game.

But there are traps in this approach as well. The most dangerous of these is something I call "The Opera Effect."

Opera has been popular for centuries, and opera foundations spend lavishly on stars, sets, costumes and orchestras. But sometimes they can offer only six performances of each work, because there aren't enough opera fans to fill the theater more than six times.

Opera audiences passionately support local productions, but they're a small percentage of the population.

The games business offers similar risks. When we focus on niche game categories, we develop passionate followers but we have little margin for error.

We have to ship in calendar quarters when similar games aren't shipping, so we don't dilute the limited audience and revenue. Every detail must be right in order to please our expert players.

If you go final three months late and a major competitor just released their game, you might as well keep working on the game for three more months. That's how long it will take for the window of opportunity to re-open.

Making money with indie games is hard to do in any case. Serving a niche audience may spawn a great business, but it will be even harder to make money.

1.16.2 And What Does the Heart Have to Say?

I just made some powerful, logical arguments. "Go for the big genres, be wary of niches!" I proclaimed.

But then again, let's go back to the topic of passion.

Your market research may identify that superhero puzzle games are a high-sales-potential category.

But your mind keeps coming back to that mobile 3D motocross

game with physics based on the gravity and atmosphere of different planets.

Is there a shortage of mobile 3D motocross games? Apparently not, since my online search just now produced multiple results.

Is there a shortage of commitment and passion in your head and heart if you choose to develop a superhero puzzle game that you find boring?

Yes, and the way to deal with it is to explore ways to instead build the game that dominates your dreams.

The world does not owe you a career in the games industry just because you love to create games. An idea isn't going to be a hit title just because you're passionate about it.

But if it's what you love to do and you can pursue it in a common-sense way, do you want to look back at age 80 and regret that you never tried?

Can this effort start as a part-time project so you can see if you want to graduate to making it your primary job?

I can't guarantee your success, but I do know that people who love a category will create far better games than people who are just doing what the data suggests is best.

After all, Steve Wozniak, co-founder of Apple and a founding member of our Board of Directors at Electronic Arts, didn't design computers because he thought it was a hot category.

He designed computers because that's what he felt like he was born to do.

1.16.3 "I Could Never Do That!" Syndrome

There are many people who have great new game ideas, but never do anything with them.

"I could never take on EA or Machine Zone or Tencent or Riot," they say, as they keep following the same boring work routine for 25 years. "You can't compete with the big publishers."

A few years later Nintendo or Wargaming or Supercell announces a similar product, and the designer grumbles that he or she had the same idea years before.

I am a passionate baseball fan. I've built several major baseball games, for big companies and for small ones.

I've had an indie baseball title win "Sports Game of the Year" awards when no one thought we could stand up to the reigning big-publisher franchise.

As rare and difficult as it may be to do so, sometimes an indie game can get noticed and become a hit.

If you have a great idea and you never explore your indie game, all you're doing is guaranteeing that someone else will develop the idea instead of you.

Maybe there really is no way for you to create this game. But I believe that you have to explore, try things, look for ways to push your idea ahead.

Trying and failing feels bad.

Never trying and watching someone else succeed feels worse.

DISCUSSING QUESTION 1.17

How would you feel if The New York Times, Wired magazine, Oprah Winfrey and your best friend's mother all said your game sucks?

This topic is most relevant for: Everyone

1.17.1 What My Mother Taught Me

Yes, the answer to this question is obvious. Any of us would feel awful, terrible, gutted, humiliated and a lot of other horrible feelings if this happened.

My mother, who was a professional artist, taught me something very important about doing work that has your name on it. In fact, it's advice I've thought of often as I write this book.

"If you sign your name to a painting, or a story, or something you build with your hands," she'd say, "you have to be ready to accept the consequences. If you love what you did and other people love it, too, that's great."

Then she'd look me in the eye and say, "But if you love what you did and other people don't like it, you have to be willing to live with that. You can't be an artist if someone criticizing work you're proud of will make you stop doing any work at all. You have to be able to learn from the criticism, get better at what you do and keep going."

I have no idea if people will like this book when I finish it, but I'm going to write it anyway. And even if they don't like it I'm going to learn from this experience, improve my work and write another book after this one.

I think some readers will criticize my advice to "take care of yourself and your family financially and emotionally while pursuing your indie game." They'll say it contradicts the Silicon Valley stereotype of complete, self-sacrificing "burn the boats after you land on the beach!" commitment.

This book reflects over three decades of Silicon Valley experience. I've seen friends become millionaires and I've seen friends lose their marriages and their families and their homes. I can live with criticism that says that the approach I recommend is too cautious, because I believe I'm giving good advice.

Having people attack your work – and you – sucks. It feels terrible. But, as my mother said, when you put something out there with your name on it you have to accept that those bad days as part of the deal.

Each time you ship something new you'll find that it gets easier to see criticism of your work. The harsh words don't change who you are and what makes you unique, and the feedback will help you grow as a creative professional and as a leader.

That's why I ask this "How do you feel…" question: to get those feelings out on the table so you can look at them, recognize them.

And once you recognize them, then your next job is to make a conscious decision not to let those fears stop you from pursuing a game you'd love to create.

CHAPTER 12

A Fun Idea (1.18)

DISCUSSING QUESTION 1.18

You just won a mega-million-dollar jackpot in the lottery! You've cleared your to-do list and taken a 3-month vacation at a series of your favorite cities and resorts.

You return happy, rested and all caught up in every phase of your life. There's no to-do list for work, and nothing at home that needs to be cleaned, straightened, fixed, watered, painted, re-arranged or put away.

You no longer need to work, nor does your spouse or partner. If you have kids, however, they still attend the same grade of school and they still have to do their homework. Some things can't be changed by money!

From this moment on you can do whatever you want to do each day. In this "perfect world" how would you spend the first month when you got back?

This topic is most relevant for: Everyone

1.18.1 Where do Dreams Come From?

Let's pretend for a moment that your indie game is a great new smartphone football game. You think it will compete head-to-head against EA's Madden NFL franchise and win.

You were playing Madden with your sister for the 10,000th time when the idea came to you, the way to change the UX and the camera angles to make the game both easier to play and more fun to watch.

Now, when you answered this question about how you'd spend your days after you won the lottery, what was it that you planned to do?

Did you see yourself sitting with your team and hand-crafting the world's greatest mobile football game?

Or did you...

- Envision yourself on a sun-soaked beach, planning your next dive in the infinite colors of the tropical reef?
- Dream of writing the Great 21st Century Novel on the balcony of a hotel suite in Venice?
- Start planning a tour of the 50 best restaurants in the world?

When you answered that question about winning the lottery you wrote down what you'd most like to do if you had all the time and all the money in the world.

How did your post-lottery-win plans relate to your indie game?

If they tie together in some way, that's a good start. You're planning to work on something you love. You'd be doing this project even if you had all the time and all the money in the world.

But what if the stories don't match?

What if your big idea is to build the world's greatest mobile football game, but your post-lottery dream is to open a bed-and-breakfast in Brooklyn?

Then you have to ask yourself some more questions.

1.18.2 Sometimes We're Stuck

There are times when we're stuck due to financial obligations and we have to tough it out for a while.

I deeply support the real-world thinking that goes into these "I can't quit this job right now" decisions, especially when we have children and other family members who depend on us for support.

If we recognize that sometimes we have no choice other than to work at a boring or frustrating job, what does that mean for our indie game? Could it be a slow-but-sure side project that gets worked on as time allows?

1.18.3 For Love or Money

Do you have more than one passion? Is one passion more financially rewarding, while another is closer to your heart but will earn less money?

Most people don't have just one narrowly-defined kind of job or project that they could enjoy doing. If your indie game is #2 or #3 on your "Top 10 favorite things to do" list you may get great joy from working on it.

Or are you horrified to realize that your indie game and your post-lottery dream just don't match? Not even close.

Doing something that you don't really care about just for the money often turns into a miserable grind.

As painful as it sounds, I know from my own experience that giving up on an ill-conceived indie game can be a good thing.

Discarding an old idea opens the doors of creativity to a different initiative that may combine both personal passion and the potential to make money.

But you have to stop working on the old dead-end initiative in order for the new dream to crystallize in your mind and in your heart.

PART II

GREAT PEOPLE, GREAT GAMES

CHAPTER 13

Great People, Great Games: The Questions

QUESTION 2.1

Will you be working alone at the start of this project, or will you need to start with a small team?

Please take your time, write down your responses, and answer fully from your deepest thoughts. Think only about your own opinions, not about what others may want you to think or do. Do not look ahead to other questions until you have finished this one.

QUESTION 2.2

If you're working solo on your indie game, is this something you've done before? How recently?

If you'll be leading a team on your indie game, is this something you've done before? How recently?

Please take your time, write down your responses, and answer fully from your deepest thoughts. Think only about your own opinions, not about what others may want you to think or do. Do not look ahead to other questions until you have finished this one.

QUESTION 2.3

If you already have an established team and successful prior games, why are you considering building an indie game instead of working through one of the established publishers?

QUESTION 2.4

Will your game require support other than standard customer service after launch? Will you be running a "live team?"

If so, what kinds of team members will you assign to the live team?

Please take your time, write down your responses, and answer fully from your deepest thoughts. Think only about your own opinions, not about what others may want you to think or do. Do not look ahead to other questions until you have finished this one.

QUESTION 2.5

Are you planning to work full-time on your game?

Is anyone else planning to go full-time with you?

QUESTION 2.6

Is there a way for you to pursue your indie game part-time and still make progress towards your goal?

Do you have potential team members who could work on the project part-time as well?

What parts of your indie game could you complete even if you were just working on it part-time?

Please take your time, write down your responses, and answer fully from your deepest thoughts. Think only about your own opinions, not about what others may want you to think or do. Do not look ahead to other questions until you have finished this one.

QUESTION 2.7

If you have a team, will your group all work together in a big room?

Or will you build a virtual team where you each live in different places and communicate electronically?

If you chose this latter option, how often (if ever) would you want to get together to meet in person?

Please take your time, write down your responses, and answer fully from your deepest thoughts. Think only about your own opinions, not about what others may want you to think or do. Do not look ahead to other questions until you have finished this one.

QUESTION 2.8

Who will design your game?

How will the design be shared with the team?

Note: With this and the following three questions you may not have answers yet, based on the stage of development you're in with your game. Answer where you can and don't worry about the blanks that aren't yet filled in.

Please take your time, write down your responses, and answer fully from your deepest thoughts. Think only about your own opinions, not about what others may want you to think or do. Do not look ahead to other questions until you have finished this one.

QUESTION 2.9

Who will do the programming on your game?

QUESTION 2.10

Who will do the art and animations on your game?

Who will create the user interface?

Please take your time, write down your responses, and answer fully from your deepest thoughts. Think only about your own opinions, not about what others may want you to think or do. Do not look ahead to other questions until you have finished this one.

QUESTION 2.11

Who will create the sound effects in your game?

Who will compose or arrange the music?

Who will integrate the sound and music into the game code and ensure that it is synchronized correctly?

QUESTION 2.12

Of all the people and teams you've worked with, who's the one person with whom you'd most like to work again?

What was it about this person that made them so special to work with?

If you're building a team, would he or she be interested in working with you on your indie game?

Please take your time, write down your responses, and answer fully from your deepest thoughts. Think only about your own opinions, not about what others may want you to think or do. Do not look ahead to other questions until you have finished this one.

QUESTION 2.13

In which past job you held was it the most fun to come to work each day?

Was it the project itself or the people you were working with that made it special?

QUESTION 2.14

What is the best-organized company you've ever worked for? What did they do that made you feel that way?

Where did you work in your career thus far where people got the most done each day, week, month and year? What was it that made the team so productive?

Please take your time, write down your responses, and answer fully from your deepest thoughts. Think only about your own opinions, not about what others may want you to think or do. Do not look ahead to other questions until you have finished this one.

QUESTION 2.15

Regardless of how efficiently the team worked, and regardless of how much you enjoyed the process, what is the project you've worked on in your career where you were most proud of the game?

What was it about that game that made you feel so proud?

QUESTION 2.16

How would you feel if you never went back to your current work environment again?

How would you feel if you never saw the people you work with again? Are there some people you'd never miss and others you'd think of constantly?

Are there other perks or activities involved in your current work that you'd be sad to lose?

Note: We are just talking about hypothetical feelings, and are not planning or taking action.

Please take your time, write down your responses, and answer fully from your deepest thoughts. Think only about your own opinions, not about what others may want you to think or do. Do not look ahead to other questions until you have finished this one.

QUESTION 2.17

What other parts of your life would bring you joy if you could just magically make them go away? Some of these may seem obvious (the IRS?), but writing them down still helps you organize your thoughts.

What other parts of your life would bring you anguish if they were suddenly taken away (e.g. your family, your church, close friends, places you like to go, activities you enjoy etc.)?

Make a short list of things you would and would not like to leave behind, and if you feel especially strongly about any of the people or items on that list, write down why.

Please take your time, write down your responses, and answer fully from your deepest thoughts. Think only about your own opinions, not about what others may want you to think or do. Do not look ahead to other questions until you have finished this one.

QUESTION 2.18

Is there anything or anyone in your life now that you need to get away from, so the idea of starting over someplace new sounds especially great?

Is there a bad memory you're trying to escape by moving to a new office or even a new town?

Is there something pushing you towards making a complete, across-the-board clean break and starting over in a different job, a different industry, a different place or with different people around you?

Please take your time, write down your responses, and answer fully from your deepest thoughts. Think only about your own opinions, not about what others may want you to think or do. Do not look ahead to other questions until you have finished this one.

CHAPTER 14

My Story: Lost Dreams and Those We Just Misplace

My father received his degree in Anthropology from the University of California. He was passionate about field research, and his future looked bright.

Then the stock market in the United States collapsed, ushering in the Great Depression. Tens of millions of people lost their jobs, and the funding for scientific research dried up. There were no jobs in anthropology for recent graduates. My dad worked his way through school a second time and earned a second degree – this time in Business and Accounting.

When I was a boy I asked my dad a lot of questions about how businesses worked. He'd give me thoughtful answers.

But then we'd watch a show about the great herds of buffalo and the lives of the Plains Indians. Or about the cultures of Athens and Sparta. Or about the Maori of New Zealand.

If I asked him about any of those topics his eyes would light up like Christmas morning. He'd walk over to the bookcase and pull out one of his old textbooks. He'd take off his glasses, balance the book in his big hands and flip through the pages until he came to the section he wanted.

He'd show me the illustrations, his face beaming, and tell me about the subject. I enjoyed those conversations, although after a while as a young boy I'd be ready to go play.

Dad's business card said he was an Accountant. But his eyes told you he was an Anthropologist.

There are lots of books about how to choose a dream to pursue in your life. I think they've got it all wrong.

Our dreams choose us. We don't have to pursue them. They're right there all the time, waiting for us to notice.

As a boy I told my parents that when I grew up I wanted to do accounting, just like my dad.

Each time I said this my father would look at me and shake his head. "You don't want to be like someone else," he'd tell me. "You want to be yourself. You want to find what *you* love to do. I had limited choices because of the Depression, but you can experiment and try things and choose what you want to do."

My mother was a professional artist who also had to change careers because of the Depression. She became a corporate executive at a time when few women were promoted to those levels. She would tell me, "Make sure you put a roof over your head, but find a way to do what you love when you go to work each day."

It's one of the great gifts my parents gave me, the idea that only I could decide where my passions lie.

We can't always pursue our passions when we want to, or in the way that we want to do so.

But if you never pursue those dreams at all, you give away a piece of yourself, a piece that can also bring joy and value into the lives of others.

That's not something we should abandon willingly.

CHAPTER 15

What to Do with Your Answers (2.1–2.3)

"THE SECRET OF MY SUCCESS IS THAT I'VE BEEN LUCKY
ENOUGH TO HAVE BEEN INVOLVED IN GREAT MOVIES
AND TO HAVE WORKED WITH GREAT PEOPLE."

— Harrison Ford

If you have not yet written down your answers, please go back and do so. Writing your thoughts down – even when you're the only one who'll ever read them – will produce far more insights than just answering silently to yourself in your head.

DISCUSSING QUESTION 2.1

Will you be working alone at the start of this project, or will you need to start with a small team?

This topic is most relevant for: Everyone

2.1.1 Solo Project or Initial Team

Some games can be solo efforts, though the design has to be highly disciplined in order to produce lots of fun from the work of just one person.

Most indie games require a team, with specialists coding, creating the art, doing 3D models. designing play mechanics, creating sound effects and music and more.

If you're building a team, hiring only the people you truly need is an essential part of your plan, since it's critical to spend as little as possible and conserve cash.

What does an ideal small team look like? In a perfect world you all would...

• Have worked together before, and done so productively

- Have complementary strengths, experience and training
- Have an individual specialty that is unique on the team and vital to the company's early success

The world isn't perfect so most teams don't have all of these advantages, but try to cover as many of them as you can.

If your indie game requires money from investors they will have other criteria as well, and we'll discuss those issues in later chapters.

2.1.2 And Now, a Word from Our Sponsor, "Cash"

A few paragraphs ago I used the phrase, "It's critical to spend as little as possible and conserve cash."

I cover this point in detail, with lots of suggestions, later in this book.

But I wanted to give you a short preview of those comments here, much earlier in your planning, because it may be the most valuable advice in this entire book if you're running a business.

It's advice that often sounds exaggerated, which is why so many first-time business founders end up in trouble.

Never *ever* personally guarantee a lease, a bank loan, a credit card or any other loaned money.

Guarantees are legal commitments (often just a single line in the small print of an agreement) where you promise to pay back money if the company you manage cannot do so. They can easily lead to unexpected problems – even financial catastrophe – for you and your family.

These provisions are routine in many business credit card agreements, which means that if you run up the card balance and the business closes you still have to repay the credit card company.

The word "guarantee" may in fact never appear in the small print, and may instead be stated as something like the clause below, where I have added some comments in brackets:

"You agree that in the event that Lender is unsuccessful in attempts to collect amounts owed it under this Agreement and any such amount is over 45 days past due, Lender may collect all such unpaid amounts directly from you and that you shall be fully and personally liable for all such debts and unpaid amounts [i.e. you guarantee the loan], which shall be immediately fully due and payable upon demand [you have to pay it back all at once], and Lender shall have the right to pursue all legal and administrative steps at its disposal to secure payment from you [they can sue you personally, seize your assets and force you to either pay them or pay big legal fees trying to stop them]."

Now is it clear why I'm warning you that these kinds of loans and credit card agreements can be disastrous? This is only one of many different ways that these clauses can be worded, some of which may look innocuous if you're just scanning the document and not carefully reading every word. If in doubt, consult an attorney.

Most companies succeed or fail based on how well they manage cash. Conserving your cash is the single most important skill to acquire for a first-time business leader.

Most entrepreneurs are surprised the day they run out of cash. They are even more surprised by all the bad things that happen in the days that follow.

Businesses can recover from all sorts of problems. But if you run out of cash and can't issue paychecks or pay for your lease the business will almost certainly close down within just a few days, if not immediately.

Most cash crises are triggered by coincidences where expected cash does not arrive and/or unexpected payments have to be made.

Late cash arrival and unexpected cash departure are both routine in business, especially indie businesses.

Avoid cash commitments as often and as long as you can.

- Adding employees adds salaries, benefits and payroll taxes, and laws require you to pay all of the above on time
- Leasing an office adds a non-negotiable cash commitment each month
- Running up your credit cards creates a later cash crisis when the payments grow into hungry monsters eating up your bank account

Cash is King. Thank God I was taught this early on by a mentor, because I would never have lasted long as an indie without this lesson.

We'll discuss all of these issues – with specific examples of how surprises happen and how to avoid them – later in this book.

2.1.3 The Thing About Terms

I attended a business class many years ago where the instructor started the day with a fun activity.

"I will pay one million dollars," he announced, "to the first person who will give me a pen."

We all had cheap pens and note pads right in front of us in the hotel meeting room. One man almost fell flat on his face leaping out of his chair to give his pen to the instructor.

"Thank you, sir!" our teacher proclaimed. "I am now obligated to pay you one million dollars, and everyone in this room heard me make this oral commitment to you."

We all looked at each other. He couldn't possibly be serious.

The man went back to his seat and the instructor approached him. "Here are my terms for the deal," he said. "I will pay you a penny every 25 years until the debt is paid off, and the debt is personal, non-transferable and non-assignable, so you can't collect from my kids after I die. Here is your first payment."

And he handed the man a penny.

"If you learn just one thing from me today," the instructor told us with a gleam in his eye, "this is it. Everyone focuses on the total value of a deal. But what really matters are the terms. Keep your eye on the terms of every deal and you'll do well in business."

I did keep that lesson in mind, and every deal I've ever done has reminded me that he was right.

DISCUSSING QUESTION 2.2

If you're working solo on your indie game, is this something you've done before? How recently?

If you'll be leading a team on your indie game, is this something you've done before? How recently?

This topic is most relevant for: Everyone

2.2.1 What Kind of Adventurer are You?

People who feel driven to create indie games are determined to achieve a goal, to build something that other people will want to play and enjoy. As a long-time D&D player, of course, I think of us as adventurers who choose to go on important missions, working diligently for something in which we deeply believe.

We all have different ways of setting out on these adventures, and it's important to understand your natural work style and how you like to get things done.

In my case, I'm good at doing solo projects but I like being around other people. Given the choice, I prefer working as part of a team over being a purely solo performer.

I have a couple of friends who are happiest when they're holed up by themselves at their computer, creating something all by themselves until it's time to get feedback on their work.

I have other friends who would go stark raving mad three days into a solo project. They simply have to be collaborating on something to enjoy work each day.

If you're considering a one-person indie game as a full-time activity and you have never worked alone before, look for an opportunity to take a practice run for at least a couple of weeks before you fully commit. It's hard to know your real preferences and limits until you try them.

2.2.2 First Time Managers and CEO's

Ask any successful game studio founder about the first time they ever led a team and you'll hear some fun stories about their mistakes.

There are some parts of being a manager that you can learn from a book. But many parts of managing you just have to learn by doing it. You have to figure out your own personal style. You'll learn from your successes, and grow even more when you make mistakes. I learned a lot of important wisdom the hard way as a first-time CEO.

It's not rare for indie game teams that are started by first-time managers to be successful. It's harder for a new manager to get to this stage than for a veteran leader, but it happens all the time.

Do you know experienced games professionals who would be willing to serve as advisors? These arrangements can be informal help exchanged by friends, or more formal arrangements where advisors are paid cash or receive stock options (which we'll discuss in a later chapter).

If a team is going to be involved in your indie game, ask yourself before you start out, "Is leading this team what I really want to do? We'll discuss these choices in more detail later in this book.

DISCUSSING QUESTION 2.3

If you already have an established team and successful prior games, why are you considering building an indie game instead of working through one of the established publishers?

This topic is most relevant for: Established game development teams

2.3.1 It's All About Leverage

I recently read an interview where a successful television producer started work on a new video game. He talked with a few major publishers, then decided to go indie and publish the game himself.

A reporter asked, "Why didn't you want to work with a publisher?"

"Because," the producer answered, "I didn't like their leverage."

The word "leverage" sums up the experience of working with major game publishers, as I've done (both as an employee and as an independent studio founder) for many years.

"Leverage" in business means "Having the advantage in a negotiation." If you have lots of leverage and negotiate a contract, the terms are likely to come out more in your favor. We discussed above how seemingly small contract terms can be supremely important.

What creates the publishers' leverage? Money and Audience.

Major publishers today specialize in internal development, and only work with highly experienced and successful external teams. If they do work with an independent team, however, they take care of the two toughest problems in game development:

- Money: They'll advance a top team the funding needed to build their game, and they can afford to spend millions of dollars
- Audience: They have millions of email addresses and permission to contact those users when a game is published

Those two benefits directly address the two biggest problems of indie studios: cash and building an audience. What do you give up in return?

Royalties. Your share goes from being the majority to being smaller than the app stores' 30% cut.

Control. You get paid advances against royalties when the publisher approves each milestone, so if you disagree on the design no cash will arrive until you do things their way.

Rights. Publishers want to own the Intellectual Property (IP) rights, including copyright, trademarks and even patents. Unless you have a carefully negotiated contract they can eventually cut you out of the deal and own the franchise.

For most teams a big publisher deal is not an option. If you're one of the exceptions, it's up to you to decide how you feel about the leverage.

CHAPTER 16

Going Live (2.4)

DISCUSSING QUESTION 2.4

Will your game require support other than standard customer service after launch? Will you be running a "Live Team?"

If so, what kinds of team members will you assign to the Live Team?

This topic is most relevant for: Everyone working on an online or mobile game

2.4.1 Business Models and How They Change

We're going to talk a lot about different business models later in this book. I want to raise the strategic issues of choosing business models, however, as we talk about building game development teams.

When you're running a business it's important to view business models as impartial, objective mathematics. They represent different ways to get paid for the work you do when you're an independent business owner.

You also have to consider marketing factors. You "position" your products and your business to inspire people to want to buy your game, and a business model that works for both the publisher and the player is an important part of that positioning.

Free to play is a common model on some platforms, less successful on others, and (despite its broad success around the world) controversial to many in the industry.

The core objections are that there's no "total all-in price" for the game, either as a monthly subscription or as a one-time sale. The in-game store offers the potential for players to spend more money over time (on skins, costumes, levels or whatever) than they ever would have spent buying a packaged game. To the traditional buyer this can feel like price-gouging.

On the flip side, players on mobile games find free to play to be a great "preview mechanism," the service that radio provides for the music industry. Users get to decide if they like a game before they start spending money on it.

I often encounter intense "Good vs. Evil" discussions over this issue. Publishers using and sometimes abusing loot boxes (or crates, or capsules or...), which I'll discuss below, have intensified and polarized opinions on this issue.

Avoid falling into these emotionally-loaded "what is evil?" debates. We have to be paid for our work or we and our teams won't be able to keep doing it... but we do have to fit the business model to our audience.

Stay focused on three aspects of any business model:

- **The math**: does it provide benefits to both the publisher (we can make money) and the player (as a preview mechanism, or by allowing micro-payments instead of a single large expense)?

- **The positioning**: is it a model that your target audience on the target platform(s) are accustomed to using? Have others tried this model and failed?

- **Player cultures**: what's customary on this platform and in the region(s) of the world where the game will be sold? Can we invent a better business model that they'll accept?

- **Budget and schedule**: Introducing new business models often means we build a game's audience more slowly than if we're using well-established systems. Do we have enough cash to pay for a longer path to profitability?

It's important to remember that we aren't always the initiators. Business models are driven by many forces, not just innovation, and will change over time. Two, three, or five years from now you may need to change how you're doing business, even if you love the ways you do things now and don't want to make those changes.

For online games, subscription models were initially popular. Then the popularity of free to play games inspired many publishers to create hybrid models, or drop subscriptions altogether. In recent years new games have once again successfully introduced subscriptions as their core model.

In the early days of smartphone games the "premium" model was popular, where users paid up front to download and own a game.

As the app stores became crowded and prices dropped, premium sales dried up and the "freemium" or free to play model became more popular. Users got the game for free, but paid for additional levels, features and personalized items.

In recent years in-game ads have become a major source of revenue, especially for simple "hyper-casual" games that users may play for only a few days.

Keep studying the market, keep studying your players, and assume that games industry business models will change over time... just like everything else in our business.

2.4.2 Living the Live Ops Loca

Ten years ago "live ops" was something that non-game software companies did. Now it's a required mindset and approach for most games that have a major online component.

Even story-driven action and adventure games, where many players may do just one complete playthrough, benefit from the monitoring of user progress, actual vs. projected difficulty of each challenge, player confusion on next steps etc.

Live ops is short for live operations, which is a simple concept. Once any piece of software goes live and people are using it there are two sets of issues that arise:

Problems:

- Bugs
- Users try but then abandon the game
- Confusing interface on a specific screen
- Incomplete or unclear documentation
- Areas of the map that no one is visiting
- User complaints about the game, app or project website
- Contact form entries go unanswered
- Contact form entries are answered, but make users angry, not satisfied

Opportunities:

- Discovering where users disappear (se we can keep them)
- Researching user paths so we find why they aren't using app

features, menus, etc.

- Announcing sales and special offers and creating "events" where users have to act within a specific time window
- Upselling users to additional features
- Testing different menu styles etc. to see which one get best user response
- Testing preliminary functions of new features with selected opt-in users
- Managing user communities to build committed relationships

You'll notice that QA, product development, marketing and community management are all involved in live ops, whether it's for game or non-game software. This theme of team collaboration will come up over and over again in this book.

Before the advent of Xbox Live, PSN, patches and the growth of mobile and browser-based games we tested every game as ardently as we could. We gathered input from all over the publisher and all over the development team. Publishers bought confidential "mock reviews" from journalists, to see if outsiders saw any weaknesses or issues that everyone inside had missed.

And then we crossed our fingers, held our breath and shipped the game.

If something confused players and they never got to The Great Hall of the Aardvark King (and thus missed the 25 other Great Halls all the way down to the grand finale with the Queen of the Zebras) there was no way to fix it. 300,000 cartridges or 300,000 CD's had already been manufactured and shipped to stores, and back then there was no way to fix them.

If your game wasn't a big hit there were no re-orders, no second and third manufacturing runs. You were screwed.

This explains why I love the modern world of live teams and live ops. We don't have to be perfect. We get second chances. And third, and fourth, and…

2.4.3 Get Off to a Good Start

Live ops is not something we start thinking about as we near completion of a game. It's something that has to be top of mind on the first day of work on the project. A few examples:

- A user data policy has to be created so everyone on the team understands how different forms of player data have to be treated under U.S., European and other regions' laws
- Data has to be tagged if it is user-identifiable under those policies
- Telemetry has to be built into the game to collect data on player paths through the game's screens and states, not just their progress through the challenges and user spending patterns
- A procedure for adding new data points and telemetry has to be defined, since even modern data bases don't like having new data classes added in many different ways
- Systems and procedures have to be created for running in-game events, so that teams can script activities with little or no modification of the game's code to support each instance
- Tools and dashboards have to be created so that when the game goes live the team can examine all the collected data, not just a pre-defined subset
- Tools and dashboards have to be created for Customer Service to examine (and potentially correct) in game user assets when questions arise

It's tempting to say, "We'll think about those things once we get the fun identified in the game and the design feels solid."

Unfortunately, that's like saying, "We'll figure out where to put the elevator shafts after we've erected all the steel and poured all the concrete in the building." You've missed the chance to do things properly and you'll be hacking crude fixes forever to get the functionality you need.

Data, telemetry, metrics and analysis all have to be planned for in the original structure of the code for the game. We'll talk more about how to look at that data in a later chapter.

2.4.4 Making a Conscious Transition

When the first version of a game is released where users are spending real world money, a transition happens. The development team that created the game integrates with the community management function and transitions (with some people swapping in or out) to become the live team that manages the product.

As they collect data on actual play patterns, user retention, what parts of the game generate revenue etc. the live team makes running improvements to the code and assets. If they do so effectively they can build an audience that week-by-week is more and more committed to the game.

If the game is a hit the live team may continue operating for years, evolving the game as they go.

The centerpiece of operations for most live teams is events. We have (at least) one official holiday in the U.S. each month throughout the year. Every thirty days in the real world you get an excuse to do something different in your daily life, energizing boring routines, and you might even get a day off.

Events have the same function in online games, and by keeping things feeling fresh and new they alleviate boredom and make players want to stay involved.

Events have these critical needs:

Motivate players to come play the game right now. They may already be playing every day or they may not have logged in for three weeks. We just want to give them a reason to come and play right now.

Marketers call this kind of activity a "call to action," because it gives the user a reason to stop waiting and act.

Fun. Whether it's a contest, a special challenge, a group activity or some other attraction, the players need to have fun. Games with boring events are deemed boring as a whole and abandoned.

A Time Limit. Players need to enter the game within a defined set of days to participate, and the deadline is real. Some aspects of the event may endure (e.g. special items may be bought in the store after the chance to win them for free has expired) but the experience ends at midnight.

Diverse Themes. A once-a-month "High Score Weekend" will lose its luster quickly. Major holidays (and informal holidays like The Super Bowl and The World Cup) give you an excuse to create themed announcements and custom graphics for users as they enter the game. When the calendar doesn't cooperate you can make up your own mythical in-game holidays to celebrate.

Reusable Assets. Our budgets aren't just finite, they're often tiny. Events have to use existing game assets whenever possible. When necessary we want to re-skin characters and re-decorate screens and settings rather than starting from scratch.

2.4.5 The Need for Strong Product Managers

Live teams for many games are built around both game developers and marketers. The latter are often called product managers or PM's, since their objective is to sell the game to players.

This is a very different structure than the way that packaged games' teams are organized, where development and marketing work as separate, parallel functions.

PM's are integrated into the leadership of live teams to drive the vital work of attracting players to the game, not to mention attracting revenue to the company. Product managers often join a dev team long before the game goes live, so they can work to pave the way for a strong initial launch.

In some companies (especially in mobile games) the PM's direct the live team's work and manage the other disciplines. In other settings PM's are paired with a producer, and there are many variants in these reporting arrangements.

The emerging role of the PM may or may not be appropriate for the kind of game you're building, but it's valuable to understand how they work on teams where they're part of the organization and leadership. If nothing else, this is an important part of learning the business of game publishing, which is vital for all indie teams.

CHAPTER 17

The Power of Part-Time (2.5-2.6)

DISCUSSING QUESTION 2.5

Are you planning to work full-time on your game?

Is anyone else planning to go full-time with you?

This topic is most relevant for: Everyone

2.5.1 The Different Kinds of Part-time

You may feel you have only one option for how to build your game, as in "I need this paycheck so part-time is my only choice." But it's good to consider what kind of part-time window you want to work with.

Start by sorting the key tasks that need to be done into categories:

• What can be done full-time

• What can be done part-time

These tradeoffs have to be based on real-world choices, not perfect-world fantasies.

One key goal: Find a way to make some kind of progress every month, and (when circumstances allow) every week.

When I say, "I worked on this project part-time," I could be referring to very different kinds of work:

- A passion project I worked on occasionally during nights and weekends while I held a full-time job
- One of several projects I was working on as part of my regular job
- A project I worked on after I reduced my hours at my primary job
- A summer project I did back when I was in school and had 10 weeks free each year

Different projects are better suited to different approaches.

If you're working part-time, start by identifying the time windows you have available. Then you can plan how you'll use that time to advance your game step-by-step towards completion.

If you have a full-time job the only free time to do project work might be on weekends or occasional late nights, which raises the issue of life balance.

The part-time work may bring you joy, but committing more hours after long days at work can impact family life and relationships, not to mention your health if you shortchange sleep and exercise.

I find it's best to plan the time collaboratively with my family, so they're part of deciding how to balance work and home life. This makes it easier to get and keep your family's support for what you're doing.

DISCUSSING QUESTION 2.6

Is there a way for you to pursue your indie game part-time and still make progress towards your goal?

Do you have potential team members who could work on the project part-time as well?

What parts of your indie game could you complete even if you were just working on it part-time?

This topic is most relevant for: Everyone

2.6.1 Part-time Planning

Sometimes I see people (including me) stopped by roadblocks on a project when there are still some ways they could be making progress.

If I were working on a game and didn't have the time or money to produce a demo, a mentor might ask me questions like:

"If you don't have the budget to hire a team, what can do by yourself?" There have been times when I pushed my idea forward by coding a simple prototype myself.

"Can you use PowerPoint to mock up the game instead of building a demo?" The ability to create multiple clickable buttons on a page in PowerPoint allows designers to mock up the logic of some strategy and storytelling games without actually having to write code.

"Can you use a website to mock up the game instead of build-

ing a demo?" You could do the same for some games with HTML and CSS on a website, the basics of which are easy to learn.

"Could you start testing your ideas by designing a board game version of your concept?" Many of the games industry's most famous designers have used a board game prototype to flesh out their thinking on an electronic game.

Sometimes we just need someone to ask us the right questions and then we realize what we can do next.

You may face barriers that really can't be avoided or broken down in this way. Nevertheless, think about alternate approaches while you're in the shower, walking the dog or stuck in traffic.

2.6.2 The Catches in Working Part-Time

There are some issues to be aware of when you're doing part-time work:

Laws vary state by state in the US and in different countries, but in most places you cannot do your own work at the workplace of your employer without their written permission. You can't use even a single pencil or piece of paper from your employer's office. If you break those rules they could claim under the law that they own the work instead of you. Most firms would never dream of enforcing such a rule over a pencil, but they have the right to do so.

IMHO Family life is a priority. No matter how busy I've been in my work life, I never missed watching our kids' weekend soccer and baseball games. If I'm not traveling or at an event I always make it home in time to join my wife for dinner. I've never had a project that was worth ignoring my family.

You can sabotage your mission by sabotaging yourself. Getting enough sleep is critical to staying sharp and using good judgment.

Getting enough exercise is vital, both for your health and to keep the right attitude when work gets stressful.

Birds don't fly when they're caged. It's hard to expand your horizons when you're immersed in a project and glued to your chair. I go to meetups almost every week to learn new ideas, new technologies and new business models. I meet new professional allies. I can't let my skills or my knowledge atrophy just because I'm on an exciting project.

One person doing all the work themselves can take a long time. I wrote my award-winning mystery novel *The Fog Seller* as a fun and fulfilling creative side project. But it took seven years to complete because I never allowed it to interfere with my game design and production work. I'd gladly do it all again, even if I knew ahead of time how much work it would be.

Some jobs do not lend themselves to sharing the space in your head. You don't want to do two things badly instead of doing one thing well.

I have friends who are engineers who could easily do one project at work and one project at home. I've seen other programmers who were just as intelligent but whose work faltered. They were consumed by endless bugs on both projects, with neither code base ever really coming under control.

If your nature is to give your whole focus to one thing at a time, your part-time project may not go well when that attention is divided.

The only real way to find out if this approach can work for you is to try it.

CHAPTER 18

Leading and Managing (2.7)

DISCUSSING QUESTION 2.7

If you have a team, will your group all work together in a big room?

Or will you build a virtual team where you each live in different places and communicate electronically?

If you chose this latter option, how often (if ever) would you want to get together to meet in person?

This topic is most relevant for: indie games that involve more than one person.

2.7.1 My Take on the Workplace

I believe that in a perfect world it's ideal to have everyone on the team work side by side in the same office. You'll brainstorm new ideas more effectively and catch problems faster than if the team were scattered in multiple locations.

Of course, we don't live in a perfect world. I've worked on success-

ful projects where parts of the team were on three different conti-
nents.

In most major urban centers there are many kinds of short-term
shared work environments, with everything from desks in an open
setting to a private room or a separate office for four or more people.

These new shared spaces offer practical options at prices that scale
based on your need for space, privacy, and access. They don't
require long term lease commitments and you pay only for the
space and features you need.

If you choose to work at one of these facilities, be sure to research
carefully and negotiate aggressively, since many will offer dis-
counts or deals if asked.

Shared workplaces are often marketed as social cauldrons where
great new products are born and where co-founders meet. In my
experience the odds of this happening are low.

Sites will offer you the chance to work for free in their office for one
or more days as an evaluation period. This is essential, since the
noise level, culture, facilities and routines for each facility are very
different.

I've been in shared workspaces that were quiet, like a library.

I've been in shared workspaces that were loud, like that bar down
the street. In fact, one place had a fully-equipped bar as the centerpiece of the room, complete with bartender!

If you need a dedicated office for a team, one cost-saving option is
sub-leasing, where you take over a space that another company no
longer needs. They may require that you stay for the duration of
the original lease, however.

Workplaces don't always have to be offices. The hit game *World of*

Goo was created by a two-person team who developed much of the title in a coffee shop where they met each day.

Your views about where and how to base your company may differ from mine. What's most important is that you conserve cash, try things and see what works with your personal management style.

2.7.2 God Bless the Cloud That's Got Its Own

Sometimes it's just not feasible to have everyone working together, even if you all live in the same region.

In the San Francisco Bay Area, where I'm based, it's routine to have team members whose homes are two hours or more apart. Founders may base the company in San Francisco since it is the hub for public transit, but "The City" boasts some of the highest rents and business taxes in the world.

In settings like this the power of the modern Cloud, with software collaboration tools we never dreamed of just ten years ago, makes it possible for at least some members of a team to work remotely.

When I advise indie teams, however, I don't say "Just have everyone work from home! It'll all be OK!"

I believe that the more scattered your team, the more management time it will take to coordinate your efforts. The more likely it will be that you have communication problems that can cost you time and money.

You can use regularly-scheduled visits and frequent Skype calls to stay in touch, but monitor the progress and results carefully. Some people thrive using these methods to collaborate. Others gradually drift apart, which is often fatal for a project.

2.7.3 Flow: What It Is and Why it Matters

In his best-selling book *Flow*, psychologist Mihaly Csikszentmihalyi described how his research identified the ideal conditions for getting work done.

This condition of *"flow"* exists when we:

- Have a clear set of goals
- See that we're making significant progress
- Get consistent, clear feedback so we know we're on track
- Work without lots of interruptions
- Do work that's challenging enough to be interesting, but not so difficult that we fail

As a game designer, producer, programmer and writer I feel like these rules absolutely apply to me.

A major goal of any product development or game publishing organization should be to create an environment where as much of the team as possible can work in that "state of flow" as often as possible.

Of course, organizational design – like game design – is a matter of balance, psychology and trade-offs.

We want the programmers and other creative leaders to have the right environment to stay "in flow" as much as possible, so we give them offices with doors and minimize interruptions.

But now everyone who doesn't have an office is upset. There's a perception that "some people are valued and get doors, and some are devalued and stuck on the floor, and it's all about your job title and whether they like you."

Wait, we can fix this. We spend more money and give everyone an office with a door. But now we lose most of the positive effects of spontaneous teamwork. In fact, we start to lose the feeling of being a team, and can start to operate as a group of independent agents on parallel missions. That usually means lots of issues over who-controls-what and increased communication problems.

Wait, we can fix this. We schedule more meetings and add more detailed procedures, so we keep people operating as a team and avoid the loss of communication. But now all the meetings are interrupting everyone, and we're disturbing that productive flow that we gave everyone doors to help them achieve.

I'm exaggerating the issues here, but it's a delicate balance and fixing one problem can exacerbate another. The right trade-offs will be different for every game project and every team.

CHAPTER 19

The Creative Crafts (2.8-2.11)

DISCUSSING QUESTION 2.8

Who will design your game?

How will the design be shared with the team?

This topic is most relevant for: indie games that involve more than one person.

2.8.1 Designing, Not Digressing

Most indie games start their lives with a designer or designers on the team, since often it's the game idea that creates the passion for the project.

But that's not always the case. I've seen successful indie games grow from different roots:

Tech Performance. The team produces the first game in a popular genre that can run at 60 fps with high quality graphics.

Special Effects. A team creates a new kind of game environment that makes players go, "Wow!" and makes engineers go, "How the hell did they get the screen to look like that without dropping the frame rate?"

Characters. The art director creates characters whose look, animations and antics are so attractive that people just naturally want to play the game.

Art direction and/or Audio & Music. The mood of the game feels compelling, often created through a combination of great visual design and great audio. Players are dying to try the game, based solely on the emotions evoked in the video.

I've seen all of these starting points produce successful games, but one rule applies:

Someone has to lead the game design on the project. It isn't enough to say, "We'll just all try stuff and figure it out." That collaboration is essential, but someone still needs to lead the design process.

I know a super-talented two person indie game team with one engineering wizard and one art direction wizard. Nominally they share the design work, but if you ask for details they'll tell you, "One person leads how it plays and the other leads how it looks. Everything's clear, and we collaborate to solve problems."

2.8.2 The Enigma of Writing Things Down

There was an era in the 1990's when the big publishers believed that "the bigger the GDD (Game Design Document) and the TDD (Technical Design Document), the more likely it is that you'll get a good game on time and on budget."

Documents grew to be fat, rigid, arbitrary and unrealistic, consuming hundreds of pages. Most teams abandoned updating these tomes in the first six months of the project, and eventually management figured out that they didn't work.

If you do a Google search on "Game Design Document" (GDD) you'll find articles with different frameworks for formal design docs.

GDD's were born at Electronic Arts and were used for large projects – our team wrote some of the first ones. I think it's a good step so long as the documents are high-level, concise and have a rigid page limit to enforce those values.

Even more important, however, is to create a strong wiki (or similar online document) to share every aspect of the design of your game and its components. These are the ultimate living reference points, and allow the leaders of every section of the game to record and continually update reference material that ensures consistency and continuity.

I believe that designers choose and plant the first seeds of game design, but the entire team tends, feeds and trims the garden as it emerges to achieve the game's overall goals. If you agree with me, collaborative documents like wikis and internal WordPress sites best support that style of development.

2.8.3 Where Designers Need to Start

Try to keep your initial game design documents short, simple and focused. I've been taught by some great designers and producers, and here are key points for what to include:

Start with the one-sentence summary. You wrote this down back in section 1, and it provides the ultimate north star for what the game experience will be.

Summarize three to five of the most important design "pillars," the handful of activities or play styles that will make the game stand out and inspire fierce player passion and loyalty.

All other decisions are judged against the rule that "these pillars are the consistent center of our game." For example, on the *Assassin's Creed* games, you might describe the pillars as:

- Exploration – It's a big, open world and to complete your missions you have to explore and investigate

- Stealth – Wading in and fighting doesn't work. You have to blend into the crowds, watch and listen.

- Vertical Movement and Jumps – Vertical travel is almost as common as horizontal inside the walls of cities. The "Leap of Faith" is part of every highlight reel.

- Living Cities in both Sight and Sound – The streets are teeming with people. You move through the crowds as in real life, overhearing snippets of conversation, surrounded by characters who make way for you and for each other.

- Story – The action is driven by an uber-story in the modern world, with specific stories and subplots that drive missions in every game.

If you worked on the teams that built this franchise, you'd know that everything the team designed in the game had to serve these five pillars of gameplay. And they can be summarized in 125 words.

Focus on player feelings and write down how the game will evoke them. If you see a great old movie you don't come home excited about mid-20th-century car design. You'll want to talk about all the emotions you felt as you lived through those experiences with the characters.

From your very first design doc, take the time to write down how you want the player to feel as they play each portion of the game. There might be one consistent feeling in a short game, or sharply conflicting emotions in a longer experience.

A Picture is Worth a Thousand Words. Chart out the flow of the game before you ever write narrative descriptions. You'll see issues faster and your summaries will be shorter because diagrams communicate more clearly.

Artists should use their pre-production time to create lots of quick concept pieces. You can save beautifully crafted imagery until after the characters, environments, lighting and palette stabilize.

Use generic models and rough animations to try out different game mechanics. If your hero's sword can morph into a club or a feather you can use a simple test bed to see how each object might feel and the controls that will operate it.

Start with Your Charts. Most games have spreadsheets at their core that determine the characteristics of many items, NPC's, locations etc. Oher spreadsheets will list things like the first estimates of how many animations will be needed for each character, how large each game level will be in real world dimensions and in its memory footprint, etc.

We all know that when you do spreadsheets at the beginning of the project almost every cell in those first drafts will change. Lists will grow, classes will be re-defined, priorities will shift.

Nevertheless, creating those core game spreadsheets right at the beginning gives you many advantages (at least for me!) including:

- All those aspects you haven't thought of yet will start to come up
- Budget and schedule estimates will get a lot more accurate
- If you're picturing a game of one scale and charting one that's much larger, the problem will jump out at you
- An engineer can look at the spreadsheets and envision the data structures they'll use to build a solid foundation for the game
- Whatever game element is being coded, it always has real (albeit first draft) data to allow it to be tested
- If you're working on a restricted-memory platform your art and audio lists can also assign rough RAM budgets to different classes

All of these benefits support the principle of "learn as much as you can as early as you can in your project, so you make mistakes before there's a lot of wasted work based on invalid assumptions."

DISCUSSING QUESTION 2.9

Who will do the programming on your game?

This topic is most relevant for: indie games that involve more than one person.

2.9.1 DIY, Partner or DOA

On every video game someone has to do the programming.

It may be a non-technical creative using a drag-and-drop tool like GameMaker. It may be a computer science major with years of game experience. It may be anyone in between those levels of expertise.

If you're able to code the game yourself, you're all set. If you have an individual or team to partner with, you're all set.

But at some point you'll need to determine who will code the game in order to proceed. In later sections I'll discuss issues that relate to selecting and working with a programming partner or team.

2.9.2 First Make it Fun

Every good engineer will tell you that software development needs to start out with a solid engineering framework, and a plan that will produce a consistent and reliable game. That's great advice.

If a pillar of your game design is that the game runs at 60fps, that initial technical plan will lay out all the constraints on memory, resolution, dimensions, formats and everything else that can make an asset or a complete level slow down the machine. This reduces the risk of wasted work dramatically.

The same is true if you're targeting an especially high peak poly count, top-end screen resolution, large numbers of concurrent users, etc.

There's a trap I see some teams fall into, however. Having their game run at 60fps is so critical to the plan that attaining that speed and never losing it – even for a single day of development — devours lots of engineering bandwidth and produces constant interruptions.

Someone checks in some new assets that haven't been optimized and the game drops below 60fps. Suddenly all other work stops until either the code is modified or the offender is required to remove and modify the assets.

This raises two issues:

"All other work stops." Having the team's work interrupted constantly can reduce productivity dramatically. Remove the offending asset so its author can make corrections (or the team can schedule time to fix the bug you just exposed), but only that one person needs to stop what they were doing.

First, Make it Fun. Yes, an engineering team needs to prove very early in production that any critical tech challenge in the game is indeed achievable. Teams that haven't proven key feature and performance assumptions early on have been known to waste months of work before concluding that the game can't be built as planned.

In that context, the first goal of any game development is to get to the point where the game is fun. Any time that the team veers from "First make it fun, then make it fast" there is a danger that diversions will cost the project lots of time and money.

Be ruthless about "First make it fun," and only make exceptions when there is a compelling common sense reason to do so.

2.9.3 If You're a Non-Technical Game Developer

If you are planning a technically ambitious game and have little or no programming experience, I'd recommend teaming up with a programmer rather than trying to code it yourself. She or he can then guide decisions like whether or not to use an engine and which one to select.

If the beauty of your game lies in some aspect of the design other than its technical challenge, I have seen non-programmers successfully master any of several different engines and produce professional looking finished games.

Just remember that for a non-technical designer the game will take far longer to develop than it would for a professional programmer. Make sure that your calendar, your personal life and your budget can handle that extra time.

It's not easy to learn any engine, since at some point you're likely to have to learn at least some aspects of programming in scripting languages or a traditional programming language.

You can take courses online, watch a wide array of YouTube instructional videos, and/or take programming classes at public universities, adult schools or (in some cities) private training operations like General Assembly and Playcrafting.

In the end the only way to learn any language or system is to throw yourself into a project and build something, which is why project work is always central to programming classes.

If you're learning on your own, this gives you a focused path of study, since you'll always be working to learn whatever skill unlocks the next element you want to add to the game. It also helps with motivation.

As with learning Spanish, German, Japanese or Chinese, there is an initial frustrating period where you're doing a lot of work and you don't have a lot to show for it.

If you stick with it, however, the clouds will start to part and you see results on the screen. That's when it gets to be more fun, even with a long way to go till you have a completed game.

DISCUSSING QUESTION 2.10

Who will do the art and animations on your game?

Who will create the user interface?

This topic is most relevant for: indie games that involve more than one person.

2.10.1 Playable, Then Pretty

It's only natural that we want our games to look great as early in the project as possible.

If you're working with a big publisher there may be political factors. You may need to emphasize having a great trailer or sizzling screen shots early in development, so that the executives get a strong first impression of the game.

In almost all other situations a very important design rule applies: Playable, then Pretty. And yes, this is the art version of "first make it fun" that we just discussed above.

Your biggest objective as you start development of any game is to reach the point where you can see that it's fun to play.

Until that moment, all the great graphics in the world don't matter. I can see "great graphics" with no gameplay at any time just by searching on Google.

If you're bringing in outside artists to create assets for your game, postpone spending that part of your budget as long as possible. Try to use placeholder graphics for your initial test versions until you start to feel good about the game being fun.

When you reach the point where you have a final list of the art assets you need on any game, you'll notice something interesting. Many of the items you thought you'd need when you started the project are no longer on the list. Nailing down the fun in a game before you start creating large numbers of animations and environments can save a lot of time and money spent on assets you'd never use.

What art assets *do* you want to create at the beginning of the project? The Art Director for the game will start by creating (or directing the creation of) concept art to define the look and feel of the game. They'll develop the color palette and the game's overall style. They'll create lots of placeholder images to let the programmers do their work without final art.

It can also be very valuable to create one example of every kind of asset (environment, player characters, NPC, enemy classes, weapons, objects, animations, sound effects, music files, etc.) to prove out production pipelines and ensure that size and memory limits can be met.

2.10.2 "Hey UI, I'd Like You to Meet UX!"

In his landmark 1993 book, *The Design of Everyday Things* (which he recently re-issued with many updates), Donald Norman shared the term "User Experience Architect." This was the title he'd chosen to replace "User Interface Architect" on his business card at Apple.

Norman defines UX — the now-accepted abbreviation for User Experience – as being more than just the functional design for software products. UX also includes graphics, the interface, the physical interaction with the computer or other device that's running the software, the documentation, and even the service you get if you contact the company looking for help.

The introduction of the smartphone, with its hyper-competitive online stores, pushed UX to the forefront of the Silicon Valley vocabulary. As games became the largest category in those app stores the term came to be critical for us as game designers as well.

UX principles instruct game teams to:

• Optimize every aspect of how the player interacts with the game, to maximize both fun and efficiency

• Reduce or eliminate every possible source of frustration a player could feel towards the game or the company that publishes the game

This is the same integration of Product Development, Marketing, Customer Service and Community Management that we discussed above in the chapter on live ops.

When you're trying to stand out among tens of thousands of competing products, every nuance of how the player plays your game becomes important. Finding every little hiccup in the experience that drives users away becomes critical. Helping new users master the learning curve is critical to retention.

Any indie game that hopes to succeed in the current incarnation of our industry must abandon the narrow objective of building a strong UI.

The only way to move the odds in your favor is to see the challenge as being one of UX: User Experience. And to do so from the very beginning of your project.

DISCUSSING QUESTION 2.11

Who will create the sound effects in your game?

Who will compose or arrange the music?

Who will integrate the sound and music into the game code and ensure that it is synchronized correctly?

This topic is most relevant for: indie games that involve more than one person.

2.11.1 The Secret of Sound and Music in Media

Games, like film, often create the impression that visual elements are what drive the definition of quality.

Games, like film, actually create much more of the user experience with music and sound effects than the players realize as they experience the work.

You can explore this for yourself. Watch a good movie you haven't seen before with subtitles turned on and the sound turned off. Then watch it again with no subtitles and the sound turned on.

The difference is striking.

Audio often gets under-budgeted, under-scheduled, under-valued and under-represented in game development. Don't make these mistakes.

2.11.2 The Secret of Sound and Music in Production

Many of the issues I've raised above under design, engineering and art have parallels in the audio elements of your game.

There's one more secret of audio. It's one reason why, year after year, (apart from our incredibly talented people) our team was nominated for Best Audio or Best Music at the DICE Awards by the members of the Academy of Interactive Arts and Sciences.

Common sense dictates that since audio implementation has to be synced with a game's animations and transitions, you'd wait for other parts of the game to be done before gearing up work on the audio.

In practice, there's a downside to this common sense approach.

In the real world of game development, anything that is started later in the project gets less time on the schedule and is completed under greater deadline pressure. It's more likely to have features or assets cut, more likely to be rushed, more likely to be good instead of great.

Early in a project we feel like we have time to do things right, but even with sophisticated project management the last half of every project can feel like a race to the deadline.

That's the secret of audio in games. As inefficient as it is, you have to start work on the sound effects, voice and music in your game early in the schedule. That's when you have the perceived luxury of time, so when the time comes to start final syncing of the assets you've got quality assets ready to go.

There's another benefit to this approach: from the earliest moments of the game your playtests and demos will have strong sound and music.

CHAPTER 20

Being a Founder (2.12-2.13)

DISCUSSING QUESTION 2.12

Of all the people and teams you've worked with, who's the one person with whom you'd most like to work again?

What was it about this person that made them so special to work with?

If you're building a team, would he or she be interested in working with you on your indie game?

This topic is most relevant for: indie games that involve more than one person.

2.12.1 You Never Know Until You Ask

I have consistently been surprised at the high quality of people who are recruited into small startups when they could enjoy greater job security in large corporations.

Years ago I sat near an engineer whom I especially admired at the game company where I worked. He didn't report to me and the only places our paths crossed were company social events and the weekly schedule-update meeting.

Fast forward several years, and I'm leading my first startup. One day I'm surprised to hear that this engineer is applying to work at our small company. We sat down together, and he told me that he was excited about finally getting to work closely with me.

This was a moment that meant a lot to me. As honored as I felt to hear a guy whom I respected so highly say this, it also made me angry at myself.

I could have hired this strong engineer several years sooner (after he had already left the company where we both had worked), if I'd just had the confidence to reach out and ask if he were interested!

You never know until you ask.

2.12.2 Co-Founders vs. Early Employees

Co-Founders and Early Employees are both critical parts of a startup, but they're very different roles when you're hiring early team members.

I'll discuss the business and legal sides of this issue in more detail in a later chapter, but here's a bullet list of the qualities of each of these vital parts of your team:

Co-Founder:

- Joins the team when the idea for the game is little more than "a glimmer in the founders' eyes"
- Works for less (usually far less) money than they could earn in a job at a mature company
- May be living off of savings, be supported by their partner, live with their parents etc. and take no salary at all

- Earns a significant stock option with special benefits (which we'll discuss later), since they're taking greater risks

- In both actions and words, serves as part of the core strategic thinking that drives the company

- Is passionately committed to the venture and will do whatever it takes to get the game completed and launched in the market

Early Employee:

- Joins the team during early stages of the development of the game

- Works for somewhat less money than they could earn in a job at a mature company

- Earns a stock option

- Plays an important role in the early operation of the company

- Is (at a minimum) deeply committed to the venture and will work their heart out to get the game completed and launched in the market

Later Stage Employee:

- Joins the team after the team has had some initial success

- Is compensated within the typical pay range for their job and the relevant industry and geographical area

- May earn a stock option — some companies give them to all employees (as I prefer to do), while others give them only to more senior team members

- Plays a valuable role in the operation of the company (otherwise you would not have hired him or her!)

- Is (at a minimum) committed to the venture and will work diligently to make the game successful

As you look through these lists you'll see that they are very subjective and general, and leave a lot of room for interpretation.

That's intentional. The one rule that trumps all others is, "Listen to the best advisors you can find, and then use your own best judgment."

2.12.3 Dynamic Duos

Many great startups began with two key players with very different personalities who each played a key role in the company's success.

The most famous recent duo was Steve Jobs and Steve Wozniak of Apple. Wozniak was the engineer who brought the machines to life, and Jobs was the visionary designer and hustler who positioned and promoted them to outperform their big-company rivals.

There are lots of kinds of these indie game "dynamic duos." The ideal (but not required) way to create that perfect partnership is to start with someone you already know and trust from having worked together before. It's even better if you can develop the idea from scratch as a team, so it feels like the vision is shared between the two (or three or four) of you.

DISCUSSING QUESTION 2.13

In which past job you held was it the most fun to come to work each day?

Was it the project itself or the people you were working with that made it special?

This topic is most relevant for: Everyone

2.13.1 Can You Analyze Fun?

Ignore the financial success or failure of the games you've worked on, and just focus on the most fun project or job you've ever been part of. It could be in the games industry, or in any other field.

Not "The Best Game" as judged by someone else, but the project or team you picked simply because you had the biggest smile on your face going to work each day.

Was this a long-ago dream job you're trying to regain? Your most recent project? The first job of your career?

Was the project well run? Was the team productive? Or did all that fun affect the team's productivity and the quality of the game?

It's critical to think about whether it was the game, the people, the environment or all of the above that made the job or project special. Then you can consider what aspects of this favorite experience you want to re-create.

What kind of daily routine did you experience in this favorite job? Founders of startups can have exciting and unique challenges, but the work often requires long hours. Issues can demand your attention at any time on any day. If that sounds bad to you now, it will only sound worse once you're leading a startup.

It's important to understand what you really want, so you chase the right dreams and find real happiness.

If it was the people you worked with who made this game and team special, try this exercise:

1. Make a short list of the best teammates you've ever had
2. List their key qualities and characteristics
3. Use that list to outline the kinds of people you want to hire

2.13.2 My Bullet List for Teammates

Here are the qualities I associate with the best people I've worked with in my career. Remember, though, that many leaders have their own unique criteria, and there is no perfect formula.

Extremely talented at their professional craft (programming, art, marketing, financial analysis, etc.)

Committed to doing high quality work at everything they set out to do.

They do what they say they're going to do, and get it done by the deadline when they said they were going to do it. No drama, no excuses, just results 99.9% of the time (because no one is perfect).

Able to kick around ideas and share thoughts with others and arrive at the best answer to any issue or question without pride getting in the way. They don't worry about whose idea is adopted, just that the best idea is chosen.

Supportive of the people around them. Your child is sick and you have to stay home for a couple of days? They'll help cover for you without complaining, and they know you'd do the same for them.

Will argue fiercely over game design or business issues, but it's the ideas, never the people, that are criticized.

Once a decision is made, they'll willingly execute the plan, even if they continue to disagree with it. No "I told you so!" Just "Let's make this work."

If they're worried about something they'll come talk to you in private. Great people openly share their concerns with their manager, but they start by doing so one-on-one. This avoids "Reality TV" style drama while making sure problems are identified and addressed.

Someone who's easy to work with, so long as the focus of the work is on quality, but...

If the focus on building a great game gets lost and things start to get sloppy they stop being easy-going. They get very focused and start looking for ways to push people and processes to get things back on track.

2.13.3 No Waiting Around

Good startup teams work hard, but they take breaks and work-home balance is also important. The comments below are not about chaining yourself to a desk. They're about what happens when you're not sure what to do next.

What do strong team members do when they finish something and aren't sure what to do next? They'll immediately ask their manager, co-worker, producer etc. for guidance or suggestions.

If they're waiting for assets from someone else, or if they check off all of their to-do list, they'll ask teammates, "How can I help?"

These rules apply to a company's leaders as well. Strong teams aren't founded by victims of circumstance. A manager never explains, "We couldn't do any important work this afternoon because we never received the documents."

Strong managers always take the initiative: "We never received the information from Acme Inc., so we worked on our graphic novel game proposal for Cloversoft instead."

If people don't display this "I'm free — how can I help?" attitude, don't add them to your team.

CHAPTER 21

The Power of Process (2.14–2.15)

DISCUSSING QUESTION 2.14

What is the best-organized company you've ever worked for? What did they do that made you feel that way?

Where did you work in your career thus far where people got the most done each day, week, month and year? What was it that made the team so productive?

This topic is most relevant for: Everyone

2.14.1 What Organized Teams Have in Common

There are many different ways to organize the day-to-day work of a company. Yet almost all successful companies are organized in a way that has been carefully and consciously chosen by their leaders.

If you've worked on a great team, there's a good chance you want to set up the same kinds of systems for your startup. So long as the game genre, tools, pipelines etc. are reasonably similar that's a very good idea.

All of the widely-used project management systems have a handful of things in common. They track:

• Tasks that need to be done

• Who is assigned to do each task

• When that task is due to be completed

• How we can tell that the task has been completed

There are systems like Agile that are ideal for game projects, since it's hard to identify each step on day one. I'll discuss these options in a later chapter.

2.14.2 The Three Stages of Production

Game development has borrowed project management processes from film, music, television and other media. One of those borrowed systems is the three-stages of production. Its components are:

Pre-production. I've worked on over 100 completed games, and many times the final game we shipped was quite different from our original vision.

The objective of pre-production is to work out all the major details of the game, and to do so before you've spent lots of time – and money — creating code and assets that you'll never use.

• The artists define the art style and create concept sketches and then samples of completed assets for all key characters, items and environments

• The engineers define the memory footprint and requirements for each element of the game, and may prove the viability of

new technology by creating initial working versions of required
features

- The designers work out the pillars of the design and the key play
  mechanics
- Audio engineers and musicians create samples of the sound
  effects and music for the game
- Producers use the data from the preliminary samples to cross-
  check the schedules for the game

A game is only ready to leave the pre-production phase when every
discipline on the team has a clear idea and concrete examples
of what they'll create for the final product. Many changes still lie
ahead, but all the major decisions will have been made prior to the
start of high-volume asset creation.

If you're working with external funding sources they may also have
a signoff that is required before you can proceed to full production.

Production. After pre-production the team has a good idea of
what the game will be, how it will play, its visual and audio styles,
and its technical constraints. This enables a transition from a planning and prototyping stage to a "doing" stage, where the assets for
the complete game are produced.

Teams often grow during this cycle, as additional in-house, contract
or external artists, audio engineers, game designers, producers,
programmers, etc. are added to the team to speed the process of
completing the game

Post-Production. In film, music and television, "post" is what happens after all the filming and recording has been done and the raw
material goes to the editors, audio engineers and other technical
professionals to complete in tandem with the director.

The games version of post-production has many similarities. We
have completed creating assets for the game and now focus on
assembling them into the final version of the game. Many or all of

the people who joined the project at the start of the production phase may spin off to other work.

Gameplay is tuned, QA scours the game for bugs, animations are smoothed, music and sound are synched, and non-required elements are cut. When the game feels like it's ready for its initial release the team ships the first version of the product.

2.14.3 The Delta in Modern Alphas and Betas

For decades the definitions of the software concepts represented by the Greek letters Alpha and Beta were relatively simple and stable:

Alpha is the first fully playable version of the game. It may have temporary artwork, missing details, no sound effects, etc., but you can play a complete game from beginning to end. If it's a level-based game you can play it to a pre-defined level. It may not be pretty, but playing it lets you figure out if the game is fun.

Beta is the first version of the game that you believe is fully tested and complete and ready to ship to users. The team has declared that it will make no more changes to the game apart from fixing bugs, and thus cannot destabilize the code other than through badly implemented bug fixes.

In practice, once this stable version is reached, continued testing will expose more bugs that do need to be fixed. When no more significant bugs are found after a full test cycle, the game is approved and shipped.

So why is it different for apps and online games? Because teams who released early versions of their titles wanted users to understand that these were incomplete and early versions of their games. Since Beta meant "not quite final," they labeled the title screens in those early versions "Beta" so users wouldn't complain about errors or mistakes in the games.

In some early social games this new kind of "Beta" lasted for two years instead of two weeks!

We'll discuss the nuances of these "betas" in more detail in a later chapter. In the meantime, just remember that the word can have very different meanings!

Oh, and that Greek letter "Delta" I referred to in the headline? It means "difference," as in, "The difference between the first and second speed tests was three seconds."

DISCUSSING QUESTION 2.15

Regardless of how efficiently the team worked, and regardless of how much you enjoyed the process, what is the project you've worked on in your career where you were most proud of the game?

What was it about that game that made you feel so proud?

This topic is most relevant for: Everyone

2.15.1 Why Pride Matters

The project that gave you the greatest sense of personal pride is a key beacon in defining how you want to design and build your indie game. It tells us what you value most in the work you do each day. For example:

If you picked the game that made the most money, that says that you derive the most fulfillment from "winning the sales race."

If you picked the project where the team completed the most difficult assignments, it suggests that you value a challenge.

If you picked the project where you liked the people best, that reinforces how much you value great teammates.

If you picked the product that got the highest Metacritic ratings, the best press reviews, or that won the most awards, it suggests not just that you value producing something of quality, but that you're looking for outside validation in addition to your own opinion.

Just remember, your game primarily will be judged on how much fun it is to play and the personal connection you establish with your player community.

2.15.2 What Motivates Top Performers?

How do we build companies where the very best people will feel proud to work? What will make it easy to recruit the best people?

I've had a lot of theories about this topic over the course of my career, and I continue to evolve my thinking.

It's certainly true that one thing that motivates top people is money. If someone's compensation feels deeply unfair, their morale is headed for the dumpster.

But there are other major motivators that will surpass the value of money for many top performers.

I've come to believe that producing a game that is widely respected for its exceptional fun and quality is a deep and powerful motivator. It can command individual commitment even more deeply than cash.

Great games pull in great people, who in turn are far more likely to build something new that's great as well.

So how do you build a team that is focused on producing games of exceptional quality? Here's my checklist:

Look in the mirror and commit to yourself that you're willing to go through all the extra hassle, time, expense and heartache of producing something truly great. When you work your heart out for months or even years just to produce a game that's pretty good, it can be tempting to declare you're done and move on. Leaders who are committed to exceptional quality keep pushing.

Hire people who have that built-in commitment to trying to

build something great. I can say from experience that once you have a few of them at the core of your team the hiring process starts to work on its own to self-select the same kinds of people.

Compete with yourself. Most companies watch their competitors and try to create new games to stay one step ahead of the pack. When they build a hit franchise they focus on growing its sales.

The best publishers then ask themselves, "If we had a brilliant, innovative and well-funded competitor, what would they have to do to build a game franchise that would outsell our biggest franchise?"

Then they go out and execute that plan themselves before a competitor does so, competing with themselves by radically improving their already-successful franchise or developing an even better new one. It's what you have to do to stay on top for an extended period of time.

2.15.3 What Comes First?

I've been asked this question many times at events and meetings around the world.

So which is the chicken and which is the egg? Do happy teams with strong cultures produce quality products? Or do high quality projects inspire happy teams and stronger company cultures?

It's like asking if your heart or your lungs play a more important part in a long and healthy life. If either operates at a less than strong level your life goes downhill fast.

If you have either weak products or a toxic company culture, your business goes downhill fast.

CHAPTER 22

Looking Both Ways (2.16–2.18)

DISCUSSING QUESTION 2.16

How would you feel if you never went back to your current work environment again?

How would you feel if you never saw the people you work with again? Are there some people you'd never miss and others you'd think of constantly?

Are there other perks or activities involved in your current work that you'd be sad to lose?

This topic is most relevant for: Everyone

2.16.1 Ventured, Lost and Gained

Whenever we decide to put time into something new, we have to take time away from something else.

Think about what (if anything) you'd miss if you decided to pursue your indie game project. If this represents a full-time change, think seriously about this list of people, activities and benefits you value most today.

There have been times over the years when I came home from work and said to my wife, "Today was awful. I just want to tell them to '*&^$%$&#*!' and quit this job."

She'd nod patiently and ask me to tell her what happened. By the time I finished (and maybe drank a glass of wine), I usually felt better and my faith in the project had been restored.

If you quit a job and later decide you want it back, there are no magical time machines. Your old boss may no longer be interested.

If you're planning an indie game to get away from your current one, make sure it's something deeper than an occasional bad day or one bad assignment that's driving you to action.

DISCUSSING QUESTION 2.17

What other parts of your life would bring you joy if you could just magically make them go away? Some of these may seem obvious (the IRS?), but writing them down still helps you organize your thoughts.

What other parts of your life would bring you anguish if they were suddenly taken away (e.g. your family, your church, close friends, places you like to go, activities you enjoy etc.)?

Make a short list of things you would and would not like to leave behind, and if you feel especially strongly about any of the people or items on that list, write down why.

This topic is most relevant for: Everyone

2.17.1 The List of Everything Else

What else is driving you to take action right now?

What other realities restrict your choices?

I know that when I start to get excited about even a small, fun project I can lose track of other obligations and consequences. Then I think about it and regain my perspective.

That's what makes these questions important. They're here to remind you of everything else that's important to you, not just the game that's currently dominating your thoughts.

DISCUSSING QUESTION 2.18

Is there anything or anyone in your life now that you need to get away from, so the idea of starting over someplace new sounds especially great?

Is there a bad memory you're trying to escape by moving to a new office or even a new town?

Is there something pushing you towards making a complete, across-the-board clean break and starting over in a different job, a different industry, a different place or with different people around you?

This topic is most relevant for: Everyone

2.18.1 Personal Danger

For most readers this section will not apply, but those cases where it is relevant are incredibly important.

First and foremost, if you are in any situation that represents personal danger, please get help immediately. I know from experience that these kinds of things happen to good people, and that they happen more often than any of us want to believe.

It's easy to rationalize someone else's behavior, explain it in an empathetic way and talk yourself out of acting. You convince yourself that a situation is OK, even though you may feel very frightened and threatened all the time.

Whether the help you seek is best offered by a family member, a friend, the local police, someone at your church, a doctor, a counselor or someone else, reach out right now. Whatever situation it is that is threatening you, there is a way to get help to make it better.

2.18.2 Magnets Can Attract or Repel

Sometimes we can feel like we're stuck in a bad work situation. Continuing in the status quo is unacceptable, but we feel like we have no alternative. I've had times when I hated going to work each day.

I've learned that whenever "getting away from something" becomes my primary motivation I need to stop and think.

If you're running away from a psychotic horror movie villain who happens to be wielding a chainsaw, any direction will do. (But do avoid attics and basements with only one door!)

But when you're planning how to regain the happiness you're seeking, you can't just pick any old direction and run.

No one but you can know how your answers to this series of questions may suggest the next steps in your life and your work. But it's important for you to think about them and about what you really want.

Only then can you fully commit to whatever you choose to do next.

2.18.3 The Power of the New

There's an old joke about a guy who dies after having broken all of the Ten Commandments multiple times, not to mention numerous federal, state and local laws and regulations. He is sent to a dark, foul-smelling corner of Hell, and wanders through its caverns in misery.

Eventually this new arrival comes across a fellow denizen who is smiling and happy, even as a tiny demon appears to be biting him on the leg.

"How can you be smiling?!" the new guy asks. "We're rotting here in Hell! That little monster is biting your leg!"

The happy man looks up at him and smiles. "You don't understand," he says. "This is the Fourth Circle of Hell. I just got reassigned from the Seventh Circle. This place is wonderful!"

Sometimes what is driving us forward is not a specific dream or a thought-out vision, but a deep desire for something new.

But remember, taking the first opportunity that comes along can take you to a worse circle of Hell than your current one.

PART III

LEADING THE WAY

CHAPTER 23

Leading the Way: The Questions

QUESTION 3.1

When you're working on your indie game what will your business card say?

Will it be your only business card or will you still "keep your day job?"

Why did you choose this job title for your card?

Please take your time, write down your responses, and answer fully from your deepest thoughts. Think only about your own opinions, not about what others may want you to think or do. Do not look ahead to other questions until you have finished this one.

QUESTION 3.2

To what kinds of people will you hand your business card? What will you want from them?

What benefit will they expect to gain from knowing you?

What will be the actual benefit they gain from knowing you?

Please take your time, write down your responses, and answer fully from your deepest thoughts. Think only about your own opinions, not about what others may want you to think or do. Do not look ahead to other questions until you have finished this one.

QUESTION 3.3

What will you spend most of your time doing each day when you're working on your indie game?

QUESTION 3.4

If there's anyone else working in the office with you, how will they be spending their day?

How will you monitor their progress?

Please take your time, write down your responses, and answer fully from your deepest thoughts. Think only about your own opinions, not about what others may want you to think or do. Do not look ahead to other questions until you have finished this one.

QUESTION 3.5

If you're planning to be a leader as the company grows, are you ready to let go of controlling every detail of the work?

If you find yourself hesitating to let go of daily control of key aspects of your project, why do you think you're feeling that way?

QUESTION 3.6

What's the one small part of your game you most dislike having to delegate to someone else?

What's the one small part of the project where you can't wait for the company to grow, so you can finally delegate that part of the job?

Please take your time, write down your responses, and answer fully from your deepest thoughts. Think only about your own opinions, not about what others may want you to think or do. Do not look ahead to other questions until you have finished this one.

QUESTION 3.7

You and a group of your leading team members are debating how to solve a major problem.

Several people favor Choice A, others prefer Choice B. People on both sides are getting angry at each other. Two days later a second meeting just makes things worse.

This is an important issue that can't be allowed to drag on. How will you resolve the debate and reach a decision?

Please take your time, write down your responses, and answer fully from your deepest thoughts. Think only about your own opinions, not about what others may want you to think or do. Do not look ahead to other questions until you have finished this one.

QUESTION 3.8

What's the project from your career where managers, teammates and players gave you the most praise for your work?

What were the specific things you did (as best you can remember) that earned that praise?

If your boss praised you for one thing and teammates valued you for something else, and the player feedback valued still another portion of your work, write down answers for each category.

Please take your time, write down your responses, and answer fully from your deepest thoughts. Think only about your own opinions, not about what others may want you to think or do. Do not look ahead to other questions until you have finished this one.

QUESTION 3.9

If you've managed people in your work, at which position did the people who reported to you give you the most positive feedback?

What specific things did you do to earn that praise?

QUESTION 3.10

What's the biggest project you've worked on start-to-finish that shipped successfully?

It may be measured in how long it took to complete, in how many people were on the project, or any other common sense way.

Please take your time, write down your responses, and answer fully from your deepest thoughts. Think only about your own opinions, not about what others may want you to think or do. Do not look ahead to other questions until you have finished this one.

QUESTION 3.11

What's the biggest role you've ever had on a project that was completed and shipped?

Examples of roles include things like artist, CEO, customer service representative, engineer, executive assistant, GM, product manager, project director, sales manager, technical writer, trainer, writer, etc.

QUESTION 3.12

What's the biggest project or component of a project you've ever led? How many people did you direct on the project?

Please take your time, write down your responses, and answer fully from your deepest thoughts. Think only about your own opinions, not about what others may want you to think or do. Do not look ahead to other questions until you have finished this one.

QUESTION 3.13

Have you ever worked for a startup or very young company that failed? If so, why do you think they failed?

Have you ever worked for a startup or a very young company that became a big success? If so, why do you think they succeeded?

CHAPTER 24

My Story: Two Lessons from a Great Teacher

My boss at my first college job was the late Pomona College Professor of Music Dr. William F. Russell. I enjoyed playing in the band under his (irreverent) direction, and earned money for textbooks working for him as a security guard at the music building.

I didn't recognize it at the time, but he had a gift for making the people who worked for him feel appreciated. My job was simple: open the locked door of the music building for students from 6 PM to 11 PM each Sunday night.

The locked door meant that no strangers could enter the building while music students were scattered, alone and vulnerable, in small rehearsal rooms on three different levels. The security guard's presence each night meant that students could still get in to rehearse after the building closed at 6 PM.

One evening in my freshman year Dr. Russell came into the lobby, looked over at where I was sitting and studying, and waved.

"It's good that you're here," he told me.

Three years later, sitting in that same chair as a senior, I still remembered that he thought it was important I was there, doing my job.

As leaders we don't have to make elaborate speeches to make our people feel appreciated. We just have to tell them that their work is important and that we're glad they're there.

And we have to mean it.

Dr. Russell's greatest gift to us was an idea he shared with the band, and later in a Pomona commencement address. "Be careful what it is that you truly want in your life," he told us, "because you're likely to get it."

You may have heard the similar phrase, "Be careful what you wish for," because (as every D&D player knows) the results may not be what you'd intended.

Dr. Russell put a new twist on this idea. His point was that whatever we truly, deeply want most of all – *whether we admit it or are even aware of it* – is likely to come to us in some form.

And, he added, often what we want most of all isn't money or something we can buy with money. But we end up making money from it anyway.

It can actually be harder to make money by chasing it than to make money by chasing our dreams.

Here's another contradiction. Silicon Valley is portrayed as being driven by venture capital and a quest for wealth.

I've been part of a startup that went public, the Silicon Valley equivalent of winning the Super Bowl. Yet as I remember working on that small team, the strongest memory is how much we all loved the products and the work we were doing, even when few people had ever heard of the company.

That's when I remember Dr. Russell's advice: "Be careful what it is that you truly want in your life, because you're likely to get it."

What we all passionately wanted was to build great games, and to be appreciated for the work we did. Because of that passion and focus we got what we really wanted: the fulfillment of having done great work that's still respected many years after the company was founded.

But it also turned out that, because we did great work, the company and the team made a lot of money.

Dr. Russell may have been a great music teacher, but he was even better at teaching us about life.

CHAPTER 25

What to Do with Your Answers (3.1-3.3)

"A DREAMER IS ONE WHO CAN ONLY FIND THEIR WAY
BY MOONLIGHT, AND THEIR PUNISHMENT IS THAT THEY
SEE THE DAWN BEFORE THE REST OF THE WORLD."

— Oscar Wilde

If you have not yet written down your answers, please go back and do so. Writing your thoughts down – even when you're the only one who'll ever read them – will produce far more insights than just answering silently to yourself in your head.

3.0.1 Diving Deeper into the Process

At the start of this book I described what I call the Passion-Process-Product Method:

- We start with our passions
- We experiment to develop a process that allows us to work on an indie game we'd love to create, either part-time or as a full-time job
- When we're ready, we launch our game as a product for our audience to play

As we reach Section 3 of this book we are well into the Process stage of the Passion-Process-Product approach. The task may at times feel daunting, but if you keep going the journey can also be a lot of fun.

Most of all, remember the single most important advice I share in this book: only you can discover and decide upon the right path to take to create your indie game.

DISCUSSING QUESTION 3.1

When you're working on your indie game what will your business card say?

Will it be your only business card or will you still "keep your day job?"

Why did you choose this job title for your card?

This topic is most relevant for: Everyone

3.1.1 Titles and Choices

What title do you put on your business card?

On one-person projects you're doing everything. Do you say "Game Designer" to emphasize your craft, "Director of Product Development" to make the business sound larger, or "President" to tell people that you're the founder?

There are only two "wrong answers" when choosing a title:

1. Never sign up for a job you won't do well.
2. Never allow yourself to take a role on your game that doesn't primarily involve doing work you enjoy. Taking a role you hate, even for the best reasons, soon erases your love for the work and for its outcome.

DISCUSSING QUESTION 3.2

To what kinds of people will you hand your business card? What will you want from them?

What benefit will they expect to gain from knowing you?

What will be the actual benefit they gain from knowing you?

This topic is most relevant for: Everyone

3.2.1 That Little Devil on Your Shoulder

How are you feeling as you hand out your card? You're almost certainly feeling proud, because this is your very personal vision of a game.

But what other emotions, in addition to pride, will you be feeling as you pull out that little piece of printed cardboard?

When I founded my first company I was very proud to hand someone my card. To start with, David Bunnett, our Art Director, had done a fantastic job on the card's design, so I usually got compliments on it. More importantly, I was really confident in the quality of our first products – both games turned out to be successful.

Every time I looked at the letters "CEO" on my business card, however, a little voice spoke up inside my head.

"I don't have an MBA," the little voice would tell me. "I've been through management training with three different companies, but that was all at the Director or VP level. I feel comfortable leading the team, but I can't stop worrying. I don't have formal CEO training, and I could be making big rookie mistakes. Next to an Ivy League MBA I look like an amateur. Maybe I'm in over my head."

What I did not know as I endlessly repeated this internal message of self-doubt to myself is that the Ivy League MBA's whom I envied were doing the same thing.

I've talked with friends who've shared that a little voice in their head kept telling them, "It's the Stanford MBA (or Yale, or Columbia, etc.) that got me the chance to start this company, and the fact that I was part of a team on a successful startup. But I was just a junior member of that team. I keep meeting CEO's who have years of experience working their way up the ladder in great companies. Next to them I look like an amateur. Maybe I'm in over my head."

This self-sabotaging dialogue is not restricted to CEO's. I've discussed the issue with everyone from Chief Technology Officers to Chief Financial Officers and from Concept Artists to Composers. The majority of them have had that same self-inflicted demotivating experience.

If this "maybe I'm in over my head" dialogue sounds like you, it's good to recognize it. Half the battle is knowing that the self-doubt is normal.

That makes it a lot easier to ignore the discouraging little voice in your head, which is exactly what you need to do.

3.2.2 A Hundred Reasons to Hand Out Your Card

The list you made of people to whom you'll hand your business cards says a lot about what you think you'll be doing on your indie game. But sometimes we can miss big opportunities.

Did you list, "people to whom we're selling, pitching, evangelizing, etc.?" In almost all businesses someone has to go out and do the selling, network-building, partner-finding and publicity. If it's you, how will you learn what it takes to be great at some or all of those roles?

Did you list, "people whom we're recruiting?" First-time CEO's or senior managers often see recruiting and hiring as a secondary part of their job. One of the secrets of Silicon Valley is that it's actually a critical and primary function. If you can't build a great team you can't build a great company.

Did you list "partners and allies?" Many young companies accelerate their progress when their game produces a benefit for a much larger company, inspiring an alliance between the two.

For example, if your 60fps shooter shows off the speed and power of Intel's or NVIDIA's chips they may be willing to feature your title in marketing programs to demonstrate the potential of their technology.

Building these alliances is a key part of a CEO's job.

DISCUSSING QUESTION 3.3

What will you spend most of your time doing each day when you're working on your indie game?

This topic is most relevant for: Everyone

3.3.1 Never Enough Hours in a Day

If I'd answered this question back when I founded my first company, my prediction would have been wildly inaccurate.

With just a few people on the team, I found that the coordination of the project and all the extra paperwork that comes with being a CEO conspired to keep me away from the game design work I loved. Being a VP at a large, established company – where much of the admin work is done for you — takes less time than being CEO of a small, lean startup.

Payroll alone was a twice-a-month exercise in hours of agony, since I had resisted paying for our bank's payroll service to do it for us (which I should have embraced from our first week of operations). Making sure the California and Federal employment taxes and deductions were calculated correctly so we didn't have to pay penalties took an hour all by itself on each cycle.

Not all such distractions are predictable. When you're leading a company all sorts of "unique events" can take your time. Some of the surprises can be wild.

One time the local police issued an arrest warrant for one of our team members. It turned out to be a mistake, but I still lost a full day dealing with the police, other freaked-out team members, and the even-more-freaked-out object of the arrest warrant.

Or the day when a key team member's spouse showed up at the office and wanted to help me reorganize our project plan. Right then and there.

Bizarre stuff happens in every group, because we are all unique and human. When you're the leader of a team, everyone's bizarre stuff (at least the public variety) becomes your stuff, too.

CHAPTER 26

Getting Organized (3.4)

DISCUSSING QUESTION 3.4

If there's anyone else working in the office with you, how will they be spending their day?

How will you monitor their progress?

This topic is most relevant for: indie games that involve more than one person.

3.4.1 Staying on Track

Your indie game may be a VR shooter, a paranormal romance adaptation of Japanese graphic novels, or a kids' educational game where all the characters are penguins. Regardless of the game genre and art style, if more than one person is involved in the process, by definition, you have a team.

A small indie team might start out with a CEO who is also the designer, one programmer and one artist. The three of them sit together in a small room and work with their laptops on a single round table.

The leader looks across the table at the co-founders and sees them working diligently. Are they doing the right tasks? Are they doing them well? Will the tasks be done on time?

How do you know that someone is half way through completing something?

As one example, I've held the job of Sr. Engineer, and I'll tell you what I learned. When it looks like you're half way there, you're often only 10% of the way to being "done."

You can fool yourself into thinking you're closing in on final code when you're not even close, which means it's easy to mislead your teammates on scheduling.

The same thing happens in other disciplines. Concept art that's been approved by the Art Director looks like it's ready to drop into the game. But users may think the "Continue" button looks like a toaster. A button may be checked in that takes 32K of memory when the app needs something that fits in 2K.

Changing the color of a button or shaving two millimeters off its size can (in extreme cases) produce a revenue gain or loss of $200,000 a year. Saving $200K isn't a task you skip past because you don't have a free day in the schedule, which is why completion dates are hard to predict.

You can't run a company just on faith that everyone's work will turn out right on the first try. You can't just assume that all tasks will be completed on time.

3.4.2 The Simple Secrets of Management

There are many excellent books on how to lead teams. Below are a few key points that I've learned working with great managers over the years.

Listen first. When I first met Southwest Airlines Chairman Joel Peterson at a Stanford Graduate School of Business Igniters event, he started our conversation by asking about my background instead of waiting for me to ask a question.

I could tell that he was really listening to me as we talked, not thinking about things he had to do when he got home. Now imagine that your boss always listened intently to you – how good would that feel? What would you need to do to be that kind of boss?

No surprise: Peterson's book, *The 10 Laws of Trust: Building the Bonds That Make a Business Great* is concise and well worth reading.

Weekly 1:1's. I believe that every manager needs to schedule a one-on-one with each of their direct reports each week. When I hear managers say they don't have time, my response is, "what's a higher priority than listening and communicating with your team?"

Most 1:1 meetings are fairly short and review key issues, but occasionally something makes a 1:1 into a very important and thoughtful meeting that runs longer. These can turn out to be some of the most valuable meetings you have all year.

In addition to reviewing key objectives, progress and potential problems, there are two key questions to ask in each one-on-one:

- "How are you feeling?"
- "How can I be of help to you?"

Expect success. Strong performers are motivated by an environment where success is expected of every individual and of the team as a whole. Everyone deserves to start out with your trust and confidence, which motivates them to appreciate and preserve those valuable assets.

Spend more time with your top performers than with less pro-

ductive team members. Most of us fall into the opposite pattern if we don't consciously alter it. Focusing on the best people is a pattern I've seen in many highly effective managers, because it amplifies the strengths of an organization rather than diverting attention to lingering problems that should already have been resolved.

Don't hire or retain weak performers. It may be a lack of the right skills, or a mismatch of person and job. Either way, continual efforts to turn a weak contributor into a strong one rarely succeed, and distract leaders from higher priorities. Both parties need to find a better fit elsewhere.

Ask before you tell. I discuss "showing respect for everyone on the team" in several different contexts in this book. There's no better way to show respect than to ask for — and seriously consider — someone's opinion.

It won't be feasible on every topic, but whenever it's possible ask your leading team members for their input on tough issues, both 1:1 and in small groups. Then take the time to really listen to their answers and consider them. When time permits, you can broaden these requests for input to more people across the entire team.

With my teams the ideas presented by team members often were better than some – or all – of the solutions I was considering before I asked for input.

Keep making new mistakes. Highly productive teams try lots of initiatives, make lots of mistakes, and then quickly utilize that learning to improve. So long as people don't repeat the same mistake, supporting this "learn by doing" approach motivates and retains top performers.

MBWA ("Management by Walking Around"). You can't lead a group of people if you're stuck in an office. Walk around every day and randomly ask team members, "How are you doing?" Then demonstrate the listening skills mentioned above. People will notice and respond.

Criticize and correct in private. Routine everyday feedback occurs in public, but if I need to deliver a strong negative message I do it calmly in private. "Treat it as a teaching moment" is some of the best advice I ever received.

I had to learn not to soften the message or "beat around the bush." Just wade in, calmly say what needs to be said, then listen to the response and move on.

Celebrate in public. People should be honored in front of the whole team when something was done well. Every Friday we give some small award or recognition for great work that week. If a small group completes a difficult challenge we praise them in front of the whole team.

If a manager praises a team member in our leadership meeting I'll practice "MBWA" and drop by that person's desk to say, "I heard about how you came up with a clever solution for [the problem]. That was great work."

Play by the same rules you declare for others. Do the things you tell people you're going to do and keep your word. Meet your own deadlines. Admit it when you make a mistake. *This single point is some of the most important – and difficult to consistently maintain – advice in this book.*

None of this is new, and most of it isn't easy. People of many cultures, generations and eras appreciate the same things from their leaders.

British Field Marshal Sir William Slim told his officers 75 years ago (and the full text is well worth reading if you search for it online):

"I tell you as officers, that you will not eat, sleep, smoke, sit down, or lie down until your soldiers have had a chance to do these things. If you hold to this, they will follow you to the ends of the earth... Spare no effort to praise and reward soldiers for outstanding performance — it costs nothing and gains everything... Soldiers are smart and can smell a phony a mile away. Get to know the soldiers in your platoon. After three months, you should know their names, names of family members, home towns, and any unique problems with which you can help... If you take good care of your soldiers they will take care of you."

3.4.3 The Most Common Mistakes of New Managers

Steve Jobs, Warren Buffett and Jeff Bezos all were first-time managers at some point in their careers. It's a rite of passage we all go through.

In this section I'll share the most common mistakes that I see managers make early in their careers, and some basic ways to avoid each trap. We'll also cover these issues in greater depth below.

Oh, and one more thing: I made each of these mistakes myself as I was learning how to lead teams.

Problem 1: Being buddies instead of being a manager with a team. This is one of the most common problems I see in my advisory work. The manager has worked for bad leaders who disrespected team members, and they're determined to act like a friend instead of a boss.

The solution: It's important to demonstrate respect for everyone on the team, but someone has to be in charge. If that's you, strong performers *want* you to lead the team and direct the work that's being done.

If the team isn't getting things done or isn't making money (or achieving some other critical goal), people won't go home each night feeling proud of the company. And they won't get the promotions, the raises or the bonuses they hope for.

Leaders who respect everyone around them and are focused on producing strong results are far more popular than the managers who try to be liked.

Respect and results are the two most important things a manager has to demonstrate, and the former is critical to producing the latter.

This "buddy" issue can also take the form of trying too hard to run the business like a family, something I did earlier in my career. Consider the following list of leadership attitudes:

- Sincerely liking the people on the team
- Wanting to do right by them
- Respecting them and showing that respect
- Helping people develop new skills and advance their careers
- Compensating people fairly
- Showing consideration for individuals with families or other obligations that may require flexibility in work times

This list represents things that good managers do, regardless of whether they think of their company as a business, a family or anything else.

But there are places where those business and family models diverge. If our young children continually failed to do things they needed to do, didn't pay attention at school, etc. we would have taken action to get them back on track.

First we'd talk with them. If that didn't work we'd try turning off the video game system, cutting back on TV time, suspending a favorite activity until they corrected the problem.

But we couldn't fire them and kick them out of the house, because they're family.

Sometimes team members who have been valuable and productive will start to have performance problems. Our senior managers and I would sit and talk with them, try to figure out what was wrong, try to help them correct the problems.

But if they couldn't fix those performance problems after we worked with them and gave them opportunities to improve, they'd be fired.

Managers who get too preoccupied with the idea of "family" take too long to challenge, discipline and terminate poor performers. By doing so they lose the respect of their top performers instead of winning the loyalty they feel their "family" attitude deserves.

A related problem is...

Problem 2: Responsibility without accountability. You may have heard of "Responsibility without authority." This means assigning someone a goal without giving them enough control or resources to achieve it. Picture someone who's directed to complete all arrangements for a team's air travel, but who's given no authority to spend money to book the flights.

Responsibility without accountability is the opposite problem: a manager has the authority and the resources to do a job, but doesn't take action to ensure that the team achieves the desired results. The individual creates problems, doesn't get things done, produces less than their peers, but nothing ever happens.

People wonder, "Doesn't the manager see what's going on?"

Let's say that Anne, Barbara and Carlos each oversee a different mobile game for a mid-sized publisher.

The teams who work with Barbara and Carlos regularly update their titles, add new content, refresh the in-game stores and run a steady stream of events, challenges and activities for players.

Anne's team has grand plans for a major new Version 2.0, and they've completed many new assets that sit ready to be integrated into the game. But many features are incomplete, the new version is behind schedule, the current version looks just like it did six months ago and their only events are sales tied to major holidays.

Inexperienced leaders may hesitate to discipline Anne for her poor performance. It's not fun to tell people that their work needs to improve, and sometimes those people get angry. It feels awful to fire people.

If she does nothing but admonish Anne, the CEO is practicing responsibility without accountability. She's not insisting that managers achieve results. The weak and the strong managers get the same treatment.

After a few months Barbara gets tired of reading nasty online reviews about the company – based on Anne's game — and she quits. Strong performers want to feel proud of the company and everything it does.

Problem 3: Not setting clear goals, objectives and ground rules in advance, and putting them in writing. I'm often hired to help young (and not so young) companies when projects start to fall behind schedule. The most common cause for these problems is that the team started doing its work without first having agreed upon some of the most basic aspects of a plan.

I'm not talking about writing a 250-page document packed with details. What's often missing is a set of answers to the most basic questions of how the project will be completed, initial answers that can be worked out in a few days at the beginning of the project. Many of those answers may change as the work progresses, but teams have to start with an initial plan to work effectively in the early stages of a game.

Let's say you're one of eight people who are working on the team. You've already agreed on the basic elements that the game will contain, and how it will be played.

As you start out, the leader and the team would sit down together and agree on:

- **Who** would direct each creative craft (art, engineering, etc.) and approve the final version of each asset, feature or milestone

- **What** elements of the game would require the approval of the project leader to be considered "done"
- **How**: The sequence of steps (pipelines) used to create each major class of asset in the game, and any requirements (e.g. size in pixels, bytes etc.) for each class of asset
- **Who** would develop each major element of the game
- **When** each major element would be due, and in what order
- **When and where** you'd meet to review issues, resolve questions, share feedback on each other's work, etc.
- **How much** you'd each be paid (often discussed individually in private)
- **When** payments would be made

If a plan meets these "who-what-when-where-why-how much" objectives for each step and has a realistic budget and schedule, it's probably a good starting point for the team.

Passion and excitement are wonderful components of creating an indie game.

Starting without a basic plan – even if it just covers the initial experiments to develop a new kind of game – makes everything much harder to complete.

Problem 4: Under-delegating and Over-delegating. There is no such thing as a perfect level of delegation. It's like driving a car on a narrow, twisting road: you have to continually watch what's going on and adjust accordingly.

Under-delegating is a fancy term for micro-managing the team and not letting go of the details. All decisions are made by the leader, instead of being distributed to the right people at the right levels of the team, and reviewed via the right processes.

Your strongest contributors will resent micro-managing the most, and I've found that it's useful to regularly ask those top people for their feedback on the issue.

Over-delegating is often a side effect of managers trying to be popular with the team. They relinquish control of day-to-day processes, allowing team members to make important decisions without the manager's review, feedback or approval. The manager doesn't ask tough questions, doesn't review and adjust where time and money are being spent, doesn't intervene until problems become big, and tries to be a people-pleaser when it's time to make tough decisions.

Team members resent micro-managers.

They develop contempt for over-delegators.

Neither extreme produces results for the teams these people lead.

Problem 5: Managing deadlines with hope instead of action. It can be very hard to predict how long any project will take unless you've already done the same job several times. So what happens when a project – as so often happens – starts to run late?

The roots of the delay can be a combination of many different factors. The game could:

- Have been started without a clear plan, so many people are unclear on what to do
- Be larger than planned and take longer to complete
- Have too few people on the team
- Have one element that is very difficult to complete
- Have lots of assets that are 20% done, but nothing that's completed
- Be discarding lots of work because it doesn't fit the project's requirements
- Any of a wide range of other issues

What should a manager do? First of all, keep careful track of progress, week by week or (for shorter projects) day by day, starting at the very beginning of the effort. I discuss methods for doing this below.

The moment you see that something is running late, investigate the reasons and then ask yourself and the team, "What do we have to do to keep this problem from continuing?"

The potential answers are diverse: cut features, add people, get different people, increase the budget, redesign things, reorganize things, cancel the project altogether, or do something else.

A steady stream of small changes and revisions can help keep a project on time. If these adjustments aren't made continually, eventually the dramatic actions needed to put the project back on schedule later on will cost lots of money, lower the product's quality, and/or further delay the completion date.

The leader's job is to work with the team to identify problems quickly, develop potential solutions… and then act decisively to do what's needed to get back on schedule.

3.4.4 "If Only We Had Known…" Project Management

One mistake I see many strong teams make is that they practice the management style I call, "If only we had known…"

One month into a game project the team leader knows that they're running behind, and so do his team members. Even with lots of experience, they fall far short of what they had hoped to accomplish in the first month.

They're already working their hearts out, but they have to catch up with the schedule so they work even harder. Nobody's getting much sleep, but it feels like they're operating in slow motion even as they race ahead.

They may suffer from "feature creep," where great ideas keep being added to the project but corresponding cuts in other, lower priority features are not made. Since the project can only become larger, never smaller, it's guaranteed that the team will miss its deadline.

The schedule continues to slip, and everyone works harder and harder and harder. They cut some small features but refuse to cut anything big and important.

With only ten days left to go before the big deadline, it's clear that disaster is imminent. The only way to make the date is to cut two of the five big features planned for the game, something they have steadfastly refused to do.

They have no choice, so they make those cuts. But even this leaves little time to polish the remaining three key items. The initial product is good, but it looks and feels rough instead of polished.

Everyone says, "If only we'd known at the start that we were going to have to make those cuts! We could have put all that time into just three features, and they would have been elegant and solid instead of sketchy."

3.4.5 Picking a System

The only way to prevent this scenario is to use some kind of a detailed project management system.

I'm a fan of the Agile project management approach (which I summarize below). I learned the basics in one night by reading the first 70 pages of *Agile Project Management with Scrum*, by Ken Schwaber.

Agile is not owned by any company and was developed by a multiple-industry consortium, although there are many different books, software systems and apps that can help you use it.

If you're working as a solo entrepreneur an understanding of Agile systems is useful, but most of its rewards come with teams.

The initial time investment in a process like this can save you weeks or even months of wasted work down the road.

3.4.6 How I Learned Agile Development and Scrum

Why did I become so strongly committed to using this system?

We tried using Agile on a project that ran for eleven months, with a team that peaked at about 60 people and a budget of close to $8 million. The game shipped on time, but our team already had a perfect record for meeting the carved-in-stone deadlines of AAA console games.

Here's the consensus we heard from our team members at the post-completion review meeting:

- Using Agile and "Scrum" processes gave us about a 10% increase in how much we produced, without feeling like we had to work harder than before
- We worked late less often and had fewer times when people felt they had to come in over the weekend to make sure we met key deadlines
- People said they felt less stress than on our prior game, even though this one on paper looked like a tougher schedule
- We wasted less time and threw away less work that was done by mistake, or that had to be cut from the game (which his may explain some of the benefits above)
- Over 90% of the team voted to use Agile on all of our projects going forward

As you can imagine, when I saw how strongly our team supported the idea I adopted it without hesitation.

When teams fully commit to an Agile system they acquire natural defenses against over-optimistic scheduling and "feature creep," the two factors that most often damage games. It's based on simple everyday processes that keep projects on schedule and focused on the highest priority work.

Implementing Agile on an established team does require a transition process. I admit that I resist changing my habits or routine, and so does the typical developer. Nevertheless, it's worth working through the issues.

3.4.7 Summary of Agile Project Management Terms

Please remember that the summary below is a super-simplified "cheat sheet" for a system that is relatively easy to learn, but where all the details don't fit on two or three pages.

I've organized the information by defining key terms, and listing them in order as they'd come up on a project:

Product Owner. The term for the person who leads the team and directs its work.

Sprints. At the start of a project the team leaders decide how long the chunks of time into which the project is to be broken should be. Each of these blocks of time is called a "sprint." A long project may have sprints that last a month each, others may go for two weeks. Projects that need very short cycles use a related system called "Kanban," which you can learn online or via guidebooks.

Sprint requirements. Every sprint has the goal of completing a planned set of features that can be demonstrated and tested, even if it's in a very basic manner. This keeps teams focused on finishing the highest priority elements of the product on each sprint. It also prevents teams from starting work on too many features at the same time and never finishing anything.

Sprint Planning. At the start of each sprint the team meets to decide what features they'll complete on that cycle. They then break those features down into tasks and people volunteer to be the ones who will complete each task and estimate how long it will take.

User Stories. Each feature is called a "User Story" or simply a Story. This comes from the idea that every product feature can be described by a sentence that starts out with, "The user will be able to…" This is part of the Agile focus on finishing something useful in every sprint.

Scrum Master. The Scrum Master organizes the lists of planned features, tasks and time estimates from the Sprint Planning process. Each task is then printed on a card with its volunteer's name and its projected duration. This may be done by a software package or completed manually by the Scrum Master.

Scrum Team. The typical Scrum Team size in Agile is about five to eight people, so in a large project the team would split into sub-groups.

Scrum Task Board. At the start of each sprint the Scrum Master prepares a bulletin board or wall in a dedicated space or room. They create columns of index cards that are tacked or taped to the wall. This is called a Scrum Task Board. Tasks for the current sprint are sorted into columns for:

- Not yet started
- Started
- In Test (or "To Verify")
- Completed

Scrum Meeting and Scrum Room. Each morning each scrum team meets in an unoccupied office or a reserved area called a Scrum Room for a maximum of 15 minutes. Everyone is expected to arrive on time, and if you're late the team will start without you.

There are no chairs in the Scrum Room and no one will sit down (apart from the requirements of a physical disability). This makes everyone want to wrap up fast and get to work.

During each Scrum Meeting each team member:

- Shares what they completed the prior day
- Describes in a sentence or two what they plan to complete today
- Moves their task cards to the correct column for "Started," "In Test" etc.

If the team realizes that a task is missing from the plan they write it down, assign it and add it to the board. Over the course of a sprint all the task cards will gradually march across the board from left to right as they are started, tested and completed.

Blockers. If anything is keeping someone from completing a task it's called a "blocker." A blocker can be as simple as "my computer's not working" or as complex as "I can't complete the level until we get all of the models for the props." Blockers are called out in the meeting and passed along to the Scrum Master, but any discussion of solutions is postponed until after the Scrum Meeting to save everyone else's time.

Burndown Chart. After the Scrum Meetings for each team the Scrum Master checks on the status of each task for this sprint and where it sits on the board. They then use their chosen Agile software system to prepare a "burndown chart," which keeps track of how much work for this sprint has been completed and how much is yet to be finished. This allows teams to recognize it immediately if they start to run behind so they can decide what to cut, what to keep and how to prioritize resources.

Sprint Review. At the end of each sprint the teams demonstrate their tested and functional work and earn applause from the project team. If all of the sprint goals are not met the meeting is not as happy, and the lessons learned are carried over into the next sprint.

Product Backlog. Any tasks that were cut from the plan during this sprint are automatically added to a "Product Backlog," which is a list of tasks that have not yet been completed. These are then considered for inclusion in the following sprint.

The Sprint Retrospective Meeting. At the end of each sprint the entire group discusses three questions in an open meeting:

- What worked well during the last sprint?
- What did not work well?
- How could we do better on the next sprint?

At the end of every project a final Sprint Retrospective is held, which covers the lessons from the project as a whole.

On the first couple of Agile projects you undertake, I recommend that you follow the standard rules in the guidebooks. It's hard to customize a recipe to your own tastes until you've made the meal a couple of times and tasted the results.

3.4.8 The Simplest System: Weekly Objectives

If you're hesitant to jump into using Agile, I've used the very basic system described below in a variety of settings. It does two things extremely well:

- It keeps everyone on the team – including the CEO – focused on the highest priority tasks that need to get done each week.
- It tracks whether those tasks are being completed.

Note that this system does not by itself keep complex projects on schedule.

Once a team gets used to the process it takes about 20 minutes a week unless an unusual issue comes up.

Step 1: Definition. Each week the leader and the team sit down together. We go around the room and each team member answers the following question:

"What are the two most important things I absolutely positively have to get done in the next seven days?"

They don't list things they hope to get done. They don't list everything they plan to do. They only list the two most important things that they absolutely positively guarantee they are going to get done in this week.

The group also discusses and agrees on the two most important objectives for the company as a whole.

Completion Criteria. Objectives always have to be worded in such a way that the question, "Did you complete it?" can be answered with a yes or no. "I'll make the presentation look nicer," is an unclear objective. What I think makes it nicer might, in your eyes, make it worse.

"I'll add at least eight new images to the presentation" is very clear: either there are eight new images in the deck one week from now or there aren't.

Review and Discussion. If anyone in the meeting sees that a key task is being missed, they can raise it.

Step 2: Writing It Down. The objectives are written down during the meeting, and afterwards they are sent out as an email, printed and taped to a door etc.

Step 3: Follow Up. The following week the team meets again. Everyone, including the leader, takes a turn answering "yes" or "no" about whether they completed each objective according to its criteria.

When everyone has answered the group then sets objectives for the coming week.

Everyone will miss an objective once in a while. If a team member has a regular pattern of not meeting two reasonable objectives in a week, it suggests that:

- They may not understand how the system works
- They may be unclear on what they should be doing that week
- They may be receiving contradictory direction or input about what needs to be done
- They may have a performance issue that needs to be addressed

Changes. Sometimes something happens during the week that changes priorities. Maybe there's a big storm and the building loses power for a day, so several people cannot complete some of the work they'd planned.

If I'm an artist, I could send a note to my manager, and say I'd like to change my objective from "complete models for two characters" to "draw concept art for two new characters," since we have no power today. The manager approves it, and the next Monday I confirm that I completed this revised objective.

If you don't have a system of your own, give this one a try. I believe you'll find it makes communication more clear and reduces wasted time. After the first couple of iterations it will take very little time each week.

CHAPTER 27

Making Tradeoffs (3.5-3.6)

DISCUSSING QUESTION 3.5

If you're planning to be a leader as the company grows, are you ready to let go of controlling every detail of the work?

If you find yourself hesitating to let go of daily control of key aspects of your project, why do you think you're feeling that way?

This topic is most relevant for: indie games that grow to employ a team.

3.5.1 Cutting the Rope

Occasionally I'll be mentoring at an accelerator when a startup team member – not the CEO – will ask to talk in private. The discussion will go something like this.

"Thanks for talking with me," she'll start out. "I've got a problem with the UX design for our educational game."

"What's wrong?" I ask her.

"It's Jeff. The spec he wrote teaches kids reading in a whole new way using a tablet. He's a brilliant guy."

"I agree," I tell her.

"But he keeps giving me new suggestions, and we've got a deadline to meet. He's the Founder so I don't want to tell him to stop, but…"

"You're afraid you'll miss your ship date," I suggest.

She nods. "I think he's just trying to make the screens feel alive with animations. That's… I like that approach and I think it's good that he keeps reminding me."

"Uh-huh," I say.

"The thing is, I get emails from him every day. He wants to discuss everything in detail. I think he misses doing the design himself and he just can't let go."

It happens all the time. I'm sure that my team members said the same thing about me when I first delegated my design role. And perhaps for a number of years thereafter!

As an organization grows the leaders have to delegate more and more of the details. The CEO and other leaders can retain control through the approvals process, but once a team grows we can't be supervising every team member every minute.

And if we could do so, they'd all get mad and quit!

If you struggle with this idea, what would you have to change about your plans in order to feel better?

DISCUSSING QUESTION 3.6

What's the one small part of your game you most dislike having to delegate to someone else?

What's the one small part of the project where you can't wait for the company to grow, so you can finally delegate that part of the job?

This topic is most relevant for: indie games that grow to employ a team.

3.6.1 Bouquets and Boredom

Whatever you chose as your favorite small thing you hate to delegate, watch this issue, because it's the place where you might find yourself "saying you're delegating but not really doing so."

Your least favorite thing? Just make sure it's something small. Every job has parts of the work day or work week that are less fun.

If what you dislike is at the core of building your game and your company, however, then your plan needs to be revised. Remember, the goal here is that much of the time you're doing work you love, not work that you think you ought to do.

CHAPTER 28

Deciding to Decide (3.7)

DISCUSSING QUESTION 3.7

You and a group of your leading team members are debating how to solve a major problem.

Several people favor Choice A, others prefer Choice B. People on both sides are getting angry at each other. Two days later a second meeting just makes things worse.

This is an important issue that can't be allowed to drag on. How will you resolve the debate and reach a decision?

This topic is most relevant for: indie games that grow to employ a team.

3.7.1 Decisions, Decisions, Decisions

In this question I'm not picturing petty rivals fighting over who gets the corner office. The topic may be something like this, where two reasonable people are deeply committed to very different and credible strategies:

Person A: "We have to put more money into online marketing. The people who buy our game love it, but awareness is still way too low and if we want to get onto the top 50 in the app stores then we have to increase sales."

Person B: "You know that at least two of the big publishers are bidding up the prices on those online ads right now because they have big new releases coming. If we buy more ads at these inflated prices we're throwing away money. We should do a flash sale for two weeks so we get more installs. That's how to make the Top 50."

Person A: "That will just make things worse, because when we revert to higher prices users will be angry and we'll lose more sales than we gained. We have to spend on product awareness, which means online display ads."

Person B: "Players know about us, they just don't like the pricing. Maybe we should just do a price cut across the board, do it once and take our medicine. Then we'll start to climb the charts."

Person A: "We can't do that! If we take our price point out of the premium category there's very little to keep it from being forced all the way down to 99 cents. We'd undermine the value of the whole brand, which means we'd undermine the valuation of the whole company!"

Which of our two debaters is right?

It could be either of them. It all depends on the game and its market position, and even if you had all that data at your fingertips the answer might not be obvious.

Neither of the debaters is driven by selfish motives. Both are trying to make the company successful. Yet as they argue they're getting more and more angry at each other.

Bob Wallace is a highly-respected software industry advisor based in Silicon Valley, and an ally from whom I have learned many valuable lessons. He has a saying that I always think about when I hear teams arguing: "Consensus is great... when you can get it."

There are many different ways to settle things when the leaders of a project, a function or a team don't readily find consensus. Some are useful, others destructive.

3.7.2 The Worst Possible Answer

If you drive north from Silicon Valley towards San Francisco, you have to decide which of the two parallel routes you'll take, Highway 101 or Highway 280.

Which one is faster? It depends on the time and the weather and whether schools are in session and...

When teams have a hard time deciding on major issues, I always remind them about that high-speed driving decision.

"If you can't decide whether to steer towards 280 or 101," I tell them, "you'll hit the concrete divider between the freeways at 70 miles an hour. Freeways remind us that on major business decisions either choice is usually better than no decision at all."

3.7.3 The Leader Decides

If you as CEO simply make a decision and tell everyone what to do, there is no danger of Death by Indecision.

But if you employ high-quality people who show initiative and think independently, making decisions solely based on rank and authority will undermine your support.

It's a strategy you can use occasionally when necessary, but there are usually better options.

3.7.4 Consensus Or Else

Here's the method I like to use on tough decisions. Note that I only handle issues this way if I'm willing to support the premise of any of the choices under discussion.

Step 1: The Leader Questions. I'll ask questions like, "What would you do if game sales in our category started to slip for one or both of the big app stores, rather than growing as we think they will?"

A logical series of questions, asked without prejudice or emotion, can create a more collaborative brainstorming mood in the room.

If this discussion does not produce a consensus answer that allows us to proceed, we move on to...

Step 2: The Leader Provides a Deadline. I'll share with the team, "It sounds like we're stuck. Let's break for now and think on it. If you guys can come up with a consensus answer to recommend to me by noon Friday I'd love to see it. If we're still stuck at that point I'll make a final call and we'll move on."

The benefits of this approach are:

> **The team has time to try to brainstorm and collaborate to arrive at their own solution**. They have the chance to make a decision on their own.

> **People are motivated to keep looking for agreement** because they prefer solving their own problems to being told what to do.

> **There is a clear, pre-announced deadline**, so when that moment comes no one is surprised.

> **Everyone knows that, one way or another, a decision will be made** by Friday.

Step 3: The Decision. In my experience even angry debaters will often work out a compromise to avoid being told what to do by the CEO!

If I'm given a recommendation I'll review it with the team members, ask questions, and sometimes I'll adjust some details. Most often the decision they are recommending is a good one and is approved.

If we still don't have agreement by noon on Friday, I'll make a final decision based on the arguments from all sides.

My decision may or may not be popular. But everyone on the team will recognize that I gave them a chance to solve it on their own, and that we're never hobbled by indecision.

3.7.5 Parkinson was Right

Many years ago an economist named C. N. Parkinson came up with "Parkinson's Law" as both a serious and a humorous commentary on our nature as human beings. It states:

"Work expands to fill the time available for its completion."

I am a great example of how this law works.

When I'm getting ready for work in the morning I try to shave, brush my teeth, shower and get dressed at an efficient pace. I don't want to waste time because I'm usually excited about something I want to work on.

Even with all that motivation, on days when I don't have an early call or meeting I may pause to hear the weather forecast on the radio, or get lost in thought as I brush my teeth.

On days when I have a deadline my behavior is different. I shave and shower more quickly. I keep moving when an interesting story comes on the radio. I throw on my clothes in no time.

As Parkinson would put it, on non-deadline days my work expands to fill the time available for its completion.

I teach CEO's how important it is to understand Parkinson's Law, because it applies to every team.

I also teach them that trying to have "perfect" efficiency under Parkinson's Law is a recipe for disaster:

Each task has its own reasonable minimum time. You could not say, "Hey Don, if you'd focused more you could have written this book in eight hours!"

Perfect efficiency squeezes all the joy out of work. In the early and mid-1900's companies engaged in "time and motion studies" to determine the fastest possible time that any task in a factory could be done. They would then push every employee to execute at that speed. Needless to say, the executives doing the pushing were not having their workdays scrutinized in the same way!

Good teams will operate effectively even if they're not being pushed. Strong project management can increase teams' effectiveness without making work feel like hard labor.

I believe that good leaders are aware of Parkinson's Law and work to minimize its negative impact... without over-doing it.

3.7.6 The Concept of Timeboxing

When we develop games, parts of the project are purely creative. How long does it take to design a title that will win the DICE Award for Game of the Year?

It depends on whether you ask the question before the game is designed or after it wins the DICE Award.

So how do we schedule things when we can't predict exactly how long everything will take?

Part of the answer is "timeboxing," and I used it with the teams that couldn't settle their argument above. By giving them two days to try to solve a problem on their own before I made a decision for them I defined a "time box" within which they had to complete their work.

This works well for resolving debates, but it also has uses in projects where teams are trying to come up with new ideas, character designs, game levels, etc.

Here's an (oversimplified) example where you need to choose a setting and story line for your next game. You could give the team:

- One week to play other game franchises that have strong settings and stories
- Three weeks to develop three potential new game settings and top-level back stories
- One week to collect comments from key team members and adjust the designs based on the feedback

At the end of five weeks, you lead a discussion about which new setting and story line will be used in your next game. If no consensus emerges you'll make the final decision based on the issues raised in the meeting.

Why is exactly one or two or three weeks the right timeline for each step? There is no magic answer, and managers will experiment to produce the best results.

When using time boxes, remember Parkinson's Law. Always look for the smallest time period that still produces good results without forcing the team into working at an unreasonable or counterproductive pace.

CHAPTER 29

Playing to Your Strengths (3.8-3.13)

DISCUSSING QUESTIONS 3.8 AND 3.9

Question 3.8: What's the project from your career where managers, teammates and players gave you the most praise for your work?

What were the specific things you did (as best you can remember) that earned that praise?

If your boss praised you for one thing and teammates valued you for something else, and the player feedback valued still another portion of your work, write down answers for each category.

Question 3.9: If you've managed people in your work, at which position did the people who reported to you give you the most positive feedback? What specific things did you do to earn that praise?

Question 3.8 is most appropriate for: Everyone

Question 3.9 is most relevant for: People who have previously managed teams or businesses

3.8.1 What Position Do You Play?

Early in my career I worked at a company that sent managers to a week-long leadership training program. Their goal was to prepare us for more senior roles.

As part of the exercise we received detailed "360-degree" reviews that the consultants conducted, gathering feedback from our bosses, peers and direct reports.

There were eight managers in our little group, from different departments across the company. We each faced different challenges.

When they handed out the reviews we all got very different feedback. But there was one pattern all eight of us had in common.

Every single one of us thought we delegated responsibility to our teams and that we did it well.

Every single one of our teams disagreed.

After a long career of leading companies and advising clients, I've learned that relying solely on self-perception doesn't work. We have to get real and honest feedback from other people.

That's why I asked about when the people around you gave you the most compliments. That praise is an independent sign of where your greatest natural strengths may be found.

So long as those strengths align with your personal passions, they're a great place to start planning your personal role in building your indie game.

(Question 3.9 is also covered by the text above.)

DISCUSSING QUESTIONS 3.10, 3,11 AND 3.12

Question 3.10: What's the biggest project you've worked on start-to-finish that shipped successfully?

Question 3.11: What's the biggest role you've ever had on a project that was completed and shipped?

Question 3.12: What's the biggest project or component of a project you've ever led? How many people did you direct on the project?

These topics are most appropriate for: Everyone

3.10.1 The Biggest Job You Ever Mastered

When you "go indie" and start a company, you're hiring yourself to do a job. In fact, you're hiring yourself to do several different jobs, and to do them simultaneously!

If the projects where you have gotten the most praise have been ones where you were an individual contributor rather than a leader, it doesn't mean that you're not cut out to manage people. All it means is that you haven't had the chance to lead yet, or haven't yet succeeded at doing so.

If your indie game involves leading a team for the first time, is there a way to move towards a leadership position in your current company? Can you hone those skills serving your present manager before you start out on your own?

Do you enjoy being a leader? Are you always on the organizing committee for the company party?

Or does being a manager feel like having to go to the dentist and get a tooth drilled five days a week?

I once worked with a really talented engineer who was also very good with people. He was a natural leader, very well-organized, and he was good at listening to people and giving them useful feedback. He earned great reviews as a leader. There was just one problem.

He hated being a manager.

This engineer wanted nothing more than to be programming on a really challenging assignment for our company. We paid managers and top non-managers similar salaries to avoid forcing them to go into management to earn more money, so there was no penalty for his decision. When he requested the change I approved it, with regrets.

If you hate managing, find a different person to do that job. Then you can focus on the work you love that will make your indie game special.

3.10.2 Learning on the Job

Or maybe it's just that you've never managed a business before and you're worried about it. It's rare that the leaders of small companies have experience in every aspect of their project.

My Master's Degree is in Education, not Business. My internship was spent teaching in barrio classrooms, not pitching in elegant board rooms. There are a lot of lessons about running a company that I learned by making mistakes. Lots of mistakes.

When I founded my first company many of the questions in this and the following sections of this book would have stumped me. My goal here is to make sure that in the future none of these questions stump you.

In a perfect world, the size of your team and your role within it should not dramatically exceed the size of your role in the largest project you've done while working for someone else.

Even if you have experience leading large teams, remember the K.I.S.S. principle: it's good to keep things a simple as possible.

Building something at a similar or smaller scale than projects you've experienced means:

• You've seen one way that people successfully tracked deadlines and managed schedules

• You understand the emotional ups and downs of working on deadline-driven teams with people who (like all of us) aren't perfect

• You've experienced what it's like to complete something and ship it

• You've lived through (and survived!) the 80-20 Rule (also called the Pareto Principle), which states: "The last 20% of the work takes 80% of the time"

(Questions 3..11 and 3.12 are also covered by the text above.)

DISCUSSING QUESTION 3.13

Have you ever worked for a startup or very young company that failed? If so, why do you think they failed?

Have you ever worked for a startup or a very young company that became a big success? If so, why do you think they succeeded?

This topic is most relevant for: Everyone

3.13.1 The Other Kind of Equity

If you've only worked for successful companies, you're working at a disadvantage compared to your less-successful peers.

As human beings we learn fastest and absorb knowledge more deeply when we fail.

In my career I've had a number of big projects that were successful, and I enjoy talking about what I learned on them.

But if you ask me, "Don, what are the most important lessons you've learned as a games industry producer and CEO?" something different happens.

I'll reel off a series of bullet points, and I can hear myself getting emotionally revved up. That's because many of the lessons I'll share come from when we as a team – and often I as an individual — made decisions that led to failure.

I'm really determined not to make those same mistakes again.

If you've been part of an organization that failed, think about what you learned. Are there lessons that you can use on your indie game?

Sometimes when I ask this question I'll get a flip answer like, "I learned not to take a job working for an idiot."

That's missing the point. A failed business is a trove of potential learning, but you have to get past the blame (and the avoidance of taking blame yourself) in order to learn from it.

I was discussing this issue recently with Bob Wallace, the veteran Silicon Valley advisor with whom I've worked for many years.

"That's the difference between entrepreneurs and other people," he told me. "Non-entrepreneurs see the failure of a game or a company as rejection. Entrepreneurs see it as experience, and a milestone on the road to getting things right."

PART IV

WHERE AND HOW

CHAPTER 30

Where and How: The Questions

QUESTION 4.1

What are the five single words that best represent your most important principles and values, the five words that tell people what you stand for?

In what order would your prioritize those five values, with the most important one, the one that takes precedence over everything else, listed first?

Since the words "values" and "principles" mean different things to different people, I'm going to start you off with 50 options from which to choose.

Please feel free to use your own words if you don't find the right concepts below. If my "placeholder" definition feels wrong, ignore it and write down your own meaning.

The hard part is picking the five most important values and principles and ranking them from #1 to #5.

Note: I use "we" in the definitions below, but most of these priorities could just as easily apply to a one-person project.

Our initial 50 options, in alphabetical order, are:

Accountability – When things go right people are praised and rewarded. When things go wrong we look to teach and correct, and if problems persist people are disciplined.

Adaptive – Our world and our market change rapidly, and we change ourselves and what we do to adapt with it. (cf. Classic.)

Aggressiveness – This can take many forms: our sales team contacts lots of potential clients and makes lots of proposals; our pricing doesn't match the competition, it crushes them; our ads are bold, proud and loud, etc.

Classic – In a world where "the fastest way" and "the cheapest way" have taken over, we create exceptional value for customers by doing it "the quality way." (cf. Adaptive.)

Collaboration – We value people and teams working together to produce the best results. (cf. Competition.)

Commitment – We're not doing one thing, then traipsing off to do something else. We're committed to our product, to our customers and to our team.

Community – We are part of communities (neighborhood, industry groups, users, etc.) and derive benefits from them, so we seek to give back to those communities as well.

Competency – We only do things we believe we can do well.

Competition – We compete in everything we do to bring out the best in everyone and everything. Our internal teams and individuals compete with each other in order to better compete with outside rivals. (cf. Collaboration.)

Courage – We aren't afraid to try things, even if they seem hard, risky or unpopular.

Data-Driven – We generate and gather data and then leverage the learning we gain from it.

Decisiveness – We investigate, discuss and evaluate complex issues, but we make fast decisions. If a decision turns out to be wrong, we fix it.

Discipline – Once decisions are made and instructions are given, everyone does what's called for in the plan.

Diversity – We want to build a team that is made up of a wide range of kinds of people.

Earth-Friendly – We don't harm the environment in any material way as we carry out our work.

Efficiency – We make the most out of every minute and every dollar, and we do it every time.

Empathy – We "walk in the shoes of the users" and focus on the quality of their experience.

Equality – We treat our team members and everyone with whom we deal in a consistent and fair manner.

Experimentation – We constantly try out new ideas.

Fair Trade – We pay our partners a fair amount in all transactions so that they can meet their basic economic needs.

Faith – Our personal religious beliefs and values also govern our business (e.g. we don't have anyone work on a Sabbath, even if the day falls in the middle of a major conference or trade show).

Fast Learning – We learn fast from our experiments and continually use that learning to try new things.

Focus – We prioritize one clearly-defined goal at a time and do whatever it takes to achieve it.

Growth – In order to prosper, the business has to grow.

Honesty, Integrity, Truth – We don't lie, we do what we say we're going to do, and we say what we really think even if it's unpopular. When we say something that turns out to be wrong we acknowledge and correct it.

Initiative – Our people come up with their own ideas and use their own best judgment when called for. They don't always wait for someone else to tell them what to do.

Innovation – We create new products or new ways to do things.

Internal Growth – Whenever possible, we look to promote people from within rather than bring in experienced people from outside the company.

Intuition – It's hard to explain, but ideas just come to us. We vet them and then we implement the best ones.

Investor Focused – We place a very high priority on creating value for investors.

Knowledge – We seek to learn from everything we do.

Loyalty – We show loyalty to our customers, partners and team members, and work to earn their loyalty in return.

Market-Driven – We see needs in the market and then we fill them. (cf. Passion-Driven.)

Passion-Driven – We create products that we are passionate about bringing to life and that we believe will inspire passion in customers. (cf. Market-Driven.)

Persistence – We don't give up just because something is difficult or discouraging on the first try.

Personal Development – We support each team member as they work to improve current skills and to acquire new ones.

Philanthropy – We give money, time or both to causes and charities in which we believe.

Price Leaders – We produce the same products with equal or better quality than our competitors at lower prices.

Professionalism – We take our work seriously and we do things in an organized, responsible and professional way.

Profitability – We're here to make money. (cf. Revenue and Users.)

Quality – Every product we ship is of exceptional quality. If something doesn't meet that goal we'll improve it till it does, or discontinue it.

Reliability – We keep our promises, whether they're about products or about how we work inside the company.

Respect –We always treat everyone with respect, even when we disagree.

Results Focused – Other things don't matter if we don't get the results we need.

Revenue – We have to generate revenue. (cf. Profitability and Users.)

Scale –We want our products to be used by millions of people.

Shipping – You haven't achieved anything until you ship. We focus on shipping things, not just talking about them.

Transparency – We do our work "in the light of day" and don't secretly do things that violate our values or that mislead communities, customers or team members.

Uniqueness – We're not like everyone else. You see our product and you instantly know it's ours. You look at our website or a video or a magazine ad and you'd know who it's from even if our name weren't on it.

User Growth – We're out to build a large user base. (cf. Profitability, Revenue.)

Please take your time, write down your responses, and answer fully from your deepest thoughts. Think only about your own opinions, not about what others may want you to think or do. Do not look ahead to other questions until you have finished this one.

QUESTION 4.2

Think of someone you've worked with where things didn't go smoothly. The reasons don't matter, and we can't work perfectly with everyone.

What are the five words that this person would say best represent your values if they're asked to describe you?

How do you feel about the words they would choose?

Please take your time, write down your responses, and answer fully from your deepest thoughts. Think only about your own opinions, not about what others may want you to think or do. Do not look ahead to other questions until you have finished this one.

.

QUESTION 4.3

We all struggle with being perfect in living our values. You may value being on time but may arrive late when traffic is bad.

Which of your five key values presents you with the greatest struggle? In what ways?

QUESTION 4.4

If you could pick any place to work on your indie game, where would it be?

Is it just down the street, or a dream destination like Hawaii or Southern France?

Is it your dream to work from your home office?

Please take your time, write down your responses, and answer fully from your deepest thoughts. Think only about your own opinions, not about what others may want you to think or do. Do not look ahead to other questions until you have finished this one.

QUESTION 4.5

If you plan to hire people to work with you on your indie game, how many will you hire in the first year? In the second year?

What skills or professions will you be looking for? Which kinds of people will be easier to find, and which will be especially hard?

Please take your time, write down your responses, and answer fully from your deepest thoughts. Think only about your own opinions, not about what others may want you to think or do. Do not look ahead to other questions until you have finished this one.

QUESTION 4.6

When you're hiring new people for your team, how will you identify great people in a sea of applicants who are "pretty good?"

What process will you use to interview people who apply to work on your team? How will you make final decisions on who to hire?

QUESTION 4.7

Are you planning to set up a new company for your indie game?

Or is it something small where (at least initially) you won't have large payments coming in and you can report it as personal income on your taxes?

If you're forming a company, do you know what legal classification of company you want to organize?

Please take your time, write down your responses, and answer fully from your deepest thoughts. Think only about your own opinions, not about what others may want you to think or do. Do not look ahead to other questions until you have finished this one.

QUESTION 4.8

If your company grows, how will you organize things? Will you have departments (e.g. an engineering department) or will you arrange people so project teams work together?

QUESTION 4.9

Are you planning to outsource any software development as part of your indie game?

Please take your time, write down your responses, and answer fully from your deepest thoughts. Think only about your own opinions, not about what others may want you to think or do. Do not look ahead to other questions until you have finished this one.

QUESTION 4.10

What kinds of business licenses will you need to operate your game studio (if any)?

QUESTION 4.11

If you're going to have employees, are there any special employment laws in your city and/or your state that add additional costs, paperwork or operating rules to your planned business?

Please take your time, write down your responses, and answer fully from your deepest thoughts. Think only about your own opinions, not about what others may want you to think or do. Do not look ahead to other questions until you have finished this one.

CHAPTER 31

My Story: Clarity Inspires Commitment

My wife and I were married very early in my career. I was finishing my master's degree in Education at Claremont Graduate University, and was working as a bilingual middle school teacher in a barrio school in Southern California.

The games industry did not yet exist. We thought I would have a career as a teacher and (I hoped) as a professional writer.

Then fate intervened. My hobby of writing computer games on the university mainframe computer had prepared me for the emerging video games industry, and my path veered from Education into high-tech startups.

My wife has ridden all of the wild ups and downs of the Silicon Valley rollercoaster at my side, as well as all of the booms and busts of the video games industry. We've experienced success, failure, and everything else, and we've always stuck together through it all.

I have told every team that I have ever led that I have very clear priorities. "I am completely committed to the company and to the project," I'll say, "but there's something you should know. There is no company, no project and no job that is more important to me than my marriage and my kids. And I'm completely cool with it if you feel the same way about your family as a member of our team."

I say the same thing at conference sessions that I give around the world on the topics of leadership, management and game development.

I've had people come up to me after those speeches and disagree strongly with my position. "There are times when everyone has to just drop everything and work their butts off as many hours a day as they can," they tell me. "You can't just give people a 'get out of jail free' card because of their families, because that just makes more work for everyone else who has to cover for them and breeds resentment."

Here are my responses to this argument:

The fact that my wife and family *know* that they come first does not make it harder for me to work long hours when there's a big deadline. It actually makes it easier. When there's no doubt about your partner's priorities it's more comfortable for families to support these bursts of effort.

Our sons are both grown men. As I mentioned in an earlier chapter, I have absolutely no regrets that I attended every weekend game the boys ever had as they were growing up (with rare exceptions if I was out of town at a conference or trade show), from kindergarten soccer through high school baseball. I made it to many of their weekday games as well.

I lost no business opportunity by doing so, though I know many companies pressure team members to skip kids' soccer games when a major deadline looms.

Even in the toughest times, when I've worked 90-plus hour weeks, I usually took time out to have dinner with my family and help put the kids to bed. I've followed the same guideline for having dinner with my wife after our children were grown and on their own.

Being part of a startup means you have lots of long days. Startup teams usually have less money than usual, fewer people than usual, and the potential for much greater rewards than usual. You know that you're not signing on for a nine-to-five lifestyle when you join this kind of team. It's a lot more work than a typical job.

If super-long hours that block out the sun of family time go on too long and too often, however, it's destructive to the goals of the company. In fact, I think that treating such long-term "crunch time" schedules as acceptable invites self-fulfilling bad planning by leaders.

It all comes back to the words that I use so often in this book: balance and common sense.

I have friends who believe that startups have to crunch continually for months or even years, and others who think that you can have a winning "nine to five" startup where extra time is discouraged.

I disagree with both of those opinions.

Whether you agree or disagree with my ideas, the most important thing is that you think consciously about your own opinion and your priorities. Then you need to honestly and openly share and discuss those values with the people who love you.

Finally, you then need to discuss them with the people who join your indie team.

CHAPTER 32

What to Do With Your Answers (4.1-4.3)

"AS YOU GET OLDER YOU BECOME THE PERSON YOU ALWAYS SHOULD HAVE BEEN."

— David Bowie, 2012

If you have not yet written down your answers, please go back and do so. Writing your thoughts down – even when you're the only one who'll ever read them – will produce far more insights than just answering silently to yourself in your head.

DISCUSSING QUESTION 4.1

What are the five single words that best represent your most important principles and values, the five words that tell people what you stand for?

In what order would your prioritize those five values, with the most important one, the one that takes precedence over everything else, listed first?

This topic is most relevant for: Everyone

4.1.1 (Almost) No Wrong Answers

This exercise is designed to get you thinking about your management style, and especially about the priorities and trade-offs that inevitably come with leading real-world teams on indie games. If you've seriously considered these 50 potential priorities – and perhaps more – you'll know a lot more about your priorities and values from the process of selecting the five ranked choices you wrote down.

If you have co-founders or collaborators, it can be fulfilling and constructive to discuss these issues with them as well.

There are very few "wrong" choices on the list, although they vary based on the goals of your new business. In that context, here are some choices that would raise red flags for me if I were advising your team:

If you did not list Profitability — If you're hoping to take home any money from your indie game, or if you're hoping for it to support itself financially for more than a few months, this goal needs to be high on your list.

As every first-time entrepreneur discovers, running even a small business involves more costs than we predict when we start out. Our first-year revenues are often lower than we expected. Even if making money is not the primary goal of your indie game, if you don't make a profit you won't be able to do the work you love for very long.

The news headlines often equate "Profit is our Goal" with ruthless magnates who pillage the world of business.

If you're running your business responsibly there is nothing wrong with making money. In fact, if you're doing great work you deserve to be rewarded in this way.

But you have to recognize the need for profit, then actually prioritize it. You have to be willing to say to yourself and the people you work with, "We're here to make money because this is work we love, we're proud of what we do, and we have to make money in order to keep doing it."

For some people this comes naturally. For others – especially those in creative or artistic fields — it requires a deliberate change of attitude. If you want to do work you love, it's a road you'll almost certainly need to travel.

If you listed Profitability as your top priority — Listing profitability as #1 implies that Honesty is to be sacrificed in the quest for money. In one recent example, Wells Fargo Bank encouraged such a results-driven culture that employees created over two million fictional new accounts in an effort to meet targets and earn bonuses. The ultimate result: millions of dollars in fines, multiple lawsuits and the resignation of the CEO.

If you did not list Quality – I discuss the issue of prioritizing Quality repeatedly in this book. After over 30 years of working in Silicon Valley I have seen very few teams succeed in business – or in any indie game – without this value being inscribed near the top position on their list.

If you did not list Honesty, Integrity, Truth or similar values – Would you want to work with someone who didn't treat these values as important? Would you want to do business with them?

If you did not list Diversity – The most effective way to reach a broad, diverse audience – and sell more games — is to build a diverse team. If photographs of your team and of your intended audience feature the same kinds of people, your chances of success grow dramatically. If you're a mostly-male team trying to build games for women your odds of success aren't good.

Historically the games business has employed fewer women and fewer ethnic minorities than the population at large, and done so at lower salaries. Improving these ratios is a matter of fairness. The teams who follow those inclusive principles, however, will be rewarded with larger audiences and increased sales as well.

4.1.2 Nought May Endure but Mutability

The famous English poet Percy Bysshe Shelley (whose wife Mary wrote the original *Frankenstein* novel 200 years ago) concludes one of his most famous poems with the line, "Nought may endure but mutability."

In modern language, we might (less poetically) rephrase that line as "Nothing lasts very long except the fact that nothing lasts very long."

Even though your principles may not change, the world around you is morphing constantly. Sometimes you have to find new ways to conduct business based on your principles.

A core value of mine is "loyalty." At one time I lived that value by keeping all of the work at our studio in-house rather than outsourcing.

My objective was to retain a stable team, rather than building and then disbanding all but the core group for every project. I reasoned that keeping teams together would produce higher quality work, and talented people were more likely to return my loyalty by staying at the studio. Many people did just that.

Years later the business environment had changed. Publishers, anxious to hold back rising production costs, had required that projects include less-expensive remote teams.

We had to cut our pricing by 25% to stay in step with these new rules, and could no longer employ complete teams year-round. We had to use more short-term and temp positions, although we openly disclosed the expected duration of temp assignments as a matter of transparency and to help people plan their search for their next assignment.

I still value commitment and loyalty very highly, both as something that I owe to others and as something I look for in return.

But market changes forced me to alter how I turn my values into action. I still try to build as much long-term stability as I can at the heart of a project, but I have to accept that I cannot manage the same way I did 20 years ago.

4.1.3 Team Values and Living What You Preach

Knowing and sharing your core values gives you a place to start with your team on any tough issue.

We once hired a team member who got off to a good start on his first day. The next day his wife called to say that he was in the hospital in critical condition with an infection, and would be away from work indefinitely.

I had a decision to make. This was an important job, one we'd hate to leave open for very long. After just one day we could easily terminate him and hire someone else.

At our management meeting that week we discussed what we should do. Most of the leaders in the room had worked together for years, so they knew what was coming.

"We always start from our values," I told them, for what was probably the hundredth time. "We expect commitment from our team, so we have to live the same values. Termination is not an option. We have to find a way to hold things together until he's back."

I didn't actually need to say anything at all. Each of our senior managers would have made the same call if they were the CEO . Sharing values is part of what holds teams together.

In fact, if I'd suggested termination our senior managers would have revolted, because it would have compromised values they held before they ever joined our team.

We cobbled together a plan to cover for the missing team member for several months until he could return to work.

When we went to visit him in the hospital, he apologized for missing work and thanked us for the support.

All I could think of to tell him were the four words, "You're one of us."

P.S.: The rest of this story is happy. He recovered and worked with us for years. We remain friends, they have a growing family, and he continues to have a successful career.

DISCUSSING QUESTION 4.2

Think of someone you've worked with where things didn't go smoothly. The reasons don't matter, and we can't work perfectly with everyone.

What are the five words that this person would say best represent your values if they're asked to describe you?

How do you feel about the words they would choose?

This topic is most relevant for: Everyone

4.2.1 Harsh Critics Can Be Our Best Teachers

The story above about following our values when a team member was in the hospital is one that makes me proud.

But we all have memories that make us anything but proud.

One time I got caught up in my own ego and confronted a combative manager in another group at the company where I was working, creating a cross-team feud.

I wasn't standing up for an important value – the issue we were fighting over was trivial. What I saw as his condescending attitude had made me angry, and I publicly accused him of being petty and political.

Of course, by saying so in front of our peers I was being petty and political myself. Not to mention making it harder for both groups to work together.

This manager (or anyone else looking at my behavior) might have written these five "values" as what they saw in my behavior:

1. Aggression
2. Competition
3. Intuition
4. Passion-Driven
5. Initiative

I'm not proud of that behavior. Those five values can be very positive in some contexts, but as a summary of the attitudes I projected that day I'm embarrassed to list them.

I've thought back many times to the moment when I picked that fight unnecessarily out of impatience and ego, and reminded myself not to make the same mistake again.

This process of reflection mirrors the two self-review questions recommended by Dr. Vijay Sathe of The Drucker School at Claremont Graduate University in his book, *Manage Your Career*:

When you do well, consider who else helped you... instead of losing perspective and becoming overconfident.

When you do poorly, consider what you can learn from the experience... instead of losing perspective, beating yourself up and losing your confidence.

DISCUSSING QUESTION 4.3

We all struggle with being perfect in living our values. You may value being on time but may arrive late when traffic is bad.

Which of your five key values presents you with the greatest struggle? In what ways?

This topic is most relevant for: Everyone

4.3.1 What I Learned from a Parenting Class

When our sons were young we went to a parenting class at one of their schools. That class taught me something that I realized was just as true for businesses as it is for families:

Your kids don't judge you by the values and rules you tell them they ought to follow.

They judge you by the values they see you live and the rules you follow in front of them. Even when you think they're too young to understand, they start to know you as you really are.

The clerk at the store gives you a ten-dollar bill as change when it should have been one dollar, and you say nothing. Your child knows your advice to "never cheat" can be ignored, because you ignore it.

You want to get home to watch the big game on TV so you drive the wrong way on a one-way alley for a block to escape a traffic jam. Your child knows your advice to "always obey the law" can be ignored, because you ignore it.

The hardest part of having kids isn't being awakened in the middle of the night or getting them to do their chores and homework.

The hardest part of having kids is having to live the values we tell them to embody, instead of merely reciting those principles and then ignoring them.

This principle applies at work as well. If you always start meetings a few minutes late you'll notice that your team stops arriving on time, even if you keep asking everyone to come at 2:00 o'clock sharp.

I'd known this in principle, of course, but the parenting class really drove it home. I had kept extra change I was given by mistake when we were at the store. I had exited through a parking lot's "entrance only" driveway onto a different street to avoid traffic.

Ever since that class, I've done a better (albeit not perfect) job of living by the rules we taught our kids. It's an important management skill that's worth the effort.

CHAPTER 33

The Home Team (4.4-4.6)

DISCUSSING QUESTION 4.4

If you could pick any place to work on your indie game, where would it be?

Is it just down the street, or a dream destination like Hawaii or Southern France?

Is it your dream to work from your home office?

These topics are most appropriate for: Everyone

4.4.1 Fun Spots

In this book the person whose feelings matter is you. In that context, here are some factors to consider when considering where you'd like to work.

Are you picturing a favorite vacation spot? I've dreamed about what it would be like to run a company in Europe or in some tropical location. I throw away the idea each time because I love where I live, and I know the romance would wear off of other places once I moved there and started missing friends and family.

Ask yourself, "Is it the project itself that gets me excited, or is it just the prospect of being in such a great place?"

Doing work that you hate in a wonderful location will, in time, wear you down and make you miserable just as certainly as doing work you hate in a boring office.

4.4.2 Local Spots

Is the location for your indie game studio someplace close to home that also works well for other reasons?

I established each of my companies within a twenty-minute drive of my home. This is both convenient and practical, since I live in the San Francisco Bay Area, a hotbed for top tech talent.

Is your ideal spot a leading business hub for the games industry? Seattle, San Francisco, Los Angeles, Austin, Chicago, Raleigh-Durham and Boston are examples of such cities in the U.S., and there are many more around the world.

DISCUSSING QUESTION 4.5

If you plan to hire people to work with you on your indie game, how many will you hire in the first year? In the second year?

What skills or professions will you be looking for? Which kinds of people will be easier to find, and which will be especially hard?

This topic is most relevant for: indie games that will grow to employ more than a small team.

4.5.1 What Size is Right?

As we've discussed, the best size for your first indie game is "as small as possible."

Growth sometimes happens by accident. A game explodes in popularity. You blink, and a team of three has turned into a team of thirty.

Some companies — especially those backed by outside investors – build a plan that will require that their brand-new startup grows their headcount rapidly. Their backers won't give them time to evolve the business slowly "like running a marathon."

These investor-backed startups are required to make an all-out sprint to create a product, blitz the market and scale the company into a large business.

Here's what's most important: pick the size of your company, don't let it pick you. Remember that some indie games only work financially for their team if the group stays small. It's your job as a founder to make sure you understand where in that spectrum your game falls.

I've seen cases where a business that made sense as a small company sabotaged its own best interests by trying to go big all at once instead of gradually and carefully. Sometimes the trigger is as simple as the CEO getting a lecture from Uncle Jimmy at Thanksgiving dinner about "what it really means to succeed in business."

The following Monday the founder stops using common sense and starts using Uncle Jimmy sense, which leads to lots of new hiring or new advertising or other expensive new things. Disaster ensues.

On the other hand, if you are a talented (and lucky) indie team that produces a breakout hit, you'll need to grow in order to earn the rewards of your hard work. Just avoid long-term financial commitments that can later drag down your cash flow, and make your growth measured instead of messy.

4.5.2 Why Growth Isn't a Dirty Word

In business school managers are taught the principle that "a company that isn't growing is dying."

I rejected this idea when I first heard it, but then realized that it's a matter of mathematics and probability. Here's how that math works:

The "status quo" for any company and for any category of business rarely lasts for long.

New products may have unpredictable ups and downs, but older products almost always have declining sales. You eventually reach the point where everyone who wants your game has already bought one. A competitor may come out with a great new rival game.

New product revenues can be very hard to predict. Your new RPG isn't the big hit everyone expected. Stuff happens.

Managers who are focused on not growing their companies arbitrarily resist responding to larger opportunities. But they *can't* control random downturns in revenue.

If you refuse to grow, the only other options are staying at the same size or shrinking. The random nature of business means that eventually something will go wrong and that downturn will happen.

It's a matter of math, and once you understand it you'll always be looking for at least some growth in your company to counteract the natural downdraft of aging products.

DISCUSSING QUESTION 4.6

When you're hiring new people for your team, how will you identify great people in a sea of applicants who are "pretty good?"

What process will you use to interview people who apply to work on your team? How will you make final decisions on who to hire?

This topic is most relevant for: indie games that will grow to employ a team.

4.6.1 Making the First People the Right People

Regardless of the size of your indie game, the choices you make when you hire people are some of your most important business decisions.

Your first three people, all by themselves, establish the core culture of your team, and if you're the leader your impact is the greatest of all.

It's critical that those first three people use the next seven hires to refine and reinforce the culture that governs how the three of you get things done. They in turn will model it for the next ten hires, who will model it for the next twenty, and so on. I've seen this approach work up to and beyond 200 people at a company.

If there are parts of the culture you don't like when you grow larger, look back at the first ten people, including yourself. Often you'll see that the roots of the large company problems were already present in those early hires.

Or you may recognize the moment when you didn't stick to your values and began to hire people who changed the culture in ways you didn't want.

4.6.2 My Law of Company Culture

I made up my Law of Company Culture as part of a conference keynote speech a few years ago. Here's how I defined it:

A Company's culture consists of:

1. How things really get done, regardless of official systems or policies, and...
2. How the people in the company feel when they come to work each day.

If you avoid hiring destructive people and show respect for team members you'll have quality teams.

If you have processes and procedures that work well at getting things done, those productive people are likely to be happy. Continually work to improve your processes and they'll be even happier.

Learning how to play the company culture game really well – in a way where everybody on the team wins — takes years of study. But it's one of the most interesting challenges I've ever faced, and one of my favorite topics when I advise indie game teams.

4.6.3 The Power of Terminology

You may have noticed that I rarely refer to "employees" in this book. I prefer to use the term "team members."

Disney calls all their employees "Cast Members." Many companies call them "Associates."

I think that what you call people as a group or a class says a lot about what you think of them.

I personally don't care for the terms "Employer" and "Employee" (outside of formal documents). The Employer has all the control and the Employee is under control. It implies that one of them is supposed to do the thinking and the other is supposed to do as they are told.

"Teams" work together under the guidance and direction of a coach or manager. But soccer, baseball or basketball players don't stop in the middle of the action to ask their boss what to do.

They operate by planning, discussing and taking direction from their manager, and then using their best judgment about what to do.

Team Members who emulate that system at work will be far more effective and productive than their counterparts who wait to be told what to do. That's why I call the people I hire "Team Members."

4.6.4 The Myth of the Warm Body

As a CEO and as an Advisor to startups I've often heard people say, "We haven't been able to find anyone good to fill this job, and the backlog of work just keeps piling up. If we don't find someone soon we're just going to have to get a warm body in here so we can finish this project."

People who've worked on our teams know what happens if some-one starts to talk about "warm bodies" in front of me.

I know it's tough. If there are major tasks that aren't being com-pleted you can feel like you're watching the long fuse on a stick of dynamite slowly burn down. When you run out of time the explosives will blow up your company.

These are some examples of the times when you'll be tempted *not* to stick to your values:

When you're trying to find a strong software engineer to code a critical part of your game. These are rare engineers, and everyone is looking for them. Hiring a good one is both very important and very hard to do.

You interview a guy who's clearly capable of doing the work, but he's obnoxious, condescending and rude. He looks at a code sample from your CTO and says, "This must have been written by an 8th grader." People would hate to be around him, but he'd solve a huge problem your team is facing.

Will you hire him or stick to your values of only hiring great people?

When you need an experienced marketing leader who knows how to get your game noticed without spending a lot of money. The team interviews a guy who has made six pretty-good games into hits with great promotional programs.

But his cologne smells worse than last night's trash. He tells one of the interviewers how good she'd look if she wore certain kinds of clothes. He's repulsive, but he could sell a lot of games.

Will you hire him or stick to your values?

When you need a controller to clean up the tangled mess of two different accounting software packages so your fast-growing company stays on top of cash management. You interview a woman who has all the skills necessary for doing the job.

But she tells each interviewer that she graduated *cum laude* from Vassar. Her resume includes the fact that her 12th great uncle served with George Washington at Valley Forge. When she hears that the Marketing Director got his B.A. at Oregon State she wrinkles her nose in contempt of his non-Ivy-League status.

She's disrespectful, egotistical and inconsiderate, but she could save you $50,000 on your next corporate tax return.

Will you hire her or stick to your values?

Many managers would disagree with me, but here's how I handle these situations.

I say no.

I would rather endure whatever consequences we'd suffer from an open position than knowingly hire someone who will be a bad fit and undermine our culture. Being consistent on this "no jerks" policy has actually made it easier for me to recruit great people.

I've made this mistake on a large scale twice over the years, when I caved in to team members who (with good reason) felt desperate for help and didn't stick to my personal convictions. And both times I ended up regretting it almost immediately.

I've always rationalized these two bad decisions in the context that our teams and I have made hundreds of great hiring decisions over many years. But each bad hire did tremendous damage to the company.

The current problems will come and go. But a bad hire keeps doing damage as long as he or she is there, until you finally fire them. Firing them is a time-consuming process that reminds you and everyone else on the team that you never should have hired them in the first place.

Worse yet, once you hire the toxic team member you stop considering alternative solutions for the problem:

- Outsourcing a portion of your programming with a company that matches your culture

- Working with a publisher until you learn how to make your game stand out on your own and are ready to become an indie publisher yourself
- Having a temp agency accountant clean up your accounting systems

None of these are risk-free options. But when you stick to your guns on only hiring quality people you're proving your team that you're committed to your values.

Your team will notice your actions, not just your words.

4.6.5 Planning and Recruiting Under Pressure

Full disclosure: I am married to a successful recruiter who has been working with game and tech companies for many years. All opinions I express about recruiting should be considered in this context.

The traditional method of recruiting is that you put an ad on a huge online website and a steady stream of resumes from qualified people piles up on your desk. That will still work for some jobs.

But for many positions you could easily get a hundred resumes without a single strong candidate. That's really frustrating when you paid a lot of money for an ad.

The best way to recruit is to have current team members recommend former co-workers whom they know and respect. These pre-screened candidates will have a much higher success rate than strangers. Many companies pay a bonus for referring successful candidates to motivate people to call up their friends.

The first place prospective hires will go to learn about your company is your website. With so many demands on your time, building a great company website early in the recruiting process is a priority that's easy to postpone, but if you are recruiting it's a necessity.

Is the position is one that a recent graduate can fill successfully? Local schools have placement offices where counselors will spend time working with students interested in applying for your jobs. This can save you significant time and money on recruiting fees.

Any schedule that assumes that several people will be hired for tech-based jobs in a short period of time is almost certainly overoptimistic and unrealistic. If any of them are especially tough hires they need to be spaced out with long lead times before they're needed. Be sure to budget in "padding" time for their training and for them to come up to speed, because even the best people don't learn the ropes overnight under new systems on a new team.

Interviewing someone for a job is not just a matter of blocking off a half hour of one manager's schedule and the candidate strolling in for a chat. Developing the right questions, preparing the team and planning who will be in on the interviews all require time and thought.

If you have several positions open there may be a significant number of interviews before you fill them, which in the aggregate can take a lot of time from people on the team. That time needs to be budgeted to avoid the process being rushed and careless, and to not impact important project deadlines.

Not everyone you hire is going to work out, and this risk has to be recognized in your plans and schedules if you're experiencing a lot of growth. In California and in many other states in the U.S. employers can establish policies saying that they have 90 days in which to evaluate a new hire and make sure they're settling in successfully.

After those 90 days separating them from the company can be

more complex and expensive. Check the requirements in your state, province or country to make sure you understand the relevant laws.

If your team gets to be twenty or more people, it can be helpful to have an outside attorney who specializes in HR law review your employment documents and procedures. The regulations are often complex, individual cities may have their own local rules, and it can be easy to try to do the right thing and still be hit with a significant fine.

Recruiters' services are often expensive, so it's worthwhile to use them only for difficult-to-find professions and specialties.

Some recruiters charge by the hour for their services. "Contingency Recruiters" charge a fee only if they bring you a candidate whom you hire, and their fee will be a percentage of the new employee's annual compensation. More experienced and better-connected recruiters charge a higher percentage than less experienced people, but are more likely to bring you high quality candidates.

"Retained Search" recruiters are paid the same kinds of salary-based commissions as contingency recruiters, but there's one big difference: they are paid in installments as they start and carry out the search, regardless of whether you hire someone or not.

4.6.6 The Art of the Interview

Many of the co-founders and early employees of Electronic Arts came from Apple, and they brought some of Apple's processes to our team at EA. One of those Silicon Valley traditions was the extended personal interview, which has become standard practice at many tech companies.

Here's a summary of how that system works:

Resumes are screened by a recruiter, by the hiring manager for the job, or by both.

The hiring manager calls the top few candidates and has a short (30 minutes, give or take) interview called a "phone screen." He or she approves a short list of candidates to pass to the next round.

In the case of some technical positions the manager may also ask the candidate to fill out a test of their technical knowledge. Engineers, for example, might be asked to write a short program to achieve a simple goal, or they may be given existing code and asked to identify problems within it.

Some companies have expanded these required tests for different disciplines into extended, complex mini-projects. In my experience this often pushes away the best candidates – who will quickly receive multiple job offers without having to jump through such hoops — and is often counter-productive.

Note: Some states of the U.S., as well as other nations, have very specific laws about how these tests can be used in hiring. If you're going to do candidate testing, get legal guidance from an HR attorney.

The candidate is asked to come in for a series of interviews, and told the process will take several hours.

The key decision makers pick people to do interviews with each of the candidates.

When we were a small company we involved everyone on the relevant project. When we grew larger we selected the relevant managers and a mix of peers and (for a new manager) potential reports to the position. We'd usually end up with six to nine people, some who interviewed as individuals, some who talked to the candidate in groups of two or three.

If the team was serious about a candidate, I would interview him or her in the last interview slot of the day. This avoided having my comments as CEO color the answers that the candidate gave to other interviewers.

On the day of the interview the recruiter or hiring manager greets the person when they come in, has them fill out an employment application form (if they haven't already done so), and gives them a schedule of the planned interviews.

It is important that every interviewer walk in to meet the candidate not knowing if the prior interviews have gone well or badly, so every discussion starts from a clean slate. If an individual interview raises big warning signs or concerns the interviewer can inform the hiring manager after the session so they can determine how to proceed.

After the last interview the candidate is thanked for their time by the hiring manager and released to go home.

4.6.7 Making Decisions

If you're the CEO, you are the ultimate and final guardian of your company culture. It's critical to make clear to teams that their role in this process is one of being advisors, not of controlling the decision, because any other approach undermines that cultural shield that only you can provide.

That said, in years of using this interview system I don't remember ever hiring someone on whom the team's consensus was clearly negative.

Once every few years (yes, that's *years*) I would veto a hire that a majority of the team members wanted to make. The fact that such vetoes are so rare tells you how well you can trust the judgment of good teams... if you start with the right people.

In interview debrief meetings we always go around the table and have everyone give their input before I speak. When CEO's speak first – even those who encourage open debate – it discourages contradictory opinions.

If the team is split in their opinions I do not act as a tiebreaker. Instead I ask questions to help reinforce the key skills we're looking for in this job, which often helps produce a consensus as people talk.

If that consensus does not emerge the CEO then makes the final decision and the meeting is complete.

CHAPTER 34

Founding a Company (4.7–4.8)

DISCUSSING QUESTION 4.7

Are you planning to set up a new company for your indie game?

Or is it something small where (at least initially) you won't have large payments coming in and you can report it as personal income on your taxes?

If you're forming a company, do you know what legal classification of company you want to organize?

This topic is most relevant for: Everyone

Note: This is a topic on which I can share my own experiences, but before you make any major decisions I'd advise contacting your attorney and your accountant. The relevant laws are different in many countries, and vary highly just among the different states in the U.S., so there are no "one size fits all" answers. There are taxation risks and other issues involved regardless of which choices you make, so understanding the individual factors and options is important.

4.7.1 Forming a Company

In many jurisdictions, if you're doing a small, part-time venture you don't need to go through the trouble and expense of setting up a separate business entity. If you're just taking in a small amount of money, you can report that revenue for taxes as personal income.

You can also inexpensively set up a very simple form of business if the amounts of money involved are not large. Be sure to research laws in your region to confirm the regulations that apply in your personal case.

If you are planning to ask for money from investors, you're unsure or there is anything else complex about your company I'd recommend a face-to-face attorney meeting to get advice before you file any paperwork.

4.7.2 When do I Need to Set Up an LLC or Corporation?

Depending on local, state and national law, you may want to take this formal step:

When your revenues reach a threshold defined by laws or regulations. In some jurisdictions there are formal requirements that apply.

When the deals you're doing involve sizable amounts of money. If you're doing work that involves larger payments you may want to have a company engaging in the business rather than accepting payment personally.

In many jurisdictions, if you are working as an individual rather than as a company someone who gets into a dispute with you can sue you personally. If the person or company gets a judgment against you, the court can force you to personally pay the penalties.

If someone on your team driving to a business meeting were in a car crash and the other driver were badly hurt the results could be catastrophic. In the United States individuals injured in accidents can receive hundreds of thousands or even millions of dollars as settlement from the person who is deemed to have caused the accident (usually via insurance) *and their employer*. Any activity that exposes you to these risks is best done from within a formally organized entity that maintains all necessary insurance.

4.7.3 The Curse of Co-Equal Partners

There are some company structures that can lower the chances of success for a startup.

When a company has three (or four or five) equal owners and no pre-arranged formula for who controls the final decisions, "Who's In Charge?" is always a negotiation.

When the partners agree, the business proceeds normally. But the moment that one partner disagrees and a discussion does not resolve the issue, there is a two-to-one vote and one partner "loses."

This tends to tear down the personal relationships that hold the company together. If one partner is always on the losing end of the debates he or she may leave. If, for example, that person is the CTO that may doom an early-stage business.

On any decision where two partners split, they may each curry the favor of the undecided partner. Partners may spend more time trying to outmaneuver each other than they spend running the company. Such teams rarely succeed.

To be fair, this arrangement is not always dysfunctional, and one of my long-time clients has three co-equal founders. One night at a dinner with their management team I asked their CFO how they made it work.

"We were aware of the problems that can arise without one final decision maker," she told me. "We'd worked together before, and we wrote down rules so we wouldn't be haggling with each other all the time."

I share this story to illustrate that equal partners is not an impossible structure for a business. But it does take the right people who share the right values in order to make it work.

4.7.4 Stock Options and Vesting

Note: I'm not an attorney and I'm omitting many details in the summary below. There are variations in laws and rules in some states, and in many of these cases there are tax considerations for both the company and for the stock option recipient, which is why you'll want to be guided by a good lawyer.

If you're looking to share the upside financial potential of a new business with team members, the typical method is to issue stock options.

Stock options give someone the right to buy a predetermined number of shares in a company at a predetermined price, usually a price that will be very favorable in a few years if the company does well. They are given to key team members, who often work for below-market salaries in the early days of a company.

Owning shares in a company means you're part owner of the company, the same way that you would be if you bought shares in Apple or Google. Shares are often referred to as "equity," another term for stock. "Having an equity stake" means the same thing as "owning stock."

Co-founders may have a stock pool with special terms for those who joined the company at the start, when the venture is most risky. They may work for dramatically lower salaries in order to earn more stock.

If the firm is a big success the option holders will have the chance to earn much more money by selling their vested stock than they could ever have received in salary and bonuses elsewhere. Higher risks yield a higher potential reward.

Stock options do not give all the stock to the person at once. Instead they have:

A Term: How long the person has to stay with the company in order to earn the right to buy all the shares awarded in the option. In my experience the most common term has been four years.

A Strike Price: The price at which the person has the option to buy each share. They are not obligated to do so. Options do not give team members shares for free. They only give the right to buy a set number of shares for the Strike Price. Regulations govern the range in which a strike price can be set to prevent such levels from being artificially high or low.

A Blackout Period: A period at the start of the option where the option is completely cancelled if the person leaves the company, in which case they have the opportunity to buy no shares. In the four year options I normally see, the most common blackout period was six months, though in recent years I've seen a lot more 12-month blackouts. If a new hire does not stay with the company until the end of the blackout period they do not earn any shares.

An Execution Date: The date when the Term of the stock option begins. This can be a team member's first day of work, can begin after they have worked with the company for three months or a year, or any other date that the company chooses. The team member also has to sign a document accepting the stock option, since there can be tax hassles (along with great joy) if the company is successful.

A Vesting Formula: This determines how many shares the team member earns the right to buy based on how long they stay with the company, or upon hitting clearly defined goals. Each time a team member hits one of the milestones, they "vest" a certain number of shares, which means they earn the right to buy them at the Strike Price.

My favorite vesting system is a "trickle formula," which is commonly used in Silicon Valley. Let's say that Susan is a key early team member at Acme Inc. and is awarded a 48,000 share four-year option. If Acme has authorized the issuance of 10,000,000 shares this represents almost half of 1% (about 1/200th) of the company if Susan stays employed the full four years.

The trickle formula I prefer is that the team member vests 1/48 (just over 2%) of the assigned shares each month for four years. In Susan's case that is an easy to calculate 1,000 shares per month.

If the blackout period is twelve months, Susan vests no shares for the first year after she receives the stock option. On the first day of the thirteenth month, she vests thirteen months of shares: the twelve months of vesting that were during the blackout period, plus the shares she vests in the thirteenth month. After that she vests 1/48th each month for the rest of the four years.

If Susan leaves after four months (voluntarily, laid off or fired), she'll have vested no shares and will not have the right to buy any shares.

If she leaves after 26 months she'll have vested 26,000 shares, and has the right to buy them at the Strike Price if she wishes to do so. The rest of the shares in her option are cancelled.

An Expiration Date: The date when the option expires if the team member does not exercise it and buy the shares. After this date the option to buy the shares at the Strike Price is lost. I've seen different periods, but the most common is ten years.

4.7.5 Cliff Vesting, and Why to Avoid It

There's another vesting system, called "cliff vesting."

Sometimes when people use the term "cliff vesting" they're really just talking about the Blackout Period described above, especially if it's a full twelve months. As part of the system described above I believe it's a viable format for companies.

But there's another kind of cliff vesting, and it can be manipulative and insidious. Under this system there are no small monthly sets of shares that Susan would vest. Instead she might vest 5,000 of her 48,000 shares all at once after one year, 10,000 more shares all at once after two years and the last 33,000 shares all at once after four years.

Some companies that practice this system have regular layoffs. People who are close to vesting a major block of shares are more likely to be cut from the payroll in these layoffs. If they miss the vesting date by even a day, they lose the right to buy what could be very valuable stock, and Silicon Valley is full of bitter stories that are rooted in this system.

I would never work for a company that offered me this kind of back-loaded cliff vesting, and I would never impose it on the people working with me to build a company.

4.7.6 Paying Royalties, and Why to Avoid It

Many indie game studio founders look for a transparent and fair way to share the financial rewards if the team builds a game that turns out to be a big hit. If they don't want to issue stock options, the most common way in which they try to do this is by paying royalties to team members.

One of the biggest advisory jobs I've ever received brought me into a mid-sized game publisher. My assignment: to help clean up the cultural mess left by their founders' well-intentioned employee royalty program.

Instead of making everyone feel rewarded, as the company's leaders had intended, it made 80% of the team angry. And that 80% included many of the people who were most responsible for turning one of the company's games into a big hit.

The changes we made in their compensation system worked, but getting everyone back to feeling good again took over a year of hard, patient work by several front-line managers.

So why do royalty programs backfire so often on the leaders who create them? There are two reasons:

Rewarding the people on an individual project creates competition, not collaboration, between teams. If Irving and Susie are leading two parallel projects and the company has just one star programmer, they'll fight each other in surprisingly aggressive ways to get that person on their team.

It isn't just a matter of Irving and Susie wanting to earn a big check for themselves. The team that gets the star programmer will believe that they have great odds of earning extra money, thanks to their manager's political skill. Their morale and their manager loyalty will both be high.

The team that gets the pretty-good programmer thinks they're doomed before they even start the project. They are demotivated, angry at the company and especially angry at their manager for not standing up for their interests.

This is why whole-company rewards almost always work better than team-specific ones.

Royalty programs require managers to identify the levels of reward for individuals in advance. If the system runs off of job titles, an art director gets this much, and a recent-graduate animator gets far less (if anything).

If the system is driven by manager decision, those calls are made in the early stages of the project. "Sandra is the lead programmer," a leader might reason, "so she'll get x% of the royalty pool."

Once you get into a game project, however, it's like watching a professional sports team across an entire season. Some established stars are distracted, lose focus and produce less. Some experienced people are given easy assignments. New recruits blossom into stars on their first projects, making a huge immediate impact.

In the case of the well-intentioned publisher I mentioned above (where I have changed many details to disguise the participants) a programmer who carried out an average-difficulty assignment and did it well got a check for an extra $100,000.

Late in the game's development schedule, however, no one knew this game would be a hit. The team was struggling, the gameplay wasn't fun, and the game was about to be canceled.

One morning, two young game designers who had just joined the team came into the producer's office and presented a series of ideas they'd been working on. The ideas sounded good, and the team implemented them.

Within a week, players at test sessions were laughing and smiling and having fun. The new designers had filled in the critical missing pieces. It was their work that ignited the game's unexpected success.

The two designers received zero royalties, zero bonus dollars, and almost zero praise. The team's royalty-vested veterans had done excellent work, but without the newcomers' help those leaders would have failed. They nevertheless got all the royalty cash and all the honors.

The company founders realized that many of the royalty dollars were going to the wrong people, but (as they should) felt compelled to honor their commitment. Once they'd spent hundreds of thousands of dollars on royalties they didn't feel they had the resources to spend a lot more money rewarding the correct people, as much as they would have liked to do so.

The two new stars left the company shortly after the game shipped. The majority of the team members, who received little or no royalties, were angry at management and at the team leads who received the cash.

The team leads were angry at everyone else for being angry at them.

I worked with the founders and managers to cancel the royalty program and replace it with stock options.

Why do stock options work better than royalties? There are several reasons.

Stock options reward the success of the entire company, not just one team. This limits cross-team competition instead of encouraging it.

Stock options usually don't have caps on their eventual value, while many employee royalty programs place limits on how much most team members can earn.

Leaders can determine rewards after a project is completed instead of publishing a royalty chart before it starts. There are guidelines in Silicon Valley for how large each kind of team member's initial stock option should be at the time they join the company. Leaders can add additional shares as a reward, and for key contributors those add-on shares can be far greater than their original grant. For true impact players you can layer on additional rewards more than once, a process called "evergreen options."

Stock options don't cost near-term cash, but deliver long-term rewards to team members if the company is successful. Leaders can give large financial rewards to top performers, and do so without depleting their cash. And you know how important it is to preserve your cash!

Stock options encourage team members to stay at a company. If the company is doing well people want to stick around to vest more shares. In Silicon Valley, if you give a key team member a big check they may quit and use the money to start their own company. That's not what we're trying to do with our rewards for team members!

4.7.7 The Catch 22 of Compensation

Cash compensation is an issue that drives strong emotions, because it has such a big impact on our lives and on our pride and confidence levels. My opinions are below for you to consider, but every experienced manager ends up working out their own preferred set of practices. Your personal values and experience should drive your decisions on these issues.

Researchers have proven over and over again that a big majority of people feel they're underpaid at work. In some cases this is because, well, because they're underpaid at work.

But there's a psychological element to compensation, too. As humans we are driven by deep instincts to always try to do better tomorrow than we did today.

- We want our kids to have a better life than we did when we were young
- We want more reserves in case there are layoffs
- We want to make family arguments about money go away
- We want to finally be able to afford that vacation (or that new car, or that bigger apartment) we've always wanted
- We want to feel proud of ourselves, not just for the money but

for the validation that we do important work

I have thought all these thoughts and felt these drives to earn more money throughout my career.

Once you have the final call on what people get paid in a company, this normal psychology becomes a Catch 22. Even when you're working your heart out to be fair, a majority of people are likely to be dissatisfied with their compensation.

And you have to learn to live with it, even as you work to make your system even more fair next month and next year.

Salaries and Raises. Once your company is well established, you'll want to have access to games industry salary data from The Croner Co. or another data provider. You can use public surveys like those done by the IGDA and websites like Indeed.com, but the respondents reflect a random cross-section that may not account for geographical deltas. As a result, numbers may be significantly higher or lower than real averages. (Note: I do not have a current business relationship with The Croner Co., but have previously been a client of theirs for many years.)

Team members generally receive a written evaluation and a salary adjustment once each year. It's best to stagger these around the year based on start dates – the companies that evaluate everyone at the same time face big all-at-once increases in costs rather than a gradual increase.

Bonuses. The great things about giving someone a bonus are:

- You can tell the person exactly what they did that was great to earn the bonus (which will make them want to keep doing that same thing)

- You can provide fast positive reinforcement for doing something outstanding, rather than having to wait seven months till their review

- A bonus can be used instead of a stock option to reward someone for their key role in building a hit game – and you can wait to determine that bonus until it's clear who made those critical contributions

- If the great performance doesn't continue no one should be surprised that you don't pay another bonus

- You can pay bonuses when the company is making money, and scale them back when things are tight

- It's a one-time expense, not one that recurs and builds from year to year

- If it feels right you can give an impact player a bonus several years in a row, so long as they understand that it's never a guarantee and is performance based

- Having more small "spot bonuses" for more people can work better to motivate teams than fewer, larger bonuses

Different states, countries and different cities have different laws about salaries, taxes, bonus etc. Once your company has more than a few team members it's wise to review your practices with an attorney.

4.7.8 Trademarks

You'll want to protect the name of your company and the name of your game with trademarks, which keep someone else from using the same name and creating confusion in the marketplace.

If you have a tag line or something similar for a game you can also seek trademark protection for that phrase. For example, EA Sports' famous "If it's in the game, it's in the game" line was registered as a trademark back in 1993 and most recently renewed in 2015.

If a name is already trademarked by someone else in the software industry (or in some cases, the broader industries of computers and electronics) you'll generally need to pick a different word, phrase etc. If the term is previously trademarked only by a greeting card company, there's a good chance you can use the word or words.

As with so many legal issues, to lock down your protection you'll need at least a short interaction with an attorney. Depending upon the complexity of the issues you may be able to save money by using a service like LegalZoom, but if your entire business is based on getting a certain trademark it's better to work with a trademark attorney. (Note: I have no business relationship with LegalZoom.)

As a preliminary check, you can do a free online simple trademark search via the United States Government Trademark Office site (do a Google search for "us trademark search tess" to find links to the TESS trademark search page). This system will identify existing and expired trademarks, but may miss valid ones that have not yet been filed or finalized, so the results are not conclusive.

4.7.9 Copyrights

Copyrights are somewhat simpler than trademarks to secure, but like any kind of legal protection they can get complicated.

You can copyright your game (or website, book, or painting etc.) just by placing a copyright notice on the title page. Many game developers don't realize, however, that this does not protect your game idea, concepts, algorithms etc. It doesn't even protect the game's title, for which you need a trademark.

The elements it does protect are the game's code, art and audio. The copyright to the code is easy to define, but how different do a copycat game's graphics have to be to avoid being sued for copyright infringement? Clear and outright copies are easy to spot, but if there are differences in the items then the issue is open to interpretation by the courts.

Many basic questions about copyright in the United States are answered at the government copyright office website at https://www.copyright.gov/help/faq/index.html.

For those games where you expect to make a significant amount of money, copyright is another one of those issues where you'll want to consult with an attorney. This is best done when your project is approaching completion, so you have a clear idea of what you'll want to protect.

4.7.10 Patents

A patent attorney once told me, "Most patents are sizzle, not steak – especially software patents. Startups get them to make themselves look good, not because they'll protect them from a well-funded competitor. But a patent is usually like a tuxedo: you buy it thinking you'll get a lot of use from it, and then it just sits there in the closet."

Those "tuxedos" are very expensive to acquire and even more expensive to keep. For most indie game teams a patent is a distraction, not a priority.

So why doesn't a patent provide strong protection for a new company?

Filing patent infringement cases costs a lot of money. If a big company infringes a small company's patent, they know it can cost the little guy hundreds of thousands of dollars — or even millions — to sue the infringers.

Aggressive competitors will not do direct copies that are no-brainer infringements, but they'll look for ways to "muddy the waters" and create questions about whether their new product infringes on a small company's patent. With so many details to argue, the case and the legal bills can drag out for years. Most small companies don't have the resources to do so and they don't sue.

Are there any cases where an indie game company should consider filing a patent application, given the high costs and potential low value? If you have a lot of funding in hand, these are some cases where you could consider it:

If you're creating unique hardware to go with your game (itself a very risky business).

If you use existing hardware in a completely new way. If you coded rumble-enabled controllers to operate in a unique way to treat some physical disability you might be able to patent the process, rather than trying to patent hardware or software.

If you create software tools that do some process more efficiently or faster than it has been done before (e.g. a unique kind of compiler) a patent may be more clear-cut than for other software.

If you elect to pursue a patent, you'll need to work through a patent attorney. Experienced attorneys will give you advice on whether an idea is worth pursuing, and will do so before you make the big up-front financial investment that a patent requires.

DISCUSSING QUESTION 4.8

If your company grows, how will you organize things? Will you have departments (e.g. an engineering department) or will you arrange people so project teams work together?

This topic is most relevant for: indie games that will grow to employ more than a small team.

4.8.1 The Internal Services Model

To explain this concept I'll use a silly example: Acme Enterprises has a website that sells three product lines: cosmetics, motor oil and baseball cards.

They could have all of their website designers work in a single department, and do the same for the copy writers and for the engineers. A manager would head each department and ensure that each project gets what it needs.

This is sometimes called an "internal services" model, because each group treats the Cosmetics team, the Motor Oil team and the Baseball Cards team as clients. These internal "clients" submit requests for services, and the departments respond to them.

4.8.2 Cross-Functional Teams

Alternatively, Acme Enterprises could assign to the Cosmetics team the necessary web designers, copy writers, engineers etc. to support all of their activity on the website. Staff members would likewise be integrated into the units that sell motor oil and baseball cards. A manager would coordinate all the work for each product category.

These self-sufficient groups are often called "cross-functional teams," because they don't need to request services from any other department. All the different professionals who would perform those services already work within their team.

4.8.3 The Patterns I've Seen

My first three years in business were spent at a large, traditional corporation. Every product line was split into marketing and product development teams, each reporting to a marketing or product development executive.

There were times when it seemed that the departments spent more time on internal politics than they spent trying to build and sell great products.

Later in my career I joined small startups where the focus was on surviving and succeeding. Engineers, artists, designers and other professions all reported to a single manager, so everyone in the group had a shared goal. In many companies Marketing has been integrated into these teams as well.

These experiences gave me a strong opinion: having everyone assigned to a project team reporting to the same manager usually produces far better results than teams divided into traditional departments.

Playing by the Rules (4.9-4.11)

DISCUSSING QUESTION 4.9

Are you planning to outsource any software development as part of your indie game?

This topic is most relevant for: indie games that are too large to be solo projects.

4.9.1 External Technical Teams

If you don't have all the necessary game development disciplines on your indie team, you'll need to make a list so you can sort out where you're already covered.

In each case below we're looking to involve someone with strong, relevant experience in game development:

- Who is providing the money to pay people as they work on the game? Or will this be a part-time side project so you don't need to pay yourself or anyone else?

- Who will design your game?

- Who will manage the game's production?
- Who will create the art? If it's a 3D game, who will model and rig the characters? Who will model the environments?
- Who will animate the game?
- Who will create 2D or 3D backgrounds and environments, sky-boxes etc. if needed?
- Who will create the sound effects?
- Who will compose the music?
- Who will do the programming? If it's an outside company, will they use a publicly available engine like Unity or Unreal, or their own engine?

If you aren't an engineer yourself it's critical that you have a strong and knowledgeable tech leader working internally at your company. Ideally he or she will be a co-founder, with a deep commitment to and passion for your game.

A tech leader inside your team can:

- Help evaluate what parts of your game can responsibly be out-sourced
- Play a key role in hiring and contract decisions relating to tech-nology
- Review the technical capabilities of outside partners with whom you may do contract work, where they can spot issues that non-technical managers will miss
- Validate the schedules and budgets proposed by internal and external engineers
- Monitor performance on all tech projects
- "Call BS" if an engineer or consultant ever uses tech talk to deceive non-tech people in the room

4.9.2 Start at the Source

Note: This section is intended for non-programmers to introduce the issue of source code, and I have summarized the issues to keep things short and simple. If these issues become important on your project you'll want to dive more deeply into the topic.

Every app, website and program has "source code," the code written by a programmer. Typically source code is then "compiled" or "interpreted" so that it works on the user's computer, console, smartphone etc. The compiled or interpreted version is called "object code."

When the game is completed you have "final source code." If you have a copy of the source code, a programmer who knows the same computer language can generally figure out how to fix most problems with your game, even if the original programmer has moved on. A programmer can read source code on the page and understand it readily.

If you have "object code" or anything else that's not source code, a new programmer has little to go on when trying to figure out why a program isn't working properly and how to fix it. If you print object code it looks like gibberish, and even formatting tools that highlight its underlying "opcodes" make it only a little easier to understand.

If you're working with programmers, make sure that you get regular deliveries of the source code to your project, and that each version of the source you receive can be compiled or interpreted to produce a working version of the program. This protects you from many dangers inherent in software development and allows your tech leader to review the work.

Contractors will want to ensure that you don't use this requirement to not pay them for their work, and the potential for clients to do so is real. An experienced attorney can help you build a deal that is fair to both parties.

If you develop software for third parties as part of your business, you will likewise want legal help with contracts in order to ensure that you're still paid after you have delivered source code to a client.

4.9.3 Who Goes Where

In my experience there is no one right answer about whether and how to subdivide work between local and remote teams. You have to experiment to figure out what will work for you.

I've seen teams that were split between Scandinavia and San Francisco who collaborated effectively with just occasional in-person visits.

I've seen teams that were split between the east and west side of the same building who couldn't meet for more than 20 minutes without bickering.

Here are my guidelines for considering these long distance relationships:

Don't Do It Just It to Save Money. If you buy a cheap used car it will break down all the time. If you pick partners just because they're cheap you'll be the one having the breakdown.

- Look for strong, quality-focused groups who will execute well, rather than just accepting the cheapest bid. The principle of "you get what you pay for" applies.
- Look for teams that have finished projects of similar size, style and complexity.
- Talk to references in your home country who've partnered with the potential team on already-completed projects.

Count the time zones between the teams. The greater the difference in the hours you're in the office, the harder it is to collaborate

The exception: if the gap is between five and eight hours or so, meetings can happen early in the day at one end and late in the day at the other. The team members who are at the beginning of their day can then do a full day of work based on the feedback they received from the team that would soon be going home.

If both teams are employees of your company, work as peers. Teams in non-HQ offices sometimes feel like they are treated as second-class citizens by the staff from the home office.

Sharing a Language Matters. I'd be an inefficient member of a project team where everyone only spoke French, because I only know about 20 words. A company from France should consider that if they consider hiring me.

In some countries of the world English is taught as a mandatory subject in schools starting at an early age. Professional conferences may be held in English, which sometimes works as a *lingua franca* when divergent groups of people share that one language in common.

Visit before you commit, and consider more than one vendor in more than one place. It is valuable beyond words to do a personal visit to the offices of potential contractors. Talking with several team members, even if some need translation, gives you a far better feel for what they'll be like to work with than just talking to the smiling face that leads the sales team.

In many disciplines external teams have been known to show the work of one very talented employee to every client. But once the contract is signed that's not the person who is actually working on your project. Meeting people in person and getting specific names whose participation can then be required in a contract can help.

Visiting more than one potential partner in person lets you compare and contrast the teams and facilities. You can visit one who is nearby and another who is very far away, and get an idea of how it would feel to work with each. This process will also give you a preview of the extra time and travel costs associated with working with distant teams.

Know the Employment Laws if You're Hiring Employees. Different U.S. States and different countries have very different laws about how companies have to pay employees, what benefits must be offered, working conditions etc. If you're hiring people, make sure to check out all these variables first.

Invest in Tools. A good Skype video setup and a fast Internet connection are essential. So is a screen-sharing system.

Keep Showing Up. Don't stop visiting a distant partner after a project has begun. Regular visits are part of good communication, as well as keeping their focus on you instead of on other clients.

Budget for the Travel and Tools Costs Before You Start. Sometimes the excitement over finding a great partner at a bargain price makes teams lose track of the extra travel costs, the time out of the office on site visits, the spending for video links etc.

Never do business in a country where citizens of your country don't routinely travel. If you can't visit without risking your own safety and can't enforce the terms of the contract through the local laws the likelihood of fraud, manipulation or extortion is unacceptably high.

DISCUSSING QUESTION 4.10

What kinds of business licenses will you need to operate your game studio (if any)?

This topic is most relevant for: Everyone

4.10.1 Looking for Approval

One of the most frustrating parts of running any business is getting governmental and organizational approvals.

In the U.S., for example, if you're going to operate a business you will need to get a "Federal Tax ID Number" so that the government can ensure that you report and pay employment taxes on peoples' salaries and calculate consultants' compensation accurately.

Most cities in the U.S. require you to have a business license in order to operate, even if you're just one person working from home. These rules are enforced aggressively in some jurisdictions, while in others small home-based businesses are largely ignored, and you only have to take this step when you open a dedicated office.

Many local jurisdictions charge an annual property tax of some kind to all local businesses.

All large publishers' console and PC titles, many indie console games and a variety of other games go through a voluntary process of being rated by the ESRB (Entertainment Software Ratings Board) to identify which titles are suitable (and which are not) for kids, and to specify required packaging and online labels. On consoles the hardware manufacturers make this process mandatory.

Most areas of the world now have laws that place legal require-ments on how you handle the online storage of user data, espe-cially credit card information, personal information like birth dates, passwords, etc.

In particular, if your game is aimed at kids or has any content that makes it not appropriate for kids, getting an ESRB rating (or its equivalent in the countries where your game is sold) is essential.

If your game is played by kids, there are strong laws in the U.S. and even stronger laws in Europe and elsewhere about how you han-dle and secure any information you may collect about your players. This issue requires that you consult with an experienced games industry attorney to avoid significant legal risks.

The key guideline here is, "Never assume." Follow up on every pos-sible issue, check out every potential problem.

DISCUSSING QUESTION 4.11

If you're going to have employees, are there any special employment laws in your city and/or your state that add additional costs, paperwork or operating rules to your planned business?

This topic is most relevant for: indie games that will grow to employ a team.

4.11.1 Letter of the Law

This is another area that requires research. Some rules will apply to all employers, while others may kick in when you reach 20, 50 or more people on your team.

In the United States, the employment laws in California and Washington state (for example) are dramatically different from those in Texas or Kansas.

Cities can have their own rules. San Francisco has employment laws that apply to businesses based there, but not to those in any of the surrounding communities.

Areas where surprises might be waiting include:

- Minimum wage requirements
- Local rules about what constitutes overtime, and formulas for overtime pay
- Required personal leave and parental leave
- Rules for who is considered an employee and who can be hired as a contractor

- Special taxes and assessments on payroll, revenues and (in rare cases like San Francisco) stock sales
- Rules for which job holders can be paid with a salary and who must be paid on an hourly rate
- Minimum required levels of benefits
- Rules for break and meal times
- Expense reimbursement policy regulations
- Legally required cooperation with a local union

If you're moving to a new city, state or country, assume that there will be lots of local employment rules you'll need to learn and follow. If you have more than a few employees, it may be worthwhile to consult a local corporate or HR attorney.

PART V

THE BUSINESS OF DREAMS

CHAPTER 36

The Business of Dreams: The Questions

QUESTION 5.1

How are you feeling about your indie game right now?

Excited? Optimistic? Worried? Disappointed?

What do you think is inspiring each of those feelings?

Please take your time, write down your responses, and answer fully from your deepest thoughts. Think only about your own opinions, not about what others may want you to think or do. Do not look ahead to other questions until you have finished this one.

QUESTION 5.2

What is the best way to share your vision of your game before it's completed? How do you get potential partners or key team members interested?

If you're an engineer, can you code a simple prototype so you can demonstrate it?

If you're an artist, can you create concept sketches?

Can you create a video trailer like those used to promote movies?

If your indie game runs in a browser, can you create the top-level screens to demonstrate its value?

With your personal experience and skills, what would be the right approach for you?

Please take your time, write down your responses, and answer fully from your deepest thoughts. Think only about your own opinions, not about what others may want you to think or do. Do not look ahead to other questions until you have finished this one.

QUESTION 5.3

How will you test your game before release to make sure it works as designed, operates in a stable manner and has no significant bugs?

Do you plan to localize the game into other widely-spoken languages?

Please take your time, write down your responses, and answer fully from your deepest thoughts. Think only about your own opinions, not about what others may want you to think or do. Do not look ahead to other questions until you have finished this one.

QUESTION 5.4

How will you test your game with real customers to see if it plays well, retains users and generates revenue as well as you expect?

QUESTION 5.5

How will you make money on your game?

What will you charge for?

Please take your time, write down your responses, and answer fully from your deepest thoughts. Think only about your own opinions, not about what others may want you to think or do. Do not look ahead to other questions until you have finished this one.

QUESTION 5.6

Exactly when and by whom will you be paid?

How will those payments be calculated, and by whom?

How far in advance will you know approximately how much money will come in each week or each month?

Will there be any cases where you refund people's money after they've paid to download or play your game?

QUESTION 5.7

Pretend that your studio has been operating for a year and you're having some success.

If someone asked you to estimate how much money your business would have in the bank in 30 days from that moment, what would you add and subtract from your company's then-current bank balance to calculate the answer?

Please take your time, write down your responses, and answer fully from your deepest thoughts. Think only about your own opinions, not about what others may want you to think or do. Do not look ahead to other questions until you have finished this one.

QUESTION 5.8

How much cash will you need to start with in order to cover all of your game's expenses until it starts producing positive cash flow and pays for itself?

QUESTION 5.9

What will you do if you complete your game, offer it to the world... and it doesn't sell?

Please take your time, write down your responses, and answer fully from your deepest thoughts. Think only about your own opinions, not about what others may want you to think or do. Do not look ahead to other questions until you have finished this one.

QUESTION 5.10

What will you do if a partner or customer refuses to pay you money that they owe you?

QUESTION 5.11

Have you ever written a Business Plan?

Do you already have one for this indie game?

Please take your time, write down your responses, and answer fully from your deepest thoughts. Think only about your own opinions, not about what others may want you to think or do. Do not look ahead to other questions until you have finished this one.

QUESTION 5.12

What would be the best possible (but realistic) financial result from your indie game?

Wealth? A salary you can live on? A few extra dollars?

A company that's doing well enough that you get to make the next game?

Is there some other ideal financial goal you're picturing?

CHAPTER 37

My Story: The Chess Game

Note: The story below comes from the experiences of my larger clients in console games, so the amount of money at risk is tremendous. For indie game teams the numbers may be smaller, but most of the issues are the same when you're selling through third parties other than the app stores, Steam and similar services. Focus on the lessons below, even if your game is far smaller than the example.

For many years of my career I worked as a studio GM or CEO, and much of what I've written in this book comes from those personal experiences.

When I started advising other companies, however, something interesting happened.

I didn't just see a few deals a year, I saw many contracts and business relationships. I learned many more best practices. And I saw more kinds of unethical behavior.

The tale that follows is inspired by a handful of client stories I've encountered over the last ten years. Unlike the other "My Story" segments in this book, the specifics I've written below are fiction, so I can give you a simplified example to cover an important topic. This also allows me to share very real business risks without violating NDA's (Non-Disclosure Agreements) on any one specific deal.

In our archetypal story the game development studio, which I'll call

"Acme," has a deal with a large corporate publisher that is head-quartered far away. The budget is about $10 million, and Acme wants the payments to come in at an even pace.

During the contract negotiations the publisher wants to hold back a sizable amount until after the project is finished, a common strategy to ensure that the developer finishes every detail of its work. But they want to hold back much more than normal.

Acme worried about this arrangement, because once you hand over your final product you no longer have the leverage of withholding delivery until you're paid

As an Advisor I can raise these kinds of concerns when I'm working with indie teams, but if a studio doesn't have another potential deal at that moment they still have salaries to pay. It might take three months or more to find and sign another deal, which could consume all of the company's cash and destroy the team.

As you've read in these pages, I always advise the leaders with whom I work to conserve cash. It's a prime directive.

Acme's team weighs the pro's and con's. They decide to sign the contract.

The final compromise they strike is that all but $362,000 of the money would come to Acme in regular intervals. The last $362,000 would be paid after the game is selling in stores.

Fast forward to the shipping deadline. Acme finishes the game on time and the publisher ships it to all the major retail chains and offers it for download. The date for the $362,000 payment arrives.

But the check does not arrive with it.

Acme's producer calls her contact at the big publisher, who is surprised and concerned. He tells the producer he'll investigate and call her back.

The next morning the producer's phone rings. Her contact has been told to direct any questions from Acme to the Finance Department. He apologizes to her, clearly embarrassed, and they hang up.

The publisher has just made the first move in a familiar game of chess, one played with cash and lawyers instead of knights and pawns. Here's how the script works:

Step 1 of the Chess Game: The publisher refuses to pay the money specified in the signed contract. Acme can complain all they want, but the publisher is already selling the game in stores and online so the studio has little leverage.

Step 2 of the Chess Game: Acme has to decide to fold or fight. Folding means giving up on the $362,000. Fighting costs money, because you have to use sophisticated lawyers to take on a big public company.

Big corporations have their own attorneys on the payroll, so legal disputes with small adversaries don't cost a lot of extra cash. A comparatively small company like Acme, which might have $5-$10 million in annual sales, would not have an attorney on staff.

Just writing a letter demanding payment requires Acme to pay their attorney to spend the time to check the full 35-page contract, at a cost of well over $1,000.

If Acme sues the publisher and the big company plays a delaying game, Acme might have to spend $200,000 to collect $362,000. If the publisher were really good at stalling it might cost Acme $400,000 to collect $362,000. Obviously, not a good strategy.

Some courts have a habit of splitting everything 50-50, so if Acme sues they could easily "win" the case but only get $181,000 after spending $200,000 or more.

To make things worse, all of the time that Acme's team leaders would spend on a lawsuit would be time taken away from working on new projects to cover the loss of the $362,000. This distraction factor, combined with the costs of a lawsuit, has destroyed more than one talented software developer.

The unnamed executive who is stepping in to take Acme's money knows about all these costs. He's betting that Acme will complain, then take a small consolation payment and go away.

Step 3 of the Chess Game: Acme calls their lawyer, spends the money and has her send a "demand letter" to the publisher.

The publisher ignores it. This is standard practice when big companies try to bully small ones.

Step 4 of the Chess Game: Now Acme faces a key decision. If they file a lawsuit they'll spend tens of thousands of dollars to try to get their $362,000, and they might not ever see a penny.

They confer with their Board of Directors, and discover that an associate of one of the Board Members has a close professional relationship with a senior executive at the publisher.

At Acme's request, the associate calls his friend and says, "This is all 'off the record,' but I wanted you to know. Acme's contract is really clear. Your company is about to get served with a lawsuit for Breach of Contract, and there may be other charges as well. I don't know how much your CEO knows about what's been happening. Maybe this guy is being a cowboy and is acting on his own. I didn't want you to be surprised."

The friend listens and makes no comment, though Acme's representative thinks he hears empathy in his friend's tone of voice. They exchange best wishes and say good-bye.

Step 5 of the Chess Game: Acme hears from an attorney inside the publisher. The attorney makes up a story about something being wrong with the game, which everyone knows is a hastily-conceived tall tale. He offers Acme $35,000 in settlement for the $362,000.

Yes, they offer less than 10% of the money they owed Acme under the contract.

Over several days and a series of phone calls between the lawyers, numbers go back and forth.

Acme ends up settling for about $215,000, and they only get that much because they have enough money in the bank to be able to afford to file and publicize a lawsuit that would make the publisher look bad. That $215,000 is more than Acme ever would have gotten after legal fees from following through on any legal action, and both sides knew it.

I don't share this story to discourage you from pursuing your indie game. In fact, I have seen few such terrible experiences in my long career.

I share this story so you'll know that such people do exist, and that they can hold important positions in large companies.

If you know that such things can happen, you're prepared to read any contract with a careful – and cynical – eye. And that's what I want to motivate you to do *every* time you receive the draft contract for a potential deal..

CHAPTER 38

What to Do With Your Answers (5.1-5.2)

"ANYBODY WHO THINKS MONEY WILL MAKE YOU HAPPY
HASN'T GOT MONEY."

— David Geffen

If you have not yet written down your answers, please go back and do so. Writing your thoughts down – even when you're the only one who'll ever read them – will produce far more insights than just answering silently to yourself in your head.

5.0.1 The Third Link in the Chain

We have discussed the Passion-Process-Product Method that forms the basis for this book:

- We start with our passions
- We experiment to develop a process that allows us to work on an indie game we'd love to create, either part-time or as a full-time job
- When we're ready, we launch our game as a product for our audience to play

In Section 5 we start diving into the Product stage, with extensive discussions of the business of games.

Before we start, however, we're going to go back to the foundation of this approach and review our passions.

DISCUSSING QUESTION 5.1

How are you feeling about your indie game right now?

Excited? Optimistic? Worried? Disappointed?

What do you think is inspiring each of those feelings?

This topic is most relevant for: Everyone

5.1.1 Pausing for a Moment

We are now well into the transition from talking about the game development side of going indie to talking about the business side.

Which of these three general cases best describes how you're feeling right now?

1. Excitement. By discussing your indie game you've gotten more and more excited about it.
2. Worry. You're still very interested in the idea, but you're also aware of problems or obstacles and you've lost some of your momentum.
3. Disappointment. You're coming to believe that this particular game is not a good idea after all. Or the fear of the "rocket launch" may have you stalled.

If it's #1, excitement, then keep reading! That excitement will help carry you through the highs and lows of building that indie game.

If you're worried, that's fine, too. Most initial ideas have strengths and weaknesses, and indie game studio CEO's will tell you that discouraging moments are always part of the process. I'll help you find ways to work through them.

If you're considering abandoning this game, first I'd like to ask you to brainstorm ways to solve the problems you've identified. Give yourself a few days, take some quiet time by yourself and consider all the issues.

If you don't come up with a way you'd like to proceed, then it may be time to put this particular game on the back burner.

You'll notice that I didn't say "discard it," or "toss it in the trash." I said, "put it on the back burner." I've had ideas I thought about for years before I ever built the game. Sometimes setting something aside and coming back to it later helps you take a good design and turn it into a great one.

There's another great benefit if you decide to set aside your current game.

Once you stop obsessing over a game that isn't right for you at the moment, your mind becomes free to come up with another idea which may be a better project.

5.1.2 Yellow Lights, Not Green or Red

There are books that tell you that being an entrepreneur requires you to "always give yourself a green light."

"Don't be discouraged! Don't be afraid! Just blindly keep rushing ahead and everything will be OK!" they tell you.

Those books are lying to you. Some ideas are a good fit for the current market and some are not. If you over-commit to a badly-timed or mis-targeted idea you can financially damage yourself and your family.

On the flip side, some "experts" are full of doom and gloom about how individuals can never accomplish anything.

"The indie era is over!" they proclaim. "Indies should realize there's nothing but red lights everywhere! Only big publishers can produce hit games!"

Those pessimists are just as misguided as the "Rush ahead blindly!" guys.

The principle you'll keep hearing from me is the concept of the yellow light. Proceed carefully, look in all directions each time you make a decision to proceed, but don't be paralyzed by fear.

If your indie game is worth doing there's always something positive you can accomplish on the road to chasing your dreams.

DISCUSSING QUESTION 5.2

What is the best way to share your vision of your game before it's completed? How do you get potential partners or key team members interested?

If you're an engineer, can you code a simple prototype so you can demonstrate it?

If you're an artist, can you create concept sketches?

Can you create a video trailer like those used to promote movies?

If your indie game runs in a browser, can you create the top-level screens to demonstrate its value?

With your personal experience and skills, what would be the right approach for you?

This topic is most relevant for: Everyone

5.2.1 How Should You Pitch Your Idea?

I'll be covering how to craft a complete pitch in a later chapter, but it's important to start thinking of how you present your game early in development.

Even before you create your first demo or teaser video, you may want to present your game to:

• Potential licensors, such as a film studio from which you want to license a popular classic movie that fits the theme of your adventure game

- Team members whom you'd like to recruit
- Hardware manufacturers, who nay give you early access to new technology that will be featured in your game
- Overseas publishers, who may license your game to sell it in their markets, generating cash to fund development

When the opportunity to do such a pitch comes up, you want to be ready. Consider how your personal skills and those of your team will best serve this mission.

5.2.2 What You Need to Know About "Lean Startups"

The term "Lean Startup" has come into wide use in Silicon Valley – and around the world — over the last few years, and refers to new "standard procedures for entrepreneurs."

If you're starting a new business you need to be familiar with this terminology, and with the steps that other business people may expect you to follow.

These concepts began to develop in the mid-1990's, and were organized in books by entrepreneurs and engineers like Steve Blank (*3 Steps to the Epiphany*, 2003) and Mary and Tom Poppendieck (*Lean Software Development*, 2003).

Many of these ideas were pioneered in the games business. In 2002 Mark Cerny was working with Sony (where he later led design of the PS4) when he introduced a games-specific version of these ideas called "The Cerny Method." I had the privilege of leading one of the early teams that adopted Cerny's approach.

In 2011 Eric Ries, who had interned with game industry veterans and studied with Steve Blank, extended Blank's ideas about how new businesses succeed in a book titled *The Lean Startup*. Although I give an overview below, I strongly recommend reading the book for yourself because its influence is widespread.

As defined by Steve Blank, startups are different from established companies because they are operating on a theory of how their business will work, not repeating and refining systems that they already know work well. Big companies like Sony and EA still face risks, but their markets are mature and their methods have evolved over time.

That means that startups have to experiment, gather feedback and then modify their ideas and products in a race to see if they can make them successful. These steps have to be repeated rapidly and efficiently in order to prove the company's value to investors with only a small amount of money placed at risk. This process is called "Rapid Iteration," and mimics an important part of the process of Lean Software Development as described by Mary and Tom Poppendieck.

In 2001 SyncDev's Frank Robinson coined the term "Minimum Viable Product" (MVP) to describe the first, most basic version of a startup's product. Customers can buy and use this MVP and then report on their experience. Their feedback and their spending patterns help the team quickly modify and re-test the product.

After many of these rapid iteration cycles the company hopes to steadily improve their MVP and ultimately demonstrate "traction." To do this they need to build a small but growing base of customers who are spending real money on the product (as opposed to free in-game currency offered in early test cycles) and generating revenue for the company.

If the game doesn't gain traction after a reasonable period of experimentation, the project is closed down. As painful as such a closure is, it's still far less damaging than completing an entire product and losing far more money.

Learning quickly that an idea isn't working represents a big win for small part-time businesses as well as big ones. Writing off an experiment after a few hundred or a few thousand dollars is a lot easier than losing $40,000 or $400,000 on an idea that was two years ahead of its time.

5.2.3 The "Standard Requirements" for Startups

If a startup is pitching to potential allies or investors in Silicon Valley today, they know before they walk into the conference room about three of the major requirements they'll be required to meet. You'll recognize them from the summary of the Lean Startup principles above.

For reasons I'll explain in more detail below, indie games are very unlikely to draw interest from investors unless they are already a big hit. But investors aren't the only targets for a pitch – all of the potential audiences I listed above may ask these questions.

Here are the goals that startup businesses are expected to pursue:

Requirement #1: A Complete Playable Game. This will be your Minimum Viable Product, or MVP, as discussed above. Remember that this isn't just a playable version of some portion of your project. It's big enough and holds enough fun that you can monetize the game and earn money from real players, even if it doesn't yet have every asset, level, mode or feature.

You may have also heard about teams developing a "Vertical Slice," which became a term of trade in the console games business in the early 2000's. A vertical slice is very different from an MVP, because it consists of a few minutes of gameplay polished and tuned as if it were part of a shipping game.

That Vertical Slice might offer gameplay you wouldn't reach until five hours into the game, so it can't be sold all by itself. They're used on larger projects so that executives at the major publishers can see proof that a game is fun to play and stunning to look at when they've only spent $1.5 or $2 million instead of $15 or $20 million on the project.

The MVP of a game is more complete than a Vertical Slice but starts its life as a much less polished deliverable. It is released for the specific purpose of getting lots of data and feedback from real users who are spending real money. For example:

- An RPG could start with a single region, and with the ability for players to advance to a "preliminary level cap" high enough to feel like they got value for their money.

- A shooter might offer an initial set of missions or scenarios. Backgrounds might be simpler and less richly modeled than they would be in the final game, and there could be a restricted range of characters and weapons.

- Other kinds of action or arcade games could offer an initial set of levels, topping out when you reached a certain point.

- An educational game could offer a series of activities built around developing one skill out of the range of skills they plan to teach to children.

You will start to gather feedback from early players long before you have a shippable MVP. The best teams start sharing small portions of their games and tracking player activity and opinions early and often. The MVP enters the picture only when the game is both entertaining enough and large enough to charge players money to play it.

MVP's may also serve as a game's "Closed Beta" (if the number of players is limited to avoid problems of scale) or "Open Beta" if anyone can play. These "Betas" are very different from "Beta" in traditional software development, which was defined as a stage where software is virtually final and going through one last phase of intense testing and corrections.

Requirement #2: Traction. Picture that you're driving your car uphill on a steep road and it's snowing. If the snow gets too deep you'll start to slip, then stop in your tracks, then start to slide backward.

Introducing a new game can be like driving that car up the hill. Your first version may not earn any revenue, and may have problems. You tinker with it, make the mechanics work better and make the game more fun. You start to get some sales.

You make more and more tweaks and changes, practicing rapid iteration. A few of these adjustments make the game less fun and have to be reverted, but most of them are improvements.

Now your Minimum Viable Product doesn't feel quite so minimal. You have a list of cash-paying players who are happy and are telling their friends. Revenue is growing every month.

That's what Silicon Valley calls "traction." You're not stuck or sliding backwards. You're moving forward, going faster and your revenue is going up.

When a prospective partner asks, "Do you have traction?" this is the story they're asking you to tell them.

Requirement #3: Team. Chronologically, of course, this requirement comes first: you'll usually need an initial core team to build the MVP of your game and achieve traction.

Potential partners want to know that you have a good game. But they also want to believe that you have a team that can create more hits, not just one, and "scale the business" to a larger size. They want to know that if you're serving 10,000 players now, you already have the technical expertise to serve 1,000,000.

If you ask any investor what's more important in a startup, the team or the new product, they'll almost always answer, "The team. Great teams can take an OK concept and hone it into a hit, but all B-level teams can do is build B-level games."

Be ready to discuss how the people you already have on your team can grow with your game and create more hits, and how you'll bring in new people as needed.

CHAPTER 39

The Final Steps (5.3-5.4)

DISCUSSING QUESTION 5.3

How will you test your game before release to make sure it works as designed, operates in a stable manner and has no significant bugs?

Do you plan to localize the game into other widely-spoken languages?

This topic is most relevant for: Everyone

5.3.1 "Quality Assurance" or "Quickly Assassinated"

QA can mean either of those two things, depending on how well it's done.

If you're an engineer or have worked on game development teams you know that bugs are insidious. Some will show up once in every 100 playthroughs. Some are in plain sight and we all look right at them and don't see the misspelling or the gap between two walls.

You cannot skip steps or get careless with QA, because the punishment is published bugs, which are at least embarrassing and sometimes expensive.

My suggestions below are all standard procedure for projects, and worth the trouble even on very small games:

Test every intermediate build thoroughly, not just advanced milestones like Alpha's and Beta's. This is part of the Agile development philosophy, and it yields big wins in time savings, budget savings and code stability. If a milestone can't be tested you need to ask yourself, "Did I actually *finish* anything?"

It may seem like overkill to have someone devote a portion of every day to QA, but that time expense is going to be offset by the time that good testing saves for everyone on the team.

Even if someone is focused on QA, the testing process "belongs" to every team member and everyone needs to conscientiously record every new bug that they see.

Deliver regular builds. Testers cannot find new bugs and verify fixes of old ones if they don't get regular new "clean" builds.

Have an organized system. Small teams may be tempted to track bugs through email or Slack. Taking the time to use a spreadsheet with big enough cells to record details or (best of all) a bug tracking system like Jira will pay off. Such systems also make it easier to cull duplicate bugs.

Write a test plan or create a test checklist or matrix. The core of any such doc is a list of every screen and every possible action on that screen, along with any instructions on where problems are likely to occur and limits that need to be tested (e.g. players can't have over 99 of something). In the latter stages of testing, those lists can then be used to ensure that everything has gotten the "once over."

Don't just check off the list. As valuable as a plan or matrix may be, good testers have to be given time to play freely on every build in the same way that users would. Some bugs defy the scientific approach, and good testers have an instinct for "breaking" games that are supposed to be rock solid and ready to ship.

Prioritize. Even if you're working solo on a project, sort your bug data base items so crash bugs are at the top and "wish we could fix these but may not have time" are at the bottom.

Assign. Write down who is going to fix the bug, and make sure each team member checks regularly for tasks that are waiting for them.

Verify fixes carefully. After I implement a bug fix I'll do a quick check and if it looks like it's working right I'll move on. That's "programmer self-checking," not fix verification. Always have someone other than the programmer play the game to verify the fix, trying to recreate the bug any way they can.

Let testers comment. I have worked with teams that told their testers, "Don't tell me what you think. Just report what's broken." This is a missed opportunity. Testers have to keep comments concise and clear, but they'll give a dev team really valuable feedback on fun and playability.

But don't balance the game to challenge testers. Game makers and testers are professional players. If we balance games to their skill levels we can lock out many everyday gamers.

Yes, it's worth testing that tiny last minute change. Every experienced developer has a story about how "the change that didn't need to be tested" led to a big problem.

Have outsiders test. Even if you're a solo game creator, buy pizza for friends and have them test your game. Better yet, have strangers (who won't worry about your feelings) test for you. "Players doing the wrong thing" produces lots of bugs that a tester who knows the right way to play will never see.

5.3.2 Localizing Your Game

Localization is the process of translating your game's text and cultural elements so it can be played in other countries. Done properly, it can boost or even multiply a game's revenue, and can turn a floundering title into a hit. Costs are based largely on word count, so translations can often be done for less money than developers expected to pay.

If you're selling through the app stores or Steam the sales increases can be especially dramatic. In 2017 Germany was the second-highest spending market on Steam, surpassed only by the U.S. (Source: Steam Spy.) Localization can also dramatically increase your chances of being featured, both in the app stores and by social media influencers on Twitch and other platforms.

A game that fails to get traction in the hyper-competitive American market might get noticed in less crowded store settings in other countries. The resulting income and rankings can in turn help the game climb the charts in the U.S.

When resources give you the option of localization, it's a process you'll prepare for early on. The translation itself will take place in the later stages of development — or even after the first version of your game has shipped.

When shouldn't you localize?

- If a target market is already crowded with games in your category
- If your game is tied to American Thanksgiving or some other one-culture holiday
- American football and baseball have far smaller markets than soccer and Formula 1
- If you're creating a big RPG with as much text as a best-selling fantasy novel

Every indie developer should prepare their game for localization, starting from the first stages of development. Do this even if you think you'll never have the money, because preparing a game for localization is a matter of process. After the first localized project (where you'll create the necessary pipelines and systems) it won't represent a significant increase in the quantity of development work.

The key steps to take include:

Place all text in separate files, not integrated in with the code. When you're ready to localize your game, deliver those text files to the translators. They'll do the translations and return the files to you in the same format, with the same number of entries. All the pointers you use to load the correct English text should work for all the other language files as well.

This allows you to set a language flag in your code that says, "Use the French version" or "Use the Korean version" so you don't have to make time-consuming (and bug-producing) changes all over the code base.

Even if you never localize your title, sorting text into files this way makes finding and fixing text-related bugs faster and easier.

I've seen teams use Excel files, Word files and unformatted text files for this purpose. All that matters is that you start splitting out the text early in development so you don't have to wade back in with changes later.

Work with your translators to code for gender, plural, tense and other differences that English ignores but that other language versions will need to differentiate. For example, in the Romance languages nouns can be masculine or feminine, which changes other words so they end with –o, -a or other variants. Text that is identical in English can have four variants (adding singular and plural to gender versions). Languages have more than one past tense, and lines that are used repeatedly by different NPC's may have to change verb forms based on the situation.

For example, if your female character converses with a male NPC, both sides of the dialogue can be different than if it's a male character talking to a group of three female NPC's. You'll need to plan for this and have flags for the localized languages to use. This helps to explain why games like The Sims use pictures instead of words for dialogue!

Resist the temptation, however, to try to swap out different words within sentences, because the Romance languages alone have traps in variable word order and pronoun placement that will sabotage your text. It's better to have two or four or even eight different complete sentences and choose the right one than it is to try to get too clever with linguistic puzzle pieces.

Don't include text in art files. Use icons instead of words whenever you can do so without losing players, a feature that calls for user testing.

When you need to use words instead of icons, it's better to avoid including them in images, as tempting as that may be. Place such text in separate files and translate it in the same manner described above. This can also make it far easier to test different UI labels with users, since swapping the text is faster than changing the art files.

Allow for different word lengths and font sizes. When designing buttons, layout and other elements of your user interface, remember that different languages and fonts can take more space than English. For example, German will produce longer words with more characters to express the same meaning, and Asian languages may use fewer characters that will be larger for legibility.

Variable width fonts will make this process a lot easier to integrate and test than fixed-width.

Plan for double-byte font support. Western alphabets can all be coded into different sets of 256 characters, but languages like Chinese, Japanese and Korean need more slots in a font. Such fonts require two bytes per character instead of just one, and can contain thousands of different characters.

This used to be a far greater problem in more primitive machines with smaller memory footprints, but you still need to allow for handling characters in two different ways and for the larger file sizes of double-byte fonts.

Quality translation is worth paying a premium. Professional translators who know how to make the localized language sound natural and local cost more money, but it's worth it. They'll also provide translation files that produce fewer bugs during integration into the game.

That intern who spent a semester abroad in France or the service that costs $19 per thousand words are not going to deliver the results you need to run a business. We're less likely to buy a game if the opening screen says something in broken English, like "Welcome to top fighting prize in the circle! Which will you commit?" Speakers of other languages are just like us, and they feel the same way about their games.

Use the same high quality translators for your online store text and marketing materials. If we have poor translations here – or none at all – we sabotage the international sales for the game.

If your game has spoken dialogue and you can afford it, record new localized dialogue. This is usually impractical for the budgets in smaller games, but if you can manage it with quality local actors it's a big plus.

If you can't afford to record localized dialogue, add localized subtitles. These can also be stored in a single file, and give you the option to also offer English (or whatever is your first language) subtitles.

Ask translators about non-language differences like colors and

fonts. Colors that draw the attention of local audiences may have the opposite effect in other cultures. Fonts may likewise trigger player reactions than are different from how the font inspires users in English.

Remember that many languages have regional differences. English speakers are familiar with the different spellings and sounds in American and British English, and offering both options can attract more players.

The same is true of other languages like Spanish, which has many differences between European speakers and those in Latin America. New World Spanish speakers are a rapidly growing games market, so if you're creating an appropriate game it's a valuable step. Soccer games are the stereotypical example, but a much wider range of titles are worth considering.

Ask your translators if this issue affects the languages they work in, and then explore whether the incremental audience justifies the extra expense.

Don't stop at EFIGS. The traditional translation targets for English language games are abbreviated as EFIGS, for English, French, Italian, German and Spanish. If you're doing mobile games, for example, the Korean market is currently larger than that of the UK + Australia, France, Italy, Germany or Spain + Mexico + Argentina.

Markets like Indonesia and Turkey are approaching $1 billion in annual value for mobile games alone. American teams in particular tend to overlook these opportunities, which enhances the potential for teams with games that fit those cultures.

If you're using Unity or Unreal, use the localization support features. It's just part of how these engines can help you build games faster and more easily. These features and developer tips are extensively documented online.

5.3.3 ESRB, IARC, PEGI and USK Ratings & More

Note: This is an area where rules and processes change frequently. I'll cover the basics below, but the websites provided by each of the organizations listed above should be considered the authoritative sources. Other world regions also have game rating systems (e.g. CERO in Japan, GRAC in Korea) with which localized versions of games may have to comply.

Games are as diverse as movies and TV series, which means that some content is intended for adults, not children. Like other entertainment media, the games industry has implemented age guideline labels. I'll focus on the American market below, but there are close parallels in other countries and each governing body has its own informative website.

Games industry ratings and marketing strategies intersect in ways similar to the movie business. Shooters aimed at players over 18 may deliberately add violence, language or sexual content that will earn them an M rating from the ESRB. It's part of their marketing plan, a signal to their target audience. Publishers of games that are aimed at teen players will manage the design carefully to make sure their rating is a T for the same reasons.

Decide early in the development of your indie game what rating you want placed on your game to reach your target audience, and which regional organization(s) you'll submit the game to. Then study the guidelines for that rating and make sure your content adheres to the rules for your chosen category.

Start the ratings submission process as early as possible, but don't start until you have a clear and final idea of all the content that will drive the ratings decision. Adding more violent content (e.g. lots of blood) after the rating has been given will require you to start the process all over again, consuming time and resources.

Although some teams feel that they have had to do extra work because of the ESRB, the clear guidance they give to players enhances the sales potential of many games. I believe that if publishers had continued to operate the way things worked without an ESRB during the first 15 years of my career (before 1994) many more families would have opted out of buying game consoles and game sales would be much lower today.

Not to mention the fact that even more politicians would be attempting to blame every piece of bad news – including the weather – on violent video games, just as they did with violent television shows and comic books in the 1950's.

Here's an introduction to how the systems work:

Packaged games. Contrary to what many people believe, games are not legally required to have ESRB (Entertainment Software Ratings Board) age ratings. The American courts have upheld that games are covered by the 1st Amendment and thus cannot have their sales legally controlled.

In other parts of the world, including Europe, systems are often a mix of voluntary and legally binding enforcement.

Like the parallel efforts elsewhere, the ESRB is a voluntary system implemented by the Entertainment Software Association (ESA), in which all of the major packaged game publishers and retailers participate. Walmart won't sell an M-rated game to a 15-year-old as a matter of company policy, not because of any laws, and almost all sellers of physical games have similar policies.

For packaged games, titles must be submitted to the ESRB via a long-form questionnaire and a video showing any moments in the game that may push the age rating to a higher level for violence, language, nudity, sexual content, drug use etc. Reviewers then determine a rating, and after publication a game is again checked to ensure that its packaging and marketing materials correctly display the right rating label.

USK ratings in Germany have a few differences from the other systems, but the number of required changes has declined in recent years. Apart from the USK itself, an excellent source for information is the website www.gameslaw.org.

Digital download games. In recent years cooperation between the ESRB (in the U.S.) and PEGI / USK (in Europe) produced the IARC system (International Age Rating Coalition). IARC is a collaborative international effort to voluntarily label the high volume of new digital games in a manner consistent with the packaged goods labeling system. National games industries involved include North America, much of Europe, Australia, Brazil and Korea.

Developers fill out a short-form IARC questionnaire and are immediately given a rating they can attach to their game. As long as the published game matches the answers on the questionnaire, you're all set.

As of this writing, the IARC system is widely used, but digital game age labels are still less consistent than those on packaged goods. Game submissions are managed in different ways by different channels and sellers:

- Google play, the Microsoft Store, the Nintendo eShop and the PlayStation Store for North America all require an ESRB rating, although some will also accept an IARC rating

- Apple does its own review of submitted titles for similar issues but has its own (similar but not identical) rating system

- The Amazon Appstore likewise has its own submissions and system

Steam is currently the least structured system, which has often made the service controversial due to its adult game titles. Game publishers whose products have been rated by the ESRB, IARC, PEGI and/or USK typically display those ratings on Steam, and community members may also label games for different kinds of adult content in a sort of user-generated informational tagging system.

DISCUSSING QUESTION 5.4

How will you test your game with real customers to see if it plays well, retains users and generates revenue as well as you expect?

This topic is most relevant for: Everyone

5.4.1 Beyond "People Like Me"

Indie games are driven by passion, which makes them very personal to their creators. Filmmakers create movies they'd want to see. Authors write books they'd want to read. App makers create apps they'd want to use.

We make games we want to play. This passion can drive a team to create a game that stands out and rises above the competition.

The danger, however, is that we can focus so much energy on building real depth in our game's play mechanics that we give only passing attention to the initial user experience.

All too often, new player tutorials and onboarding are done at the end of the project, when the team is tired, deadlines are looming and most attention is being given to final debugging and tuning. When a producer says, "We have to have someone build the tutorial," the whole room groans and the least experienced person may be handed the job.

The top mobile and online game companies in the world, teams like Supercell and Riot, will tell you that this is doing things backwards. You can't retain users if you lose them in the first two minutes after they start to play. The focus on initial user experience has to start early in the project schedule and remain a priority all the way through.

5.4.2 Good Listeners are Good Watchers

I discussed above how the most critical characteristic for marketers is being a great listener, and how game developers can gain great benefits from practicing this key skill.

Part of the wisdom that you can gain from listening to players extends to watching silently as they play. Find ways to invite strangers of all gameplay skill levels to play the first twenty minutes of your game, with no help or comments from anyone except each other.

You don't get to walk over and tell them what to do next. You don't applaud when they do well and frown when they do something wrong. If they're stuck you leave them to figure it out for themselves. Because that's what the experience will be like for the real, paying players you're trying to serve.

Although you can simulate this experience with metrics, sitting silently and watching people play is just as valuable a tool because you'll see what went wrong, how it all happened and how it affected the user.

The first test sessions often don't go very well. It's not fun to watch a cross-section of players try to learn your game with nothing to work from except the on-screen instructions. A few veteran players get it immediately, but everyone else struggles.

And everyone else is 80% of your potential market.

Even with experienced teams, these first walkthroughs normally produce long lists of notes and corrections that need to be made. It can take many iterations to reach the point where the first twenty minutes of the game unfold in the way you want.

This is why the best teams test the first few minutes of their game with real users early and often, when they still have time to make changes to get the high-retention results they need.

This exercise, however, is the culmination of a series of research projects you do to prepare for the launch of your game. Long before you start playtesting there are many other kinds of research you can do.

5.4.3 Research and Feedback on a Budget

Big companies have specialized research groups, but here are some ways for indie teams to do early-stage research and get consumer feedback on a budget:

Look at your Facebook, Instagram, Twitter, YouTube friends etc. and at your LinkedIn contacts. Make a list of a handful of people whom you respect and who you think would give you honest feedback on your idea (or your sketches, or your demo, etc.).

You don't need many advisors. If you have more than a few such people, save some of them for later iterations.

Invite each friend to coffee or lunch and tell them in advance that you want to ask them for their feedback. Some people will pass, but many will agree.

Share your idea, and be sure to take notes on their comments. It shows your respect for their opinions, and you'll never remember all the details the next day, even if you think you will.

Once your game is playable you can repeat the process, and ask the same and other people to play and then give you their feedback.

These people know you, so the comments will not be as impartial as the (sometimes brutal) honesty you see in strangers. But I've gotten really useful advice in this way.

It's best to get feedback individually. The dynamics of talking with a group changes participants' patterns of expressing their ideas.

5.4.4 Online Research

Online research can uncover valuable data that is freely available to everyone, but that most people never look for, let alone find.

Read Competitors' User Forums. Competitors' forums can be a gold mine of information. You'll have the chance to read criticisms, praise and suggested features for rival products, some of which may relate to your game as well.

Remember that many users visit forums only when they have a problem, not to say, "I love level 47 of the game!" Long lists of complaints on forums don't necessarily mean that competitive games don't have passionate audiences.

Read Games Newsletters and Websites. I subscribe to four different games industry news sites and four different tech newsletters, each with a different focus. Each sends me a daily or weekly email with links to current articles.

In recent years the long-standing game sites (many descended from earlier game magazines) have been joined by specialized sites for mobile and other new platforms. Examples of these new resources include App Annie, Gamezebo and Pocket Gamer, but there are many more.

It's free to subscribe to many professional news and game review sources, and you'll quickly see which are most useful. You can easily unsubscribe from the rest.

Although the top game websites are well known and appear at the top of Google searches, there are many more sites with significant audiences where you can gain useful insights. Use platform-specific Google searches like "top game review sites iPad" to dig deeper on your target devices.

For PC and console games Metacritic (for all of the faults inherent in its scoring schemes) lists all of the publications whose reviews it currently considers, and the "most popular" filter on that list will almost certainly introduce you to sites you are not currently reading.

CHAPTER 40

Making Money (5.5)

DISCUSSING QUESTION 5.5

How will you make money on your game?

What will you charge for?

This topic is most relevant for: Everyone

5.5.1 Ways to Make a Buck

In recent years the games industry has experienced explosive growth in the kinds of platforms, interfaces and games available to players and in the variety of business models being used to sell them. And it's not just indie game developers who are exploring these new opportunities.

For decades the video game business has sold games in boxes on consignment to retail stores, so the publishers had to take back any product that didn't sell.

With their sales heavily impacted by retail chains' used games programs, publishers have now worked to find ways to deliver additional value via online play to the original or current owner of the boxed game.

Companies may sell "Season Passes" to their games, so players can download each new episode of games like *The Walking Dead*, *Batman* or *Game of Thrones* as it's released.

Publishers of online games, mobile games and social games have a choice of business models. They may:

- Charge a monthly subscription, like World of Warcraft ("subscription model")
- Sell people a game or add-on content and then download it to their device ("premium model")
- Allow users to play a limited version for free as a "preview mechanism" and then upgrade to a full-featured game ("freemium model")
- Sell in-game items to players for real world money ("free to play model")
- Some combination of the above choices

Virtually all of these models require indie games to be sold through some form of online store or app store, who serve as distributors and retailers.

Don't just default to using the standard or common business model for your game category and platform. If you come up with a better value-for-money or a more convenient way to pay, it can magnify the success of a great game.

The success rate of different business models also ebbs and flow over time. Mobile games have flip-flopped between rewarding premium, freemium and hybrid models. The best choice varies, based on the kind of game, the target system, its audience, the geographical region of the world and other factors.

5.5.2 Different Publishing Strategies

There are lots of strategies that game publishers try to use to create hit games:

Create the best game. This is the gold standard that gives you big advantages, though it still doesn't guarantee success if no one ever learns about your title.

Lower your prices. Usually a bad idea, because the resulting "race to the bottom" of price competition is suicidal unless lower costs are built into your business. This is why the prices for mobile games collapsed early in the smartphone era, spurring the growth of free to play games. A gradual downward trend has likewise appeared on Steam.

Out-market and out-support your rivals. If you have a great game and interact more effectively with players, you win. Your community outreach and customer service are outstanding, so once-unhappy users become loyal fans who promote your company to their friends.

Invent or perfect a new business model. As noted above, Telltale Games successfully executed the episodic game subscription model, an approach where all prior entries had failed.

Invent a new category. Most "outlier" games are doomed to failure, because they're unfamiliar and hard to describe. But the exceptions – like *Minecraft* – can be massive hits.

5.5.3 Pricing Your Game

The psychology of how we decide to buy things is complex. There are no simple answers on how to price games, and the right price today may be the wrong price three weeks from now.

You'll have to experiment. Whether you're selling your game in a premium model or operating an in-game store, start by doing research on the games that you believe are the most similar to yours.

Set your prices to match theirs, then experiment with trying slightly higher or lower prices for a few days at a time to see what effect the changes have. Experiments that are too short may be like visiting the desert on a rainy day: the data is accurate but not representative. Over time you can zero in on the best price points, though they'll continue to evolve.

In open markets the "race to the bottom" drives prices down to almost nothing. As I described above, inexperienced marketers keep trying to undercut each other one penny at a time until they reach the minimum allowed price.

Don't get caught in this race to failure. Set prices in a reasonable range and stick to that range, or use an alternate business model to make money from your game in a different way.

Players who have played and enjoyed your game will describe it as being worth a higher price than people who have never played it. This is the "preview mechanism" principle behind the freemium business model, where users can preview part of the game before buying the entire product or incremental content.

Pricing your game too low makes people assume it's a lower quality title. This is why it's better to start out matching the price range of competitive games, not undercutting them.

If your game's a hit, you can raise your price. This works in some categories and is harder in others, but in many cases a $2.99 hit won't lose a lot of sales if the price is raised to $3.99.

One team I advise moved their price from $2.99 to $4.99 once their game became successful, without losing sales volume. You can also release a special edition with extra content and charge more for it.

Don't feel guilty about making money. If your price is too high people won't buy and you'll know you have to lower it. If your price point is working well, it means you built a really good game and you deserve to be paid for it.

5.5.4 Key Performance Indicators

For many years our primary KPI's (Key Performance Indicators) in the games industry were for boxed games (also called packaged goods):

- Average wholesale price per unit
- Manufactured cost per unit
- Sell-in (how many copies were sold to stores)
- Sell-through (how many copies the stores sold to consumers)
- Returns (how many copies were returned to the publisher by stores after they didn't sell).

Today games are programmed with telemetry to collect and send data to the team on many kinds of key metrics. That data can then be analyzed in search of problems that are lowering results and opportunities that might give the game a boost.

If you are working with a game that has online features it's critical that you become comfortable with calculating, interpreting and using the relevant KPI's for this segment.

Once you understand the relevant KPI's, you'll be in a position where you'll know the right kinds of experiments to undertake to move those numbers in the right direction.

The critical KPI's include:

DAU and MAU: Daily and Monthly Average Users. This describes the average of how many people enter and play your game online each day, and the average per month.

DAU is a better indicator of how active a game community is, since it only measures players who signed in today. Someone only has to log in once every 30 days to be counted as MAU, so the higher the ratio of DAU/MAU the better the game is doing at attracting player commitment.

CCU: Concurrent Users. This number is especially critical to MMO's, MOBA's and other multi-player games. The more concurrent players in these games, the better the matchmaking and social interaction will work.

CPI: Cost per Install. Cost to acquire each new user (all marketing expenses divided by the number of product downloads; online advertising costs are the big variable that can inflate this number).

Large games that (unlike most indie games) can afford online banner advertising will track what ads and what sources produce the most valuable players. They will then break down the analysis of these patterns at a high level of detail to guide how and where they spend advertising dollars.

LTV: LifeTime Value. Average revenue received per user who downloads the app, whether all at once in an initial sale or gradually over a period of months or even years. LTV must exceed Cost per Install to be profitable. LTV could represent:

- The wholesale price of a boxed game sold through a retailer
- The price of a premium online game sold via download
- The sum of a series of microtransactions where the user buys items in the game store
- The sum of a) the purchase price for the base version of the game, and b) additional in-game purchases made to add features or additional content to the game

Conversion Rate. The percentage of people who are "converted" and pay money to upgrade, add extra items or features, eliminate ads etc. A user who pays even a few cents for an item is counted as being "converted" and "monetized."

This applies both to free to play games that are downloaded at no charge and to premium or packaged games that sell incremental content to users after that initial sale.

Cohorts. Cohorts are not a KPI, but a way that users' purchase and behavior patterns are calculated in order to better study the numbers. Users may be broken up into different groups called cohorts so that the data on their activities can reveal more detailed patterns:

- Users who respond to one ad may be placed in one cohort and those from a different ad placed in a different cohort, to test if one ad or the other attracted users with a higher LTV, etc.

- Users who enter the game after a major expansion may be tracked in one large cohort, while those who were playing before the new content was added are tracked in another cohort so their retention rates and LTV can be compared

ARPU (Average Revenue Per User) and ARPPU (Average Revenue Per Paying User). These calculations may be described by the day, month or lifetime value.

ARPU is total revenue for the period divided by DAU (for the daily rate, called ARPDAU, for Average Revenue per Daily Average User) or MAU (for the monthly rate).

ARPPU counts only the revenue from those users who have been converted to paying customers, so total revenue is divided not by all players, but by the count of how many have been monetized . If it's divided by DAU it's called ARPPDAU.

Minnows, Dolphins and Whales. Companies with free to play games often use ARPPU, LTV or both to sort users into these categories, which are borrowed (unfortunately) from the gambling industry. Minnows spend very small amounts, and dolphins are the committed players who spend more.

I absolutely hate the term "whales," which refers to people who spend larger amounts. I've seen LTV windows that started at any-where from $25 up to hundreds of dollars for this group, and it's common for a relatively small number of players may account for 50% or more of all revenue.

All the teams with whom I work are familiar with my insistence on the term "Most Valuable Players," so our best customers are hon-ored instead of being derided. Some of these valuable users are actually spending money for other players by buying items for fel-low members of guilds, clans, etc. in MMO games to enhance their success as a team.

Traditionally both game and app developers pursued Most Valu-able Players above all other users because of their disproportion-ate share of revenue. In recent years, however, researchers have shown that these MVP's now provide a significantly smaller share of overall games income. This is a great reminder that we need to focus on all of our players, not just some of them.

Average Session Length (or Average Session Duration). How long the typical player stays logged into the game after they arrive. In general, mobile games do best with short session lengths and con-sole game players prefer game design styles that support much longer sessions. There are game-specific exceptions to all the usual patterns, however.

Player Progress. There isn't one set term for this, but we always want to measure how far into a game a player has gotten. In open world games this could be total hours of play, a checklist of loca-tions visited and a checklist of events triggered. In sequential level games it would be the highest level attained, and you can gather more valuable data such as number of tries to complete a level, days spent at level, etc., last level attained by churned players (defined under Retention below), etc.

Any event in your game that produces increased churn is a high priority for tuning, since players who disappear rarely return.

If a level is more difficult than you intended you'll see more attempts per player, more days at level and a higher churn rate from that level. This data can help you tune it to the difficulty level that fits its place in the overall game.

D1, D7, D30: Retention Rate. The percentage of users who are still entering the game a set number of days after the initial download. D1 is the percentage of players who came back the next day, D7 is after a week, and so on.

The opposite of retention is "Churn," the percentage of people whom you don't retain. The sum of the percentages of retained players and churned players always equals 100%. Different games use different formulas, but "no play sessions for 30 days" or 45 days are common. Churned players almost never return to being committed players.

Every team needs to calculate, "After how many days without logging in should we assume that we've lost a player forever?" Once a user hits that "we're losing them" the team can then reach out to them by email or other means to offer incentives for them to return to the game.

One secret of making these business models work is to start with the retention rate when you're trying to push up your numbers. Improving retention (along with its mirror image, reducing churn) is the gatekeeper to success with any game.

People leave if they can't figure out how to play, if it feels unfair, or if the game doesn't feel like fun. We need to get them past the initial learning curve so they'll fall in love with the experience.

5.5.5 KPI's for Online Advertising

Note: If you experiment with online advertising, start with tiny budgets and short experiments. On some dashboards new users have misunderstood forms and spent thousands of dollars on useless ads in just a few hours without realizing they were doing so. Proceed with caution.

If you're buying online ads and trying to figure out if an ad increases revenue or wastes money, remember the rule of "mobile first." More people consume content and surf the web on cell phones than on desktop computers.

Sophisticated "responsive" ad systems attempt to address this by having one arrangement of content and ads when displayed on phones, and another when displayed on a PC or Mac. Ads placed inside games would have their own unique format.

If you review your ad placement on a desktop monitor it might look like you have a great spot, but when the content is displayed to the larger smartphone audience it might be far, far down the page and thus invisible. Since mobile users are far less likely to scroll through long articles such placements are doubly useless.

An in-game ad might be shown on a menu that users visit all the time, or a screen that people rarely visit.

For ad performance measurement additional KPI's are relevant:

Impressions. This measures how many times an ad was shown, BUT it doesn't tell you whether the ad was displayed in a prime spot "above the fold" (the portion of the screen that shows before you scroll down) or far below.

Different sites use different calculations of impressions, and advertising sales teams are famous for inflating their impression totals. Market leaders like Amazon, Google etc. use more reliable processes to measure user activity.

Clicks. How many times someone clicked on your ad, which should bring them to a page where they can immediately buy your game.

CTR (Click-Through Rate). The percentage of impressions that produced a click. Higher rates can indicate either of two things: you have a well-designed ad, you're getting prominent placements for your ad, or both.

ACPC (Average Cost per Click). Online advertising systems award each ad slot to the highest bidder. If you're an advertiser and bid 25 cents per click and the second highest bid is 20 cents, most systems will charge you 21 cents (one cent more than the second highest bid) for each clickthrough to your page.

Be sure to check each deal and make sure they use this system for bidding and don't charge more than the one cent premium.

The ACPC reports the average amount you paid for each click, which can vary based on what screen the ad was on, its page position, time of day etc.

Bid. The maximum you'll pay for each click. If the ACPC you're paying is 42 cents, don't just put in $2.00 to make sure you get the best slot on each page. Someone could come along and bid $1.95 and blow out your budget.

Budget. How much you're willing to spend on a given day (or over a longer period) before your ads stop running. This is an important protection since ad prices and results can fluctuate dramatically.

The data for impressions and clicks may be updated at a different rate than the financial data (which goes through legal checks) so if you pause or stop an ad you may still see additional sales continue for a few days. Only after all of that revenue has been reported can you calculate the ad's actual performance.

Always start with lower budgets as you're developing your ads and experimenting with systems. Discontinue any ad that doesn't earn a profit after getting an initial round of clicks, and increase your budget slowly and carefully if an ad is working.

There are many sad stories of new users who thought they were entering $10,000 as a rough guess for their planned annual budget. What the system expected, though, was their budget for one day.

Spend. How much you've spent on ads during a certain period.

Sales. Make the link for each ad unique, so you can measure how many sales you made from each one. You can then calculate how your Spend compares to your Sales and determine if an ad was profitable.

CoS or ACoS (Average Cost of Sales). The ratio between what you spent on ads and how much money you made. It can be expressed as a dollar amount (a $100 spend yielding 50 units sold has an ACoS of $2.00 per unit) or as a percentage (a $100 Spend that produces $200 in sales revenue would have a 50% ACoS).

5.5.6 A/B testing

Another key method used to gather data and figure out how to improve a game's results is A/.B testing.

The classic (and oversimplified) example is that you are trying to decide whether to make the button that says "Play!" green or blue.

Using one of several software packages, the team selects 200 random players and shows them the green button as they enter the game. The system selects a separate 200 users and shows them the blue button. Advanced systems will ensure that the demographics of the two groups are similar. If the A and B groups start out with different kinds of users, the results are usually meaningless.

If groups A and B produce a fairly similar number of "Play!" button presses it may be that there is no material difference between the colors.

It might also happen that more people proceed to try out the game by playing with the green button. In this case the team would make the button green for all users.

5.5.7 How NOT to Use KPI's, Analysis and A/B Testing

There are some aspects of LTV that even big, sophisticated publishers can forget. Several large social and multiplayer game publishers went through a period a few years ago when they damaged their businesses even as they increased sales.

Companies that that have gone public or that are hoping to be acquired or go public, can feel intense pressure to rack up ever-improved financial results each quarter. Financial TV channels and websites dissect each detail of every quarterly report, and investors bid shares up or drive down their value based on those analyses.

With those big stakes on the table, publishers turned to their game management teams and asked them to start running "end of quarter sales" to boost the numbers just before the financial reports went final.

Over time, the need to regularly invent new compelling offers led teams to adjust the overall balance of their game economies. Key items became harder to earn by "grinding," playing for a longer period without spending money, so users would feel more pressure to buy instead.

The difference in gameplay between paying players and those who had not been converted and monetized grew, as did the difference in success and rewards between higher-spending players and those who spent less.

As the sales pressure grew, so did the backlash. Some players complained that the business model had become "pay to win," and left the games. Initially publishers dismissed the losses as "the people who weren't paying anyway," but another pattern started to emerge.

I'm summarizing some very complex math here, but what the most aggressive publishers found in many cases was that emphasizing short term revenue with aggressive time-based sales had three effects:

• Positive: Near-term revenue grew as users took advantage of the special deals

• Negative: Average Lifetime Value declined, as users accelerated purchases they would have made and by doing so paid lower prices

• Negative: Average Lifetime Value declined further, as frustrated users left the game and therefore spent no further dollars

The net effect: using a flurry of sales to pull revenue into the current quarter lowered revenue in several subsequent quarters, damaging the value of the company instead of enhancing it.

The best-managed games now look to build a long-term balance in how they price and promote digital items. They have events and sales, but work to avoid imbalancing the game as a whole with special offers.

5.5.8 Different Kinds of Value

I hear marketers from app and game companies say, "Users who never pay for anything have no value, so we show them ads to make money and ignore their usage patterns so we can focus on paying customers."

Prioritizing paying users over those who don't pay is inherently reasonable, though some games still make a lot of money via selling advertising. But there are other ways for users to "pay" for our games.

The arrival of companies like Ninja Metrics has made it possible to research and pinpoint exactly which kinds of "non-paying" players do and don't provide real financial value. (Note: I have no business relationship with Ninja Metrics, but have worked with members of their leadership team.)

What the new research showed was that some non-paying and lower-budget users do in fact attract higher-spending players:

A clan or team in an MMORPG or shooter may have a mix of non-spenders and different levels of monetized players. If the non-spending players move to another game, some (or all) of the paying players may go with them. The non-converted players have financial value that can be measured.

Some players are natural recruiters, always telling their friends about what they're playing, even if they never become paying players. They have financial value, and receive valuable in-game rewards in many games that offer the option to invite friends.

Socialites. In games that feature a chat window or similar function some players make the experience more fun – they're just great to hang around with. Although some of those players may not be paying users, they still generate revenue by attracting and retaining more players when they play.

Not-Yet-Converted Paying Players. Some people just take longer to convert, and some titles naturally convert users later in the process of learning the game. Dismissing players as non-paying too readily can throw away revenue.

The moral of this story is that we need to remember that almost all users are valuable in one way or another. It's our job to create so much fun in our games that they want to pay us even more to expand and extend their play.

CHAPTER 41

Getting Paid (5.6)

DISCUSSING QUESTION 5.6

Exactly when and by whom will you be paid?

How will those payments be calculated, and by whom?

How far in advance will you know approximately how much money will come in each week or each month?

Will there be any cases where you refund people's money after they've paid to download or play your game?

This topic is most relevant for: Everyone

5.6.1 Invoice Terms and Contracts

Note: Most indie game studios don't send invoices because their income comes via online stores. Some studios, however, also do work for hire projects or have financing arrangements that require them to submit milestones, so I have included this section for reference.

If you earn money by any method other than direct online sales to consumers you'll need to send customers invoices.

When you send anyone an invoice, it's normal to have the "terms" listed on the document. Common choices include:

- Net 30, Net 15, Net 10 (or any other number) – You're asking them to pay you within that number of days
- Due Upon Receipt – This means you want to be paid immediately

Of course, just because you state those terms doesn't mean the recipient will comply. In practice, the larger company usually imposes its terms on smaller partners.

I have sent many an invoice marked Due Upon Receipt or Net 10 where I knew that if we got paid in 30 days we should count ourselves lucky.

When small clients and individual customers owe you money there may be even more surprises and delays, since they may have to wait for cash to come in before they can write a check.

Invoices only have meaning when they are tied to a contract or other *written* agreement that describes the work that you'll do and how much you'll be paid for doing that work.

I can give you an overview of how contracts work, but I'm not an attorney. If there's any doubt in your mind about a contract or business deal or document, an introductory meeting with an attorney specialized in the field is usually an inexpensive way to get good legal advice. You can then decide if you need additional services from the law firm.

We once retained control of a successful game when a publisher tried to illegally take it away from us. We prevailed solely because of *one sentence* **that our attorney had advised us to add to the contract.**

This was many years ago, and ever since that moment I have never underestimated the importance of having an experienced attorney review contracts.

5.6.2 A Note About Boxed Games

Many of us go home to houses filled with our collections of boxed video games and traditional board games. It's only natural for us to dream of looking up with pride to see our own boxed game on the shelf.

With very few exceptions, for indie game teams manufacturing and selling boxed games is a shortcut to losing large sums of money. The need to pay in advance for products you have no assurance of selling – and which can be returned to you even after you have sold them – makes this a rigged game where only the retailers and the big publishers can win.

The exceptions to this rule:

Short Run Collector Editions. If the digital version of your game is a hit on the PC you may have the opportunity to create a limited number of copies of a boxed "collector's edition" with special items included. Such projects are time-consuming and cash intensive, since you have to acquire everything that goes in the boxes before you ever sell anything and you'll need to pay for shipping. Keep the parts list simple and don't order too many copies in your first run to reduce risks and you could make some money.

Breakout Hits. If your game becomes a breakout hit and starts selling large numbers of copies, it may be appropriate to add boxed versions, especially for console platforms. If you reach this stage either a publisher or the hardware manufacturers like Sony, Microsoft or Nintendo will help you with the process. Even with a major hit, be careful not to make big financial commitments where you could easily lose $1,000,000 just by placing too large a manu-facturing order on one occasion.

Partners will often be willing to share this up-front risk with you in return for revenue splits, and those tradeoffs are often worth doing. If you do have a breakout hit you'll have an experienced attorney who will help guide you through these opportunities.

This will be the last you'll read about boxed games in this book, since in today's games industry the vast majority of indie games are sold as digital downloads for any of a wide variety of platforms.

5.6.3 Working with Game Publishers

In the early years of the indie "wave" the established game publish-ers were not interested in smaller-scale PC games, because their only PC titles were adaptations of their AAA console hits. They were not interested in mobile games, because they weren't sold through the established channels served by console publishers.

Then the app stores started generating billions of dollars in game sales each year. Steam reignited a PC game market chilled by rampant piracy by moving the platform from physical to digital products. Non-console revenues in the games industry grew at phenomenal rates.

In their eternal quest for revenue, the publishers opened their doors to indie game developers, reaching beyond the small group of large AAA studios that for years had been their sole outside part-ners.

Today indie game developers with strong teams have the option of pitching their projects to publishers. If your team is just starting out and has little experience, such pitches are far less likely to succeed.

The good news in this story is that this represents an alternate path to game publishing for strong game studios.

Publishers can provide developers with:

- Financing (as advances against royalties), sharing the risk on the cash invested in the game
- Production support, providing guidance, feedback and training to the indie team
- QA and playtesting, where publishers divide expenses across many projects and operate more efficiently
- Localization and porting to other platforms, where the publisher may have expertise, partnerships and connections that would be difficult for the developers to acquire themselves
- Marketing, PR & Cross-promotion, where a publisher has expertise, connections with the press, and (most importantly) other hit games through which it can advertise your title for free
- Distribution, where the publisher can reach additional sales channels that indie publishers are not large enough to deal with themselves

The bad news is that when you work with a publisher you're not just sharing the risk. You're also sharing the revenue.

An indie game that a developer "sells direct" through the app stores, Steam etc. typically will receive 70% of the money paid by users to buy the title, with minimal deductions for electronic delivery etc. The indie developer is paying for all of their own marketing and promotion, so a lot of that 70% will be consumed by expenses.

Depending on the deal, the developer who sells that game through a publisher may get far less: 7% to 14% of what the user pays (10% to 20% of the 70% passed through by online stores). If the game fails, it's the publisher (and perhaps also the developer) who absorbs the losses.

The publisher, not the developer, has to pay for the up-front marketing costs. But – as I'll cover in detail below – the publishers get to subtract those expenses before paying the developer any royalties.

It's not uncommon for the developer who reduces their risks by working through a publisher to net 3% to 6% of what the user paid for a game. A $15 PC title might bring its creators $0.50 to $1.00 after all the deductions. And that's before you have to pay taxes on the revenue.

So why would anyone ever want to work with a game publisher?

For teams that have no other way to raise money this can be an effective way to start out in business. Shipping a successful game will build your reputation and open new options over time.

If you need the services I listed above, then working with a publisher can be a good idea. As you do so, you'll learn more about the industry and become less dependent on the publisher's expertise.

Some publishers will "unbundle" these services, and let you choose only the support you need from a menu of available options. The fewer publisher resources you require and the lower the financial risk the publisher is taking on the deal, the higher your royalty will be.

Hardware makers will offer better deals to indie teams if they want a game for their platform. Microsoft, Nintendo and Sony will offer better terms for strong titles than other game publishers, especially if a game will be exclusive to their platform for some period of time.

Successful indie games may earn licensing offers to publish or distribute a game in additional markets like Korea or China, or on additional platforms such as consoles.

Important Note: Regardless of the initial terms offered to you by a game publisher, it's imperative that you have an attorney with games industry experience review the contract. There are many issues in these deals where seemingly innocuous language can have a major impact on your game, your revenue, your company and your career.

Game publishers have very different, styles, priorities and ethical standards. All are driven by a need to earn profits. Some are straightforward, open and trustworthy. Others look to bury poison pills in contracts that they can use to take money, rights or even entire products away from their creators. A good games attorney will be able to identify early in the process where in this continuum of ethical-to-sleazy the publisher you're working with may lie.

It's not cheap, but having an expert in your corner will cost far less than the consequences of signing such a deal without that help.

Talk to teams with successful games and ask them for referrals to strong game attorneys. Talk to more than one attorney to determine whom you like the best.

The Video Game Bar Association (vgba.org) is a trade organization led by experienced industry veterans in North America and in Europe. (Note: I am friends with and have worked with several principals of the VGBA, and have worked in particular with the law firm of Fenwick and West (Mark Stevens and Jennifer Stanley) on my own projects. I do not have any business relationship with any firm, attorney or group where I receive money or other compensation for any referral or recommendation.)

5.6.4 Advances and Royalties

If a publisher finances your game by paying you while you're developing it, you'll be given "advances against royalties," which are loans that will be subtracted from the royalties earned by the game after it is released.

The publisher starts paying additional cash royalty payments to the creators only after it has "recouped" enough royalty money to pay back the advances that funded the development.

Note: I discuss sample royalty rates below, but these numbers can vary widely based on other terms in the contract. The numbers I quote below would be very fair under some deal terms, and terrible (for one side or the other) under another set of rules. This is one of many reasons why it's imperative to have a games industry attorney work with you on these kinds of deals.

For example, a game publisher might pay a developer 20% of the Net Revenue it receives from sales of the new game. They could advance the developer $200,000 (in a series of payments tied to the completion and delivery of pre-defined milestones) to finish development of the game. They would then subtract that $200,000 from the royalties before paying the developer any additional cash.

If and when the game had $1,000,000 in Net Receipts, the 20% royalty rate would have paid off that $200,000 advance (since 20% of $1,000,000 is $200,000). After that point the developer would start receiving their full royalty, usually via payments made on a quarterly basis.

Advances come in two flavors: refundable and non-refundable. Non-refundable advances are in effect a "guarantee," the minimum payment you can count on. If your game generates only $100,000 in Net Receipts (and thus earns only $25,000 in royalties), you still get to keep the $200,000.

Refundable advances can be "billed back" by a publisher if sales targets aren't met or under certain other circumstances. Since those circumstances can be manipulated and manufactured by publishers I never sign any deal that includes refundable advances. I advise you not to sign any such deals yourself.

You'll notice that I keep saying "Net Revenue" for calculating royalties. Each contract's definition of "Net Revenue" can be even more important than a difference of several points in the royalty rate.

"Gross Revenue" means the total amount of money the publisher received for the product. This is also called revenue that is "above the line."

"Net Revenue" is what's left after the publisher subtracts expenses "allowed" under the contract. Each company has its own "typical" deductions, and what is routinely accepted for console games might be an unheard-of deduction for mobile, and vice versa. Net Revenue can also be referred to as revenue "below the line."

Hollywood studios are famous for subtracting every cost imaginable – and some that are imaginary – from Gross Revenue before they pay producers and actors a royalty on Net Revenue from their films.

Here's a list of some of the items that in a negotiation publishers may ask to subtract in their calculation of the game's Net Revenue:

Delivery Costs – Digital publishers will charge back the bandwidth and data fees for the download that sends your digital game to the user. How these costs relate to their actual expenses may be unclear, but at least such costs are far smaller than traditional shipping charges for packaged games.

Returns – Game "returns" are relatively rare for digital products (unlike boxed games in the big publisher retail channels), but do happen in some online stores if users claim they were deceived into buying the wrong game, etc.
Some such claims are sincere user error, others are fraud, but the online store will exert unilateral control over which claims are accepted and which are ignored. The publisher will subtract any money they refunded from Gross Receipts before paying royalties.

Taxes, Duties, Tariffs etc. – These can vary widely depending on the kind of transaction, the state or country, etc.

Marketing Costs – This is an example of a wide-open term that can be used to charge back anything and everything, including the new carpet in the marketing department's offices. Relevant costs need to be narrowly defined, not generic, and some contracts only subtract the more narrowly defined MDF (defined below). The parties may also cap any broad deduction like this at a pre-determined percentage of Net Receipts to curb abuse.

QA – Another wide-open term, since large numbers of salary dollars can be classified as meeting this description. This is another contract provision to limit or cap.

Marketing Development Funds (MDF) or "Co-op Funds" — Different online channels handle these costs in different ways and refer to them by different names. MDF or co-op funds are amounts that publishers pay to subsidize promotion of their games, or to pay for optimum online slots such as a major landing page. These programs may be very effective in helping to sell your game or a terrible waste of money, so there is no easy definition of what to accept.

Costs of Currency Exchange – If revenue is received overseas, different fees and commissions may have to be paid in order to exchange it for dollars, Euro etc.

In general, a major part of negotiating any game contract is defining which of these deductions from Gross Receipts are allowed before royalties are calculated from the Net Revenue.

5.6.5 Selling Through The App Stores, Amazon & Steam

The Apple App Store, Google Play and Amazon are all open systems where anyone can sign up to sell their products. There are basic restrictions (e.g. no inappropriate sexual content, no unstable products that crash etc.) but those are the only requirements.

Steam is rapidly morphing away from a curated marketplace to this same kind of wide-open online store as the mobile app marketplaces, and the console makers' digital stores are moving to create special categories for self-published indie games.

Once you've signed up and published your title these systems by and large run very smoothly and auto-deposit money in your bank account each month.

The challenge that dominates every indie publisher's thinking, as noted many times above, is user discovery. In a world where hundreds of thousands of games all compete for players' attention it's easy to "throw a big party and then realize that no one is coming."

We could fill the pages of an entire book just discussing these issues. Below is a top-line overview of major factors, and online searches on each topic will uncover many additional resources on the web.

There is no one checklist of steps that will negate the problem of player discovery for any game. Many indie games do find a way to stand out in a massive crowd, but every game is different and each needs its own custom plan of attack.

Please use these suggestions as a place to start, but challenge yourself to seek out every article, every web post, every event speaker who can give you insights on what ideas may work in your unique situation.

Enter a Contest or Competition. Winning recognition in indie game festivals and competitions can increase your visibility and grow support. If you win a major competition the effect can be dramatic. Games as diverse as *World of Goo, Minecraft, Fez, Papers Please* and *Her Story* received major boosts from indie game awards programs.

Many kinds of contests are listed online, and the winners can label their game, app store description and website with accolades like, "Winner, Spring 2018 Best New Game Award" or "Bronze Medal, Best Mobile Game of the Year."

Plan and execute a PR campaign when you release your game. Many small teams assume that the major game websites and their local media won't care about the release of their new indie game.

If a game sounds unique and is getting strong early reviews many outlets will in fact write about indie titles.

Take the time to prepare a professionally written press release, guidelines for which are readily available via online search. Virtually every major games and news media site has a "Contacts" page that lists where to send that press release, and the app stores have special reviewer promo code systems you can use to give journalists free copies or free items for review.

ASO (App Store Optimization). If you've ever worked on websites you know about SEO, alias Search Engine Optimization. It's the process of making sure you use the right words in the right way on your site so search engines guide your target audience to your page in the most competitive way.

In the online stores we have now seen the growth of ASO, or App Store Optimization. This is the art of picking the perfect words, illustrations and video to encourage the right players to download and try your game.

You'll notice that I said "the right players." If you're selling a mobile puzzle game but users think your title is a hidden object game, you may get lots of downloads. But those players will abandon your game quickly, may give you low ratings, and you'll never monetize them. The description of your game and the images you chose caused the wrong people to download your app.

Good ASO therefore has two objectives:

- To describe in very few words why your game is special and worth trying when so many other games are vying for attention
- To clearly communicate what kind of game you have and what kind of audience will enjoy it, so only the "right" people download and try it

Become a Student of User Acquisition. I see excellent new articles on this topic almost every week, because the marketplace remains fluid and evolving. Read everything you can, seek out war stories of what does and doesn't work.

Your goal is to avoid paying for expensive ads for user acquisition by using every alternative method possible to find new players who will love your game. As discussed above, PR is the first method teams use to achieve this goal.

If you do buy ads, find an experienced advisor or team member to manage online ad buying. Choose your spots very carefully and keep your bids low. Start with Facebook, which for many games has proven to have a strong ability to pinpoint and target the right game audience with ads.

Monitor which ads produced players who monetize and who stay in your game, and which ads inspire fewer, less valuable downloads.

Many teams who were not experienced with online ad buying have blown a game's entire promotional budget in two hours when they did not realize how big a spend they were authorizing on an internet portal. The big players will sometimes bid ads in some networks up to suicidal levels of several dollars per click to freeze out all but the largest competitors. When this happens you want to take your spend in those networks down to zero.

There are many companies that offer "incentivized user acquisition" programs, where users earn some form of reward if they download a version of your game for free, or are offered a free download of your game for watching a video ad, etc.

Avoid these programs – it may sound like a cheap way to get thousands of new players, but the games that use these services rarely retain those players and indie publishers who use incentive programs are often left with a depleted budget and very little to show for it.

User Ratings. All user rating systems are flawed, but if managed properly over time they will help good games get noticed.

Teams typically identify players who return for extended and repeated play sessions. These users may be given a link to go to the app store and leave the game (hopefully) a five-star rating. Like all user requests, these need to be made in non-irritating ways to avoid angering or losing players.

Design the Right Icon. We may joke about how the top-selling mobile games have similar icons with the faces of male characters shouting, but that pattern emerged from user research rather than conspiracy theories. Your game may fit this profile or call for a very different icon, but it's worth it to take the time to test different images and see which one spurs the most downloads.

Always evaluate icon ideas by displaying them unmagnified and surrounded on screen by the icons of other hit games. If the colors and image don't grab your attention on that crowded screen they won't work on users' crowded screens either.

Banish all bugs. If your game is submitted to app stores with crash bugs or with obvious mistakes (even misspellings of text) it will probably be rejected. If the testers miss the bugs the problems will affect your user ratings and doom your hopes of being featured.

Update often. A game that sits there without additions, improvements or expansions soon starts to look like it's been abandoned by its creators. You'll notice that the best-selling games are updated regularly – that's one of the reasons they're best-selling games.

Virality as a Game Mechanic in Microtransaction-Based Games. This tactic can't be over-used without chasing away users or creating perceived game balance problems, but when implemented carefully it can drive growth if a game is fun to play. Examples:

Offer players in-game rewards if they invite friends to download the game and those invited players do so. Rewards can be increased if the invited users later become regular players.

Use your metrics to identify users who continue to play the game actively but are unlikely to convert to paying players. Offer these users game assets they wouldn't otherwise buy, in return for referring friends. Emphasize personalization assets like skins, badges etc. and assets that only slightly increment their abilities rather than items that can significantly alter their level of play in the game.

5.6.6 Getting Featured in App Stores

Every indie game developer – including me – hopes to see their game featured. The net is full of articles about how to earn these positions, with advice that ranges from sending flowers to app store managers to choosing the right colors for your app's icon.

There are no magical answers. In that context, here are some headlines to keep in mind.

Build a really fun game that people love to play, that is easy to learn, and that earns high user ratings. Games that meet these qualifications have a good chance of being featured, because among hundreds of thousands of games only a small percentage meet all of those criteria.

Pick an initial exclusive platform. If you roll out your game to multiple platforms at the same time you miss an important chance to be featured. If you are exclusive to one platform when you first launch your game, you are far more likely to be featured on that system's app store, and it can make tuning and debugging easier than it would be if your fork the code too soon.

Support the new features and peripherals. If a major platform maker like Apple or Microsoft unveils a great new feature or a fun new peripheral in the same quarter that your game is released, do your best to support their new offering. Teams that promote the system owner's hardware are far more likely to be featured in that company's app store.

Be international. On most platforms each nation has its own "Featured" list in app stores with this function. Localizing text to other languages is a big plus, and "EFIGS" (English, French, Italian, German, Spanish) are the most common western languages, but there are several other large game markets in locations as far apart as Turkey and Indonesia. Chinese localization can create a big win if (and only if) the game style matches those popular in China.

Translations need to be done by experts, not by AI or semi-fluent friends. I speak Spanish fairly well, but I would never do the Spanish translation for my own game.

Register early for developer events for each platform you intend to support, and seek out all appropriate contacts via their developer websites. If your game and your professionalism impress the company representatives you may be given access or referrals to local app store decision makers.

Hey, I know someone there! Some of the app stores are secretive about their staffs, while other manufacturers make it easy to find a local developer support person to work with.

You'll notice that I placed "find someone on the inside" suggestion last on my list of app store strategies. That's because developing a personal connection only works if you have a great game that's fun to play and that already attracts and retains users.

CHAPTER 42

Working with Money (5.7–5.8)

DISCUSSING QUESTION 5.7

Pretend that your studio has been operating for a year and you're having some success.

If someone asked you to estimate how much money your business would have in the bank in 30 days from that moment, what would you add and subtract from your company's then-current bank balance to calculate the answer?

This topic is most relevant for: Everyone

5.7.1 Calculating Cash

When I started out as a CEO at my first company, I thought I was pretty good at being conservative with cash.

If a client told us on September 1 that they thought a deal would close by September 15 and we'd have a check by September 30, I'd put that cash in the budget for October 30. That was being conservative.

Over time I realized that in the games industry it typically takes 90 days for small deals to get from an agreement-in-principle to a final, signed contract. The check that was supposed to arrive on September 15 might come on December 15. Or, as happened recently, the September 15 "promise" turned into a check on February 24 of the following year!

Or, as happens sometimes, the deal falls through and those dollars never arrive at all.

Always remember, "If the money is not already in the bank, don't just be cynical about when it will arrive. Assume that it may never arrive at all."

5.7.2 There's Always a Surprise!

In my years as a GM and CEO I have almost never had a month in which a significant unbudgeted expense did not appear.

- A computer dies and has to be replaced
- A game publisher has a new exec who wants a status report, so four of us have to fly to Los Angeles and stay in a hotel overnight for a 9:00 AM meeting, then fly back that night
- We need specialized insurance for a project because it's required by a new client, and now we have to spend an extra $2,180... or $21,800

Stuff happens. Your calculation of how much cash you'll have in 30 days has to include an allowance for those unpredictable expenses.

5.7.3 The "Nut"

There are some things, however, that are predictable:

If you've hired a team, you're paying salaries and payroll taxes every two weeks, give or take a few days. You might be able to stall on replacing that computer or buying that insurance, but...

Payroll and payroll taxes always MUST go out on time.

In many jurisdictions businesses can pay their employees either 24 times a year (twice a month) or 26 times a year (every two weeks). If you pay your team every two weeks each paycheck is a little smaller, but in two months of every year you have to make payroll three times instead of two. Those can be extra tough months for a business.

If a payroll date would naturally fall on a Saturday, you may have to release those paychecks a day earlier than usual.

If you've rented an office, the rent is due on a certain date and if it's late you're going to have to pay a hefty penalty. Get too far behind and the landlord will change the locks and you'll be locked out of your own business... with all your equipment and files inside.

You'll typically have to pay business property taxes and quarterly corporate tax deposits. Penalties for not doing so can be steep, and can open a Pandora's Box of legal issues. Don't miss these key payment deadlines.

This collection of "must do" expenses is often called "the nut," the amount of money a business absolutely positively has to come up with each month. A more genteel term for this, which includes provisions for unexpected expenditures, is "the monthly burn rate."

If you take your current cash and divide it by your monthly burn rate, you'll get a number that represents your "runway," the number of months that the company can currently operate without generating or receiving more cash.

So let's recap:

1. You have to be very skeptical about every dollar of revenue you think will be coming into your business until it actually reaches your bank account.
2. Every month you'll have unexpected expenses.
3. Every month you'll have to cover "the nut," expenses you absolutely positively must pay, no matter what.

Yes, it's not fair. The money coming in is unpredictable, while the money going out is already-committed dollars plus more unexpected costs on top of it. That's what you need to remember when you forecast the cash in your bank account thirty days from now.

Protect your cash and you'll always have a big advantage over your competitors.

5.7.4 The Three Kinds of Cash

Sometimes the defining line between success and failure is painfully simple: those who manage cash carefully are the ones who live long enough to survive their mistakes and make their business a success.

Those who cannot manage cash run out of money and close their doors.

That's why experienced mentors and advisors for startups always teach their entrepreneurs the phrase:

"Cash is King"

That's why we give our accelerator companies lectures about how hard it is to earn cash, and how easy it is to watch it slip away in ways that you never expected.

And that's why you absolutely, positively must understand the three kinds of cash, whether you're a tiny startup or working in a large corporation.

Here's the list:

1. Cash that Someone Else Cannot Take Back

We think of the money in our business and personal bank accounts as "ours" and are used to the idea that so long as we pay our taxes no one can take it away.

In reality, if you're running a business, especially a young business that has not built up cash reserves, it's likely that most or all of your company's cash can be taken from you.

How special is "non-refundable" cash? To appreciate it, read on about all the different ways that cash that should be in your bank account can end up somewhere else.

2. Cash that Someone Else Can Take Back

There are many cases in business where this can happen:

If a business takes out a bank loan it will come with covenants and restrictions. These may include things like maintaining a certain average balance, a certain minimum balance, having a minimum total amount of new deposits in a given quarter, etc.

If a business falls out of compliance with those covenants the bank has the option (but not the requirement) to "call" the loan, which means you have to pay back all the money immediately. All that loan money in your account is not free and clear. It's money you could have to give back.

As in all of it. As in giving back all of it at once when you weren't planning to do so.

The moral of the story: try to avoid taking bank loans. This is why you hear the phrase, "The only people who can get bank loans are the people who don't need the money!"

If you guaranteed the loan personally (something often required of small business owners or CEO's to get a loan) they can sue you personally if the business cannot pay back the bank.

Never (and I mean *never ever*) **personally guarantee any business loan or lease! It's always better to find an alternate path than it is to guarantee a loan or lease.**

If your personal account is in the same bank as your business loan they can take your personal cash without your permission and without giving you notice if the business cannot pay back the bank.

In some jurisdictions they can do this via the fine print in the loan agreement without you explicitly guaranteeing the loan. This is another reason to avoid taking business loans and to maintain strong discipline with cash.

Companies that have raised funds through friends and family, from small "Angel Investors" or from VC's (Venture Capital firms) do so under different kinds of contracts. Some are structured as "convertible notes," loans that can be converted into equity (shares of stock) in the company by the investor if they wish to do so. Others may be straight stock sales.

These arrangements are not common for indie games, but when they do happen they can be either very beneficial or disastrous for the founders.

With many of these deals, if the investors don't like how the company is doing they can "call the loan." If the loan cannot be repaid some deals give all of the company's property – including intellectual property ("IP") like patents, copyrights and trademarks – to the investors in lieu of cash. That means that you no longer own the rights to your game.

In the hands of very aggressive investors such deal terms can be used to take over ownership of a promising young company and its products.

I have seen ruthless investors privately engage in such maneuvers after publicly giving speeches about how they mentor entrepreneurs. Don't assume that every investor is trustworthy just because they sound nice and have worked with other game developers.

Investors are often given voting seats on a company's Board of Directors. If the company does not repay money that investors are owed the board members who hold those voting seats can fire the CEO and take over the company, which gives them control of the bank accounts, physical property and intellectual property.

So all that money that came from investors is not cash that you control. It is money that you could have to give back: Always read the deal terms carefully (the lawyers will give you very long documents), always hire your own, separate lawyers to review the deal, and go into the process with your eyes open if you take investors' money.

The IRS and other tax authorities. In the United States the Internal Revenue Service as well as state and local tax authorities can in many cases contact your bank and have them deliver your company's cash to the Government without your permission. If you have not formed the right kind of corporation they can do the same with your personal funds, even if it is the company that owes the taxes. You have the right to appeal if you think there's been a mistake, but in the meantime that cash is unavailable to you.

Not paying any legally imposed tax is a mistake that can snowball into big debts, but not paying employment taxes is often the most punishing mistake of all. Penalties, fines and fees can multiply dramatically in a very short time. Always be fanatical about paying payroll and employment taxes on time.

Checks, Certified Checks and Cashier's Checks. We all know that checks can bounce, and that if they do so the money we thought we had received will be subtracted from our account.

But cashier's checks and certified checks ought to be OK, right? Unfortunately, even these checks can be forged, so the value added to your bank account can later be subtracted.

3. **Cash You Are Owed or Promised**

Here's a list of things that can happen to money before you receive it.

Late Delivery. You can't sell your game until it's ready to place in an online store. Even experienced teams that work incredibly hard often deliver a completed product later than planned. Whether it's a week, a month or a year late, all the money you would have made does not come in until the work is completed.

Unless you start with a lot of cash in the bank, a small company that falls behind schedule can run out of runway and have no money to pay the team or creditors before the project is completed.

If you have partners, licensors or investors of some kind they may add money to the value of the deal, but do so only in exchange for severe concessions on issues like royalties, ownership rights etc. If you're running out of cash some partners will extract very harsh concessions to bail you out.

Late Milestone. Maybe you've partnered with a game publisher or distributor on your indie game, and they're financing development by paying you cash each time you complete a major milestone. If you're late delivering a milestone or in gaining their approval of the milestone you won't get those cash payments.

Some publishers will deliberately use pending milestone payments to pressure teams into doing additional work that is not called for in the contract, and to do it without getting any additional payment. This is why developers always want to add to the approvals section of any contract, "Approval not to be unreasonably withheld."

Even with a well-written contract, the only way to prevent unilateral publisher add-ons is to make the wording that describes each milestone very clear and impossible to misunderstand, and to refuse to add significant features to the game without a formal process of agreeing on additional advance payments.

Late Payment. Some late payments by your partners are deliberate stalling to hold onto cash as long as possible. CFO's in large companies are judged by the average number of days it takes them to pay an invoice, so they're rewarded for delays.

Other times a partner company may have their own cash flow problems. They may be waiting for a big check from somewhere else, and until it comes in nobody outside is going to get paid.

Currency transfer exchange rates, regulations and delays. If you are being paid by an overseas company or you're a foreign company dealing with a partner in the United States, your bank account and the partner's account will be in different currencies.

The exchange rate for those currencies fluctuates each day. Large banks try to do exchanges at moments when the exchange rate favors them by a few cents. I've had checks that were anywhere from $75 to $7,500 smaller than I expected because of exchange rate fluctuations that were exploited by our bank.

Large wire transfers of some currencies can be delayed by regulators in one or both countries. This may involve collecting data for tax authorities, and some reviews are intent on preventing money laundering by criminal interests. But if your money arrives two days later than planned it can cause big problems.

Stalling for advantage. I have seen large companies drag out negotiations with small partners in an effort to induce the other company to use up its cash reserves. Once the small company looks like it's starving for cash the large company unveils harsh new conditions for the deal.

By that time the small company may have no choice but to accept terrible terms in an agreement.

If you assume in every negotiation that the other side will try this tactic, you'll manage cash, time and negotiations very differently. Never cut off your discussions with alternate partners and clients until a deal is signed with the desired funder, the check is cashed and the money is in the bank.

Note: There have been times when I thought a partner or client was stalling a payment to bully us. I later found out that the team was working on paying us, but were drowning in their company's red tape. Accusing people of treachery usually makes things worse, and your best defense is to deliver no work to the other party until you're paid.

Real bank error. Like the game of Monopoly, on rare occasions there will be bank errors. Unlike Monopoly, they are often not in your favor, so you are missing some of your money. It can take from 20 minutes to several days for the bank to correct the error. In the meantime that cash is gone.

Change in management. You have a great relationship with a client or partner. Then your ally leaves and they bring in a new person.

Often your deals will continue to operate normally. But other times the new executive may cut away existing products, services or vendors. The revenue you've been receiving from this partner ends, suddenly, with very little warning.

The new leaders may renegotiate your deal so they get $2 per unit instead of $1, or they pay you a 5% royalty instead of 10%. You may have a choice between sharply reduced cash coming in from this deal, or no cash coming in from this deal. Neither choice is attractive.

Partner or client acquired by new company. The people, projects and products in the acquired company are perfectly good, but the acquiring company only wants some of them. Everything else is closed down, released or given away.

Your contract or relationship could be terminated. All the unpaid money that you were scheduled to receive from that deal disappears.

Bounced Check. When you're dealing with businesses rather than individuals you're unlikely to receive a check that bounces, but it does happen once in a while. In most cases someone just mistimed when a deposit was going to hit the bank and you get paid 24 to 48 hours later. Or it could be a sign of impending...

Bankruptcy. Sometimes that bounced check is the harbinger of even more damaging news. The company that owes you money could go bankrupt.

When a company that owes you money goes bankrupt they have two kinds if creditors.

- **Secured Creditors** have some form of collateral secured by signed legal documents, like the bank's right to repossess a car for non-payment.

- **All other creditors are Unsecured Creditors** who get paid only if there is money left over after the company's employees (in many states) and the Secured Creditors have been paid.

I have had a client go bankrupt once in my career. As unsecured creditors we never received a penny. All the cash we had planned to receive disappeared.

5.7.5 Companies Train Managers to Value Cash

When people pitch to big companies like Microsoft, Google and IBM, I often hear the phrase, "I'm going in and asking for top dollar. They have tons of money!"

This is actually a terrible approach. Here's why:

Large firms are very aware of the fact that managers might be more generous with cash when everyone knows there are billions in the bank. To offset this psychology, they make spending and budgeting controls *more* rigorous than those at a typical firm. Managers have to work extra hard for every budget dollar at most of the mega-corporations.

When you inflate your prices for the rich company, they know you're bidding high just for them, and you're less likely to get the deal.

5.7.6 Don't Sell Yourself Short

There's a flip side to this story of how much to charge customers and clients.

Many of us tend to sell ourselves short. We say things like, "They'd never pay me that much per hour," even though we know that our rate is normal for this assignment.

Underpricing high quality work makes us look like we lack confidence in ourselves.

So how do you figure out what to charge so you're neither greedy nor self-defeating?

Do your homework. If you don't already know, research the typical rates for the services you provide at your level of experience. Do online searches. Talk to people you know in the industry.

Make that research a continual process, so you track changes based on economic changes and the circumstances of different deals. Especially for indies, prices can go up and down with the tides of the economy.

There is no "right answer" for anyone on how much to charge for their work. Just do your research, make your best estimate, and adjust those fees regularly to match the market rates as they evolve.

5.7.7 Lessons from Las Vegas

Stories about hit indie games generating millions of dollars ignore the tragedies of people who mortgaged their homes to raise money to build their dream game, and who then ran out of cash.

If someone is going to Las Vegas you may hear them say, "I've budgeted $200 (or whatever number) for gambling. If I lose it all then the gambling part of my trip is over."

That same principle works well for how much of your own money to risk on developing an indie game. As they say in Vegas, "Don't bet more than what you can afford to lose."

Entrepreneurs often end up risking far more than they intended to risk. Success seems to be just weeks away, or a pending deal suggests that a short term loan will quickly be repaid. The Founder steps in, writes a check from her savings account, and everyone marches on.

Too often, all that happens is that the deepening financial crater swallows more and more of the entrepreneur's personal and family resources.

Don't do this.

So, if I'm warning you about all these perils, how can I be so optimistic about encouraging you to explore and launch your indie game?

Because there are many ways to launch an indie game without taking these extreme risks.

5.7.8 A Million Ways to Build a Dream

Here are some alternate ways to build your indie game that don't require these (often ill-advised) personal risks.

Some will apply to your project, others won't. Please use them as inspiration and idea-starters.

Start by Doing "Work for Hire." You can reduce risk by not striking out on your own until you have one or more paying publishers or other clients for whom you do some form of software development, art services, music composition etc. It could be anything from game design to mobile apps to website development to concept art, but if it helps pay the bills it can be part of the solution.

Typically the business terms of such deals mean that the client owns the Intellectual Property ("IP") in the final product. This is why such projects are called "work for hire," because the team that builds the title does not own it. In some deals the team may receive a royalty or bonus if the product sells well.

The danger of work for hire deals is that a small team may never have time to work on their own game. This can produce a vicious cycle where a group that wants to do their own title is always stuck chasing their next contract and never earning enough to have time to do what they started their company to do.

How do you break that cycle? Develop a steadily improving set of tools so that every project is faster to create and more reliable. Learn how to create better schedules and more accurate bids based on the results of every project. Most top teams also use strong project management processes, whether they be "Agile" or some other system.

Use Your Vacation as a test case. For the first few years after graduating from college I was a teacher and had ten weeks off each summer. Although I got my M.Ed. during that time and then taught at Claremont Graduate University (where I shared a classroom with the legendary business author and professor Dr. Peter Drucker), I used some of those summer breaks to pursue personal creative projects including my 1975 mainframe RPG, *Dungeon*.

If you have a job where there is a longer break each year, you have the perfect opportunity to experiment. Spend part or all of the time working on your indie game. See how you feel and what you're thinking after completing the goals you set for this block of time.

Take a Sabbatical. If you work in education or in some large companies, every few years you qualify to take a sabbatical and be paid during your time off.

Some organizations define what you can and cannot do during the sabbatical, since the idea is that you use the time to learn something that you bring back to share with the team. But you may be able to meet these requirements and make some progress on your indie game as well.

Build Tools and Assets. Unity, Epic and Crytek are all large companies that have been built entirely or in part on providing game engines and other tools to developers and publishers.

In particular, there are a number of individuals and teams who are currently making a living providing various kinds of projects, add-ons, modules, art assets, audio and music to users via the Unity Store. If you can generate a large enough stream of revenue from such assets that income could fund your indie game.

Start Out Part-time. As we've covered in depth, this can be an especially effective strategy if you have a job that leaves you with enough free time to make progress on an indie project. By not giving up your primary job you avoid the worst financial risks of a new venture.

I've seen people carve out two hours an evening three times a week for an indie game. Or every Saturday. Or an hour every morning before they go to work. Or a full weekend once a month.

The schedule doesn't matter. What does matter is:

- The time you're spending is not adversely impacting your personal relationships and family life
- The time is not chain reacting into negative effects on your performance at your primary job
- You can make enough progress each week and month that you feel it's realistic that you will complete work that you are proud to have done

Never finishing anything feels awful and makes every day torture. But finishing just a few of the right things part-time, if you're really proud of them, can feel downright wonderful.

Turn Your Student Project into a Business. Many universities with undergraduate and graduate game development programs have students work as teams on major projects. This allows them to work in the same kinds of organizational structures as the ones they'll encounter in their games industry careers.

In general, I think it's best to start our careers by working for great established companies and soaking up all their best practices and effective principles of leadership.

In that context, I have seen successful small companies launched when a student project was so strong that the team turned it into a shipping product and formed a business. The most famous is That Game Company, but even with all their success with *Flower* and *Journey* they also went through some very tough times as a business.

There can be a catch, however. Depending on the university, student projects have different kinds of status:

The project may belong to the students themselves.

The IP (Intellectual Property) rights may be owned by the university, since the project was created under faculty direction using school facilities. The team is free to make it a commercial product, but they may have to pay a royalty to the university.

The university may both own and control the project. The students cannot commercialize it without first getting permission to do so and negotiating a royalty agreement with the school.

In some cases university policies may prohibit the commercialization of student projects. This is done to keep students' focus on the learning, experimentation etc. and avoid the distractions of money.

If you're considering turning a school project into a business, be sure to check with your program's Director to understand what rules apply at your institution.

DISCUSSING QUESTION 5.8

How much cash will you need to start with in order to cover all of your game's expenses until it starts producing positive cash flow and pays for itself?

This topic is most relevant for: Everyone

5.8.1 Your Initial Funding

Most entrepreneurs find that as a company gets up to speed their initial estimate of cash requirements was low. If you have an experienced advisor or friend in the industry, ask them to look through your spreadsheet to catch omissions and overoptimistic budget items.

In the pages that follow we'll discuss how to build a basic Business Plan, which will give you a much better projection than any "guesstimate" spreadsheet.

What's the classic Silicon Valley advice?

"Take your first, best guess. Then double it."

5.8.2 Your First Company Budget

Making a projected budget for the first time may seem intimidating, but it's actually a straightforward process.

You can find a variety of models to work from by doing a Google search for "sample company budget." Focus on plans from game companies or software companies, which may have unique categories you'll want to include in your plan.

If you've done lots of internal game project budgets at established companies that's a great start. But there are lots of expenses that are buried in the "Overhead" line on those budgets that you'll need to break out for your own business plan.

What is overhead, as defined in business accounting?

- Product development cost is considered to be all the costs that go into creating your game (and operating a live team if necessary), including the salaries of the people on your team.

- Everything else is considered to be overhead: rent; equipment; salaries and expenses for marketing, sales, HR, finance etc.

It is critical that as you make your budget you make a column for each month of expenses, because they're not evenly divided throughout the year. There are bulges, often at the end of each quarter, where more money is going out the door. Some annual expenses that cannot be broken down into monthly payments will also produce spikes in spending.

For your first budget, treat everything as a simple expense, since this works best for managing cash flow and, as I keep repeating, Cash is King.

Later you can work with your accountant to "capitalize" large purchases, which spreads out the tax impact of the expense but doesn't affect when the cash is actually spent.

Be sure to research all the different kinds of taxes and fees you'll have to pay, and budget them into the months when the money will need to be spent. There may be multiple certificates or licenses you need to acquire, and these costs should be budgeted as well.

Lay out your projected revenues on the same monthly basis that you used for your expenses, remembering all the ways we discussed above for payments to be delayed or to never appear at all.

You'll then be able to track your "cash flow," which consists of:

Cash at start of month + Cash received this month
– Cash spent this month

This lets you project how much cash you'll have in the bank at the end of each month, quarter and year.

In the first drafts of your budget it will be routine to see that your month-end cash goes down to zero at certain points in the year. You'll need to cut or postpone expenses to get past those choke points, and it's best to do so from the very start of your planning.

It's tempting to spend a lot of money up front to get your office set up perfectly. Focus on doing things well, not perfectly, and always preserve as much of your cash as possible.

CHAPTER 43

Dealing with Downsides (5.9–5.10)

What will you do if you complete your game, offer it to the world... and it doesn't sell?

This topic is most relevant for: Everyone

5.9.1 Living with the Dark Side

I've said at several points in this book that I'm here to encourage you.

The first reason for asking, "What if we fail?" is that you may answer, "That would really suck, but I'm controlling the risks so life would go on and I'd find a way to build an indie game again."

You may have a different answer, and we'll discuss a range of these issues below.

Having a project or business fail can be heartbreaking, even if the lessons learned later prove to be valuable. Considering failure and concluding that the downside is an acceptable risk is a step that encourages us to keep trying, to keep moving forward.

In a later chapter we'll also discuss "pivoting" when the original plan doesn't work out.

5.9.2 All Sorts of Answers

The second purpose for this question is to consider failure and make sure we're making decisions based on all of the available information.

For example, some reasonable answers to "What if we fail?" would be:

"I'd have to go look for a new job. And I'd have to do it while I had enough savings left to make sure we were covered financially while I looked, since finding a good job takes longer than finding any old job."

"I'd go back to making games as a hobby and keep an eye on what's selling on Steam. If I see a good opening I could always try making it a part-time business again."

"I'd take a long hard look at what I needed to change about the game or in how I'm selling it. But it's just part-time and I'm not spending much money on it. I can tolerate the cost for another year, keep experimenting and see what happens."

As the investors of Silicon Valley will tell you, "Failures are where you learn what you needed to know to finally achieve success."

5.9.3 When We Lose Perspective

On the flip side, here are some answers to "What if the idea fails to make money?" that set off fire alarms and sirens in my head:

"I'd borrow $100,000 against my house (or $5,000 against my car, etc.) and use that money to fund the company so we can keep going."

If you didn't know what disease you had and nothing the doctor prescribed was working, would you spend $100,000 to buy more of the same medicine? Please don't do this.

"I'm putting in the last cash I've got so we can keep going, and if we fail I may have to declare personal bankruptcy."

If things are going this badly why would we keep going? In fact, it's clear that we should not keep going, because doing so will only make things worse for you.

"I can't give up. I have to go all in, put up every dollar I can get my hands on. I've come too far and this is my only chance. If I don't bet on myself, how am I ever going to get someone else to bet on me?"

Not all of our ideas are going to work out, and we all get more than one chance. Instead of going all in, it may be time to take the chips you have left and cash them out.

You may say, "Who'd mortgage their house (or borrow against their car or sell their late mother's engagement ring) to chase an idea that's not working?"

My answer: Someone who's worked so hard and so long and is so determined that they've lost perspective. They stop thinking and are ruled by passion and commitment.

And it happens to intelligent, thoughtful, experienced people all the time.

That's another reason why I ask this question. Sometimes talking about the consequences of failure opens our eyes and stops us from doing something foolish.

DISCUSSING QUESTION 5.10

What will you do if a partner or customer refuses to pay you money that they owe you?

This topic is most relevant for: Everyone

5.10.1 Forewarned is Forearmed

If the only partners you work with are Steam, the App Store, Google Play etc. this is a small-scale issue, limited to rare cases where users try to "return" a digital game.

If you do work for hire projects or license your game to an overseas publisher in return for royalties the stakes can be much larger.

I told the story of "The Chess Game" at the beginning of this section, (a fictional case amalgamated from several real stories) where a large publisher refused to pay a game developer as required by a contract.

How can you avoid the same thing happening to you? You can't avoid all risk, but here are my suggestions for reducing your exposure:

On all but the smallest transactions, take the time to negotiate and sign a written agreement that makes the terms of the deal clear. If most of your deals are similar you can pay an attorney to give you a "boilerplate" contract (one with the most common terms and conditions already spelled out) and then only pay for legal advice in the future if you make changes to its provisions.

Honorable partners almost always accept when you say, "We like getting everything clear in writing so there can't be any mistakes or misunderstandings that will get in our way later."

The other party may ask you to start with their contract draft instead of yours for the negotiation, which is common and reasonable if they're the larger company.

If the deal is of any scope and the other side wants to avoid a written contract, walk away from the deal. As bad as that sounds, what follows when you work without a contract will be much worse. Anyone who asks you to do so usually has dangerous intentions.

5.10.2 Letters of Intent

If a contract negotiation looks like it will take a long time you can suggest a Letter of Intent (often called an "LOI"). An LOI states only the major terms of a deal, and says that the parties will negotiate a full contract in good faith later. It can define basic steps for each party to follow, and payments that will be made.

For big, slow-moving companies that are dealing in good faith, this kind of Letter of Intent is done all the time. They'll often help you get one signed quickly to get the deal going and buy time for the contract negotiation.

Although a Letter of Intent may look simple and straightforward, you still want to have it reviewed by your attorney.

Even if it says, "This LOI is not binding upon the parties..." there are exceptions in how that word "binding" is interpreted, so don't let those words stop you from involving your lawyer.

If a company that is moving slowly says, "We don't do Letters of Intent," proceed with caution. They may be playing the stalling game to try to delay the real negotiation until you've depleted your financial reserves.

There are also some cases where an LOI can work against you. An LOI that gives you a little money but prohibits you from negotiating with anyone else for a given period of time (a common provision) can put you in a worse position than you'd be in without the LOI.

This may be part of a legitimate strategy to have both sides focus on closing the deal, or the publisher or investor may be using stalling tactics to gain leverage over you if your cash is being depleted as negotiations go on. If you have multiple parties interested in the deal don't agree to this provision, because cutting off discussions with all but one potential partner will probably cut off the other opportunities permanently.

Use your common sense, and in sizable deals do research on the people with whom you're dealing. If your intuition is telling you not to trust someone, it's usually best to follow those instincts and proceed very carefully, or not at all.

Don't automatically trust big, well-known companies. They may, like the "Chess Game" corporation I described, have a few rotten apples on their well-respected tree.

If you have not been paid for your prior work and the payment is overdue, do not conduct or deliver additional work. In software development it is standard practice to decline to perform services for clients until they have no outstanding invoices that are more than thirty days (or whatever limit feels right to you) past due.

On a work for hire contract, you should be paid an amount up front for a milestone called "Contract Execution." This "kickoff payment" means you start with cash in the bank instead of doing work for free in the hope that you'll be paid. Advancing money for the first 30 days of work is common practice.

Get paid for direct costs up front. Building contractors normally are paid at the start of the project not just for their first period of work, but for all of the wood, steel and other materials they'll have to buy to begin the project. This same principle should apply to any initial up-front expenditures you'll be required to make.

CHAPTER 44

Businesses, Plans & Business Plans (5.11-5.12)

DISCUSSING QUESTION 5.11

Have you ever written a Business Plan?

Do you already have one for this indie game?

This topic is most relevant for: Everyone

5.11.1 Writing the Right Plan for the Right Reasons

A Business Plan is a document you write to help plan the founding and the running of your game business. Its most important purpose is to help you budget intelligently, develop an effective strategy, and maximize your chances of success.

There are several good sample business plan outlines available online if you Google "game company business plan template." Look at multiple examples to see which one best suits your game and business model.

More general (but worthwhile) business plan templates are also listed on the Inc. magazine website. (Note: I have been honored as a 3-time Inc. 500™ CEO, but I have no business relationship with the company.)

If you are creating a part-time one-person business and selling your game via Steam or an app store, the plan will not be long and complex.

If you and your team have produced major games industry hits and are planning a large-scale startup, your document will be significantly longer and more detailed.

You don't have to write your Business Plan all at once – it's often better to assemble it piece by piece as you experiment and figure things out.

The building blocks of a strong Business Plan are:

Define what kinds of games the company will create, the audience to whom it will market its games, and how it will make money from those players. You have already answered all of these questions as you've worked through the earlier sections of this book.

Describe, step-by-step, each important phase of organizing and funding the company (e.g. file papers to form company, get bank account, get business license etc.).

Describe each step of creating the game, testing and launching it.

Describe how you'll acquire players and generate revenue.

Define who will carry out each of the steps you just listed, a summary of how they will do it, a schedule for when they will do it, and what the company will have achieved or acquired after those steps are completed. If this is a small, part-time project this list will serve as your personal action plan.

Estimate the costs involved, and when those expenses will have to be paid. You did this in your monthly budget.

Estimate projected revenues, and when they are expected to arrive. You've likewise done this in your budget.

Combine those two projections into a spreadsheet that shows if the current draft of the plan is likely to produce a profit or a loss. (And early drafts are very likely to show a loss.) You already did this as well.

A good Business Plan does all of the above steps concisely, with just enough detail to allow you and your team to confirm that you all agree on the key aspects of the plan. Since it's primarily for you and your team no fancy sales pitches or marketing talk are required.

The plan should neither be overly aggressive nor artificially pessimistic. It may include alternative financial estimates on the aggressive and on the conservative side.

Finally, you have to sincerely believe that you can do what you write in the Business Plan. It helps no one if you make up a story to impress someone, and such fantasies will become readily apparent in any pitch.

DISCUSSING QUESTION 5.12

What would be the best possible (but realistic) financial result from your indie game?

Wealth? A salary you can live on? A few extra dollars?

A company that's doing well enough that you get to make the next game?

Is there some other ideal financial goal you're picturing?

This topic is most relevant for: Everyone

5.12.1 Again, Almost No Wrong Answers

My object in asking this question is to get you to think about what you really, truly want to achieve financially with your indie game.

Those goals may change as you work through the process of building your game, which is not a problem so long as any team members at your side agree.

As I mentioned in an earlier section, the only answer that concerns me is if your primary goal is an "exit strategy" of selling the company and becoming wealthy. So few games bring such rewards to their creators that starting out with this as the only standard of success is simply asking for disappointment.

The theme of this book is "Do work you love, love what you do and build your indie game."

If what you're focused on achieving is an environment that only comes into being after the game is completed, it's going to be almost impossible for you to love the work you're doing along the way.

As Thoreau said, the joy is in the journey, not the destination.

PART VI

RISK AND REWARD

CHAPTER 45

Risk and Reward: The Questions

QUESTION 6.1

Do you have a paying job you're giving up, or can you pursue your indie game in your spare time?

Please take your time, write down your responses, and answer fully from your deepest thoughts. Think only about your own opinions, not about what others may want you to think or do. Do not look ahead to other questions until you have finished this one.

QUESTION 6.2

If you're starting out in your spare time or working part-time, how many hours a week can you devote to your game now?

How much of your income (if any) will this loss of time impact?

How much will the additional time impact your family and social life?

Please take your time, write down your responses, and answer fully from your deepest thoughts. Think only about your own opinions, not about what others may want you to think or do. Do not look ahead to other questions until you have finished this one.

QUESTION 6.3

If you're starting out in your spare time and plan to go full-time on your indie game later, what are the criteria for making the jump to full-time?

If you feel you're ready to make the jump now, what is it that makes you confident that this will be a good move?

QUESTION 6.4

How much money do you need to bring in FOR SURE each month in order to keep up with your bills (including taxes)?

If you're factoring living off of savings to any degree, how long can you live on this "minimum income" before those savings are exhausted?

Are those savings intended to be used for something else? What is the impact and what are the potential risks of using them on your indie game?

Note: Please do the research, study your bills and take the time to really understand your financial position. It's critical to making good decisions.

Please take your time, write down your responses, and answer fully from your deepest thoughts. Think only about your own opinions, not about what others may want you to think or do. Do not look ahead to other questions until you have finished this one.

QUESTION 6.5

How many people depend on your income?

Did you factor their needs in your total monthly financial obligations?

Please take your time, write down your responses, and answer fully from your deepest thoughts. Think only about your own opinions, not about what others may want you to think or do. Do not look ahead to other questions until you have finished this one.

QUESTION 6.6

How does your partner feel about the financial risk?

How does he or she feel about how this will affect your personal schedules and the free time you may have for social or home activities?

If you don't have a partner right now, how could working on your indie game affect your likelihood of finding someone? How do you feel about the issue?

Are there any other risks that are a source of concern?

Please take your time, write down your responses, and answer fully from your deepest thoughts. Think only about your own opinions, not about what others may want you to think or do. Do not look ahead to other questions until you have finished this one.

QUESTION 6.7

Have you ever worked on a team developing a project that started out to be one kind of game and ended up being another?

Example: A team is developing an RPG that has side-scrolling mini-games integrated into the transition between levels. As people start playing the game they tell the designers that the RPG is boring but that the side-scroller feels new and that it's addictively fun. They decide to drop the RPG and expand on the mini-games to create a full scale side-scrolling action title.

Please take your time, write down your responses, and answer fully from your deepest thoughts. Think only about your own opinions, not about what others may want you to think or do. Do not look ahead to other questions until you have finished this one.

QUESTION 6.8

Have you ever "pitched" a big game to a publisher or boss in order to get budget approval and a formal signoff?

If not, have you pitched other kinds of projects in different settings?

If so, how well do you think you did?

Please take your time, write down your responses, and answer fully from your deepest thoughts. Think only about your own opinions, not about what others may want you to think or do. Do not look ahead to other questions until you have finished this one.

QUESTION 6.9:

Is raising money from investors part of your plan for your indie game?

Have you ever pitched to investors to raise money for a game?

If not, have you pitched to investors for a different new company or project?

If so, how well do you think you did?

QUESTION 6.10:

Have you ever tried using Kickstarter, Indiegogo or other crowdsourcing website to raise money for a project?

Is that part of your plan for your indie game?

Please take your time, write down your responses, and answer fully from your deepest thoughts. Think only about your own opinions, not about what others may want you to think or do. Do not look ahead to other questions until you have finished this one.

QUESTION 6.11:

What's the biggest risk your team faced on the largest game project you've ever worked on?

QUESTION 6.12:

What were the three biggest risks at the start of your most recent game project?

What were the three biggest remaining risks when your team was nearing completion on its most recent game?

Please take your time, write down your responses, and answer fully from your deepest thoughts. Think only about your own opinions, not about what others may want you to think or do. Do not look ahead to other questions until you have finished this one.

QUESTION 6.13

Does your game have any elements that require import or export controls, etc.?

Is there anything potentially controversial about your game that could create problems if you release it in other cultures?

CHAPTER 46

My Story: Re-Launching the Sinking Ship

When you go through something traumatic early in your career it sticks with you.

Electronic Arts is now one of the largest game publishers in the world, but when I joined the company in 1983 we were an endangered startup, with our market threatening to disappear beneath us.

EA was founded in 1982 by Trip Hawkins as a game publishing company. While Atari, Mattel and Coleco fought for the multi-billion-dollar console games business, EA set out to establish its beachhead in computer games, a far smaller market with only a few entrenched competitors. If we gained the #1 position there, we reasoned, we could then move on to challenge the bigger players.

But it was the first generation of video games and something went wrong. Sales peaked in late 1982 and started to plateau. The toy store chains concluded that video games were a fad and that they would soon fade away. Retailers started marking down prices and offering game blowout sales on discount tables.

Soon there were newspaper headlines that read, "The Video Game Boom is Over!"

I was Director of Game Development for Mattel's Intellivision console, the #2-ranked video game system in the world. In a period of nine months in late 1982 and early 1983 we went from generating over a billion dollars in annual revenue to being able to sell almost nothing.

Atari and Coleco went bankrupt. Mattel Toys went through a "crunchdown" that gave control of the company to investors in return for the capital infusion needed to save the company. All but five of the 1,200 people in the Mattel Electronics division lost their jobs.

I was very fortunate that Trip Hawkins recruited me into EA. The computer games business, where Electronic Arts was focused, had weathered much of the storm affecting Atari, Mattel and Coleco. EA sold products through computer stores rather than toy stores, but the bad publicity from the toy business wasn't helping.

We had another problem at the young EA. The company had predicted that the Atari 800 home computer would be the best-seller of 1983-84, but the Commodore 64 was the runaway winner on the sales charts. Atari, beset by the toy store disaster, ran far behind.

We had an initial round of products with one big hit (Bill Budge's *Pinball Construction Set*) and a couple of other successful games including Jon Freeman, Anne Westfall and Paul Reiche's *Archon* and Dani Bunten's *M.U.L.E.* But few of our titles were available on the red-hot Commodore 64.

We did what today in Silicon Valley is called a "pivot" and redirected most of our resources to adding new Commodore 64 games to our lineup.

By early 1984 much of our original investment cash was gone, and we were still operating at a loss. Trip called everyone into a conference room – about 40 people — and announced that we had a hiring freeze, a spending freeze, and any other kind of freeze that would help save those remaining dollars. It was a very tight year.

Fortunately, the pivot worked. More Commodore 64 games came on line and we produced new hits. We started to earn a profit. We all started breathing normally again.

As an advisor to startups today I see many cases where an initial idea doesn't work and the company needs to pivot.

Some teams consider moving into completely new business models in different genres, changing every detail about their game and their company.

I always remind teams not to look for a random new idea if their original game doesn't get traction.

"The category you already know is where you'll have the greatest strengths," I'll tell them. "What would you do if you could start from scratch, leverage or re-use existing work, take advantage of what you've learned, and harness your team's passion?"

That strategy worked for us back then at Electronic Arts, it's worked for recent hit games like *Pokemon Go*, and it can work for you as well.

CHAPTER 47

What to Do with Your Answers (6.1–6.3)

"YOU SHOULD NEVER DOUBT
WHAT NOBODY IS SURE ABOUT!"

— Willy Wonka

If you have not yet written down your answers, please go back and do so. Writing your thoughts down – even when you're the only one who'll ever read them – will produce far more insights than just answering silently to yourself in your head.

DISCUSSING QUESTION 6.1

Do you have a paying job you're giving up, or can you pursue your indie game in your spare time?

This topic is most relevant for: Everyone except those with the financial means to self-fund a full-time project without incurring significant financial or relationships risk to themselves and their families.

6.1.1 Limiting the Downside

This is a central and critical question, one you've heard me discuss in several different contexts in this book.

If you plan to go full-time on any job where you may not be paid enough to support yourself and your family, the risk to your personal financial health is the biggest risk in pursuing your indie game.

Working from a pre-defined budget that you can stick to and be OK is far better than "spending money you can't afford on a project that may not earn it back," which I absolutely, positively warn you not to do!

There's no harm in saving up a war chest of "money you can afford to risk." But before you spend that war chest, I want you to consider every other alternative.

As we've discussed, the simplest and most universal option is to work on your game part-time so you can keep your existing income.

For many people this is fulfilling and as far as they want to go. Others will be seeking that moment where they can jump to full-time, but in the meantime they can learn a lot about what works and doesn't work by trying out their indie game part-time.

Can all indie projects be pursued part-time? No. If you're trying to build the next *Call of Duty* or *Fallout*, you'll need to build a (big) team and work full-time on the project. But until you've raised enough money to support your team, be sure to explore how far you can get part-time until that moment comes.

DISCUSSING QUESTION 6.2

If you're starting out in your spare time or working part-time, how many hours a week can you devote to your indie game now?

How much of your income (if any) will this loss of time impact?

How much will the additional time impact your family and social life?

This topic is most relevant for: Everyone except those with the financial means to self-fund a full-time project without incurring significant financial or relationships risk to themselves and their families.

6.2.1 The Different Costs of Time

If part-time work is the path you're considering for advancing your indie game, look at the number of hours you think you can spare. Then consider the financial and personal impact of that time.

The money part of the equation can be calculated on a spreadsheet.

The personal costs of working extra-long hours, days and weeks, if that's what you're considering, are more complex and call for a different kind of evaluation:

Family: Will the extra work time invade the parts of each day or week that you most enjoy sharing with each other?

If you have kids is there a way to schedule your work on your indie game so it does not impact your time with them unnecessarily? If your kids are older, have you discussed the idea with them?

Social: How much time do you spend with friends and on outside activities, and how important is that time to you? Will your part-time game project inhabit those same time slices each week? If you're used to being social, placing yourself in work-imposed solitary confinement may be a bad way to proceed.

Emotional: For some people working on their indie game is like having a hobby. It doesn't feel like work, so the time flies by. For others the extra hours, no matter how fulfilling, start to wear them down. Eventually the routine steals all the joy and a dream project turns into a nightmare. Could that happen with your game?

Physical: If you work on your game late at night but still have to go to work early the next day, could lack of sleep impact both your health and your performance at your current job?

If your indie game has you sitting at a desk, is there still time for you to get enough exercise to support your health? Do your moods change when you don't get a chance to engage in physical activity, as happens for many people? Any of these issues can affect your physical health, or the emotional health of your most important relationships.

DISCUSSING QUESTION 6.3

If you're starting out in your spare time and plan to go full-time on your indie game later, what are the criteria for making the jump to full-time?

If you feel you're ready to make the jump now, what is it that makes you confident that this will be a good move?

This topic is most relevant for: Everyone except those with the financial means to self-fund a full-time project without incurring significant financial or relationships risk to themselves and their families.

6.3.1 Decisions Based on Something More than Faith

There are many different ways you might answer this "when will I go full-time?" question:

- "When I've worked out all the details in my plans for the game, and I have time to pursue it, and everything is in order on the home front so I can dedicate the time needed to make this a success"

- "When my part-time income from my indie game reaches $X, so even if that's all I make I can still pay the mortgage and put food on the table"

- "I can go full-time right now, because we've been lucky and achieved a level of financial security where I can commit fully to my game without risking my family's financial future"

- "When the kids have all graduated from college, so we have more financial freedom"

- "When I've saved up enough to fund the initial costs and a few

months of runway, so I can give the idea a fair chance to succeed"

- "When I've raised enough money from investors to give us a twelve month runway"

- "When I feel like I'm finally ready to let go of my old job"

- "When my Dad is feeling better and we don't have to spend as much time helping my parents"

- "Never, because I love developing this game as a part-time activity, but I realize that I'd never want to do it full-time"

- "Never, because I realize now that I'm not as committed to the idea as I thought I was"

What matters is that you've considered this question both logically and emotionally. That's how you give your ideas and feelings a chance to gel and become clear.

As with so many questions in this book, the only one who knows the correct answer is you.

6.3.2 My Baseball Friend

While I was in college I wrote computer games as a hobby, before there was a video games industry.

When the industry began my hobby became my profession. I became one of the original five game programmers at Mattel Toy Company for their new Intellivision video game console.

Almost five decades after I coded my first primitive program I'm still designing video games. Sometimes your hobby can turn into a wonderful career.

But that isn't always the case.

When our sons were young we collected baseball cards together.

There was a baseball card shop in our area where a really nice older man would treat kids kindly, and the boys and I would stop by once or twice a month to buy some cards.

Over the course of two or three years I noticed that the owner progressively got more and more serious. One day I stopped in by myself and there were no other customers in the shop.

"How are you?" I asked the owner.

He looked up at me from behind the desk where he'd always sit, and he just said, "I'm tired."

"Long day?" I asked.

"Long day. Long week. Long year. Bratty kids who steal stuff. Grown men who argue for half an hour about how a $50 card is only worth $20, then walk out without buying anything."

"That would drive me crazy," I told him, and it was the truth.

"Baseball cards used to be my hobby," he said. "Every time I looked at them they brought me joy. Three years of doing this as a business... Now all I want to do is go home and watch TV. Right now I think I'd be happy if I never saw another baseball card again."

I've always remembered that conversation. If your indie game is turning a hobby into a job, both the upside and downside have to be considered.

My college hobby turned into a wonderful career.

My friend in the baseball card shop had his hobby turn into a nightmare.

CHAPTER 48

The Money Side (6.4-6.6)

DISCUSSING QUESTION 6.4

How much money do you need to bring in FOR SURE each month in order to keep up with your bills (including taxes)?

If you're factoring living off of savings to any degree, how long can you live on this "minimum income" before those savings are exhausted?

Are those savings intended to be used for something else? What is the impact and what are the potential risks of using them on your indie game?

This topic is most relevant for: Everyone

6.4.1 Your Minimum Acceptable Income

This is a key part of the spreadsheet you'll build that shows how much money you need for you and your family to be OK, and how much (if any) you'll spend on your indie game.

If you have a partner or initial team members who are joining you on this project they will need to ask themselves this question, too.

This step has no emotional component. It's all about numbers, money, costs and obligations. Please don't manipulate the spreadsheet to make it say something you want to hear if that projection really isn't true.

I hear people say, "Well, my monthly expenses are $3,500, but I can probably get by on $2,500 if I just stall out some payments." After late payment fees and interest charges and lowered credit ratings, a person can turn a $3,500 monthly "nut" into $4,000 or even $5,000 a month. Instead of getting by on less they could be spending even more.

Avoid self-sabotaging approaches like, "I've got a lot of room on my credit cards. I can run them up and gain a few extra months." There are lots of ways to get work done if you plan in advance, and do so without running up your credit cards until you start drowning in debt.

For every dramatic story I've read about someone launching a company using credit cards, I've heard many, many sad stories of financial disaster and broken families. Using credit cards or retirement savings "just to get past one last hurdle" almost always doesn't work. Please don't do these things.

When you're calculating all of these numbers, be sure to research all the taxes you'll have to pay if you found a new business or are working for yourself. In the U.S. this can include self-employment and "minimum required" taxes of different kinds for all levels of government.

6.4.2 The Even Bigger Picture

I cringe when I hear someone say they're borrowing from their retirement account or their kids' college fund to fund any kind of project.

401-K's, IRA's and other systems work because putting in comparatively small amounts of tax-free money for *decades* adds up to enough to give you some retirement security in a challenging economic world. The money you put in when you're young has a long time to grow, and even the money you add in middle age adds up to a lot more than it would have in any other way.

College funds work because you may start with a nest egg from family members and then add to it for fifteen years or more. The money has time to multiply and to rise with inflation if necessary.

Any experienced investor will tell you that most new ventures fail to make a profit.

If you take money from your retirement fund to risk on a new venture, you're not just losing money. You're paying extra taxes on what would have been tax-free income.

If you use your kids' college fund, you may be adding risk to their entire working lives, not just their college years. In a society where professional and/or technical training often has a dramatic impact on personal income and career opportunities, the chain reaction can be even worse.

Worst of all, you're making a bet with low odds that doesn't represent "money you can afford to lose." $20,000 in retirement money when you're 38 years old may equate to $200,000 or $300,000 when you really need it.

Would you borrow that much money from your parents' limited savings and then make a low-odds bet with it?

Borrowing that money from your older self or from your kids is just as bad an idea.

Would you borrow that much money *anywhere* for a bet where the house usually wins?

You can create and publish your indie game without taking these risks. It will take longer and represent more work, but there are ways to do it and we've discussed many of them.

If you don't fund your indie game the wrong way there's another benefit. You won't have to face yourself or your family years from now and regret being careless with money that had a more important mission in your lives and that can never be recovered.

6.4.3 Don't Get Caught Betwixt and Between

There are many ways to raise money for an indie game, a number of which we'll discuss in the pages that follow. However it is that you acquire the funds to create a game, there are three rules that will lower the risks for everyone concerned:

1. Don't spend significant amounts of money until you've developed a playable prototype of your game and strangers can have fun playing it... even if the experience is only a few minutes long
2. Don't agree to any budget or schedule that doesn't allow you to build a high quality first "complete" version of the game
3. If you're creating an online or mobile game, reserve cash in the initial budget for the live team to operate long enough for the game to reach profitability and fund itself

Let's break down each of these three guidelines and cover what they mean, and why I'm giving this advice:

1. **Don't spend significant amounts of money until you've developed a playable prototype of your game and strangers can have fun playing it... even if the experience is only a few minutes long.** This may seem impossible,

because even a short playable version of many games can cost hundreds of thousands of dollars.

It all comes down to, "What does 'significant amounts of money' mean to you?"

If you control the license for Star Wars or Harry Potter, or if you're building a sequel for a popular franchise like Call of Duty, Clash of Clans or Halo, you can predict that a new game you build will probably be a hit. The cash you spend creating the game will be at risk, but if you control your costs and schedule well it's likely you'll make money.

As we discussed in Section 1, the games industry is a tough business. If you're building a brand new game without the powerful bloodlines of a major license or a previous hit, it's almost impossible to predict if a game will be financially successful. And with over 100,000 new games appearing each year across so many different formats the odds aren't good.

Research, experiments, planning and all the stages of preparation I discuss in this book can take time, but for most businesses they don't have to take a lot of cash.

If you build a game prototype, the first version often isn't much fun to play. Some of my most celebrated game designs were boring when we got a first playable version going.

You make changes, tune the game, add features, cut things that aren't working. After a period of experimentation you may start to like the results you're seeing. You can give the game to strangers, let them play and see that many of them are having fun.

Once you reach this "strangers play it and think it's fun" stage, you still have a long way to go before you have a hit. But your odds of success have climbed dramatically, and experienced games industry producers can give you feedback on how good those odds might be.

Spending a "significant" amount of money before you reach this pointy means putting that money at great risk. That's why, throughout this book, you've heard me advise you to do experiments, work part-time or find other low-cost ways to get to the point where your game is fun to play for strangers... not just for you, your family and friends.

It's like buying expensive tickets to a Broadway show that hasn't been written yet. Not only do you not know much about the show, you don't even know who the stars will be and whether it's a musical, a comedy or a tragedy where everyone dies at the end!

2. **Don't agree to any budget or schedule that doesn't allow you to build a high quality first "complete" version of the game.**

First of all, I want to point out that on some large projects it can feel like goals 1 and 2 in this section are contradictory: you have to spend a lot of money just to get the game to the point where you can convince someone to fund the complete project. For most indie teams working on smaller projects, however, this issue should be manageable.

Raising money for your startup is a very time consuming process, and many entrepreneurs spend long hours on this one task alone, often more than half their time. You can make a lot of pitches (and learn a lot of valuable lessons) before you get your first "yes."

That's time you can't spend designing the game, interviewing potential hires, leading your team, monitoring the schedule and budget, or any of a hundred other important things. Without you spending time on these key tasks, the company may fail even if it raises the money.

If you start with only half the money you need, you may get half way through your project and find that you can't raise that second half of the funding. All the money that you and your allies have invested will be lost. You'll have to lay off all your team members.

Your company will close, and all of your time will have been wasted, because you raised too little money to have a chance of succeeding.

3. **If you're creating an online or mobile game, reserve cash in the initial budget for the live team to operate long enough for the game to reach profitability and fund itself.** We've discussed in previous sections the importance of live teams to modern online games. Often you're releasing an initial version that includes only the most critical features for players. In the weeks and months that follow you'll add content and assets based on the play patterns and spending of your users.

I have seen many cases where teams used up their budgets on version 1.0 of a title. When the game wasn't an instant hit that produced enough money each month to run the studio, they had a big problem. There was no way to run the live operations that would build an audience – and the needed revenue. Layoffs followed, and the game failed.

DISCUSSING QUESTION 6.5

How many people depend on your income?

Did you factor their needs in your total monthly financial obligations?

This topic is most relevant for: Everyone

6.5.1 Timing is Everything

Have you factored into your plans the financial needs of those who are dependent on you, such as kids, older family members, etc.? If not, please go back and adjust your chart or spreadsheet now.

There was a time in my career when my wife and I were both working long hours supporting ourselves and our two kids. Those children were depending on us.

Later in my career our sons were grown and off on their own. The list of people we supported was a lot shorter.

The simple fact is that if other people are dependent on our income, our financial options for pursuing an indie game are reduced.

If no one else depends on me and I risk my well-being chasing after a dream, then I'm the only one whom I place at risk. Even if I make foolish choices, I'm the one who'll face the consequences.

In my view, if kids or others depend on me I need to put their well-being first whenever I have the power to do so.

This doesn't mean that an indie game has to be abandoned. It does

mean that sometimes it has to be pursued more slowly and con-
servatively, and that some risks will need to be postponed.

DISCUSSING QUESTION 6.6

How does your partner feel about the financial risk?

How does he or she feel about how this will affect your personal schedules and the free time you may have for social or home activities?

If you don't have a partner right now, how could working on your indie game affect your likelihood of finding someone? How do you feel about the issue?

Are there any other risks that are a source of concern?

This topic is most relevant for: Everyone.

6.6.1 Talking About the Risks

How you manage your communication with loved ones is solely between you and them. In that context, I'm going to share some personal experiences for you to consider.

There are two stages of thinking about setting out to build indie games, which I like to refer to as the dreamy stage and the serious stage.

The dreamy stage is where we consider something without thinking it through. Every time my wife and I go to Hawaii we think about saving up and buying a condo there. By the time we've been home for a week we remember that not going to Hawaii as often as we'd like makes it more special.

I don't think you need to talk with anyone about dreamy thoughts unless you want to do so. You're just sorting out your feelings.

Once you get to the stage where you're seriously considering any major project, however, my opinion changes. If this could dramatically affect someone who loves you, someone who's dependent on you, then I think you need to talk to them before you put dreams into action.

How you respond to their feedback is up to you.

If no one else depends on you emotionally or financially and no one else is responsible for your debts then the only one who can be hurt is you. In that case I'd still ask a close friend or family member to provide critical feedback on your plans. Ideally this person will have significant games industry experience.

If you have not yet discussed your indie game with anyone else, I hope you'll do so before you put any of your dreams into action.

CHAPTER 49

Pivots and Pitches (6.7-6.8)

DISCUSSING QUESTION 6.7

Have you ever worked on a team developing a project that started out to be one kind of game and ended up being another?

This topic is most relevant for: Everyone

6.7.1 To Pivot is Human

Games have always evolved and changed as teams developed and playtested their works. For most of the history of the industry these changes were so routine that we'd simply refer to it as "doing a redesign" or "shifting the focus of the gameplay."

Silicon Valley has re-invented many of its traditions over the last twenty years, and coined a number of new terms to describe events.

One of those terms is "to pivot." A startup executes its original idea but has limited success. They have a strong team, no one has panicked, and they still have money in the bank.

Instead of continuing on a suicide mission until they run out of cash, the team uses its remaining resources to create a different product. They leverage the team's passion, expertise and the lessons learned on the first pass. If the new idea works, the company "pivots" to follow its revised strategy.

Some legendary pivots have worked out well. The team that produced the popular photo sharing website Flickr originally set out to create an RPG! YouTube was originally a dating site and Twitter was a side project for a podcast network.

6.7.2 A Near-Perfect Pivot

You've read my story above about how we pivoted the company focus in the early days of Electronic Arts, but there are many modern examples as well.

Pokemon Go is one of the highest grossing mobile games of the last several years. The *Pokemon Go* team at Google had developed a prior game called *Ingress*, which had a big budget and lost a lot of money. They were spun off into a separate company called Niantic, where they needed to create a profitable game before they ran out of the initial cash investment Google made when they were founded.

Ingress was a science fiction adventure game where you played by going to real places in your home town or current location, where special gameplay sequences would be triggered on your smartphone screen. In addition to being fun to play, it was designed to get you to exercise.

Google has a tradition of putting up a fun or interesting image on its home page every day, with many of them being interactive.

One such link was a game where Pokemon were scattered on your Google map and you could go out into the real world to search for and collect them. The game turned out to be one of the most popular mini-projects the company had ever done.

The Niantic team recognized the potential of this idea. They didn't start from scratch on a completely new full-scale version of the Google Maps game. Instead they took all of the real-world geographical locations used in *Ingress* and turned them into *Pokemon Go* related sites, saving months of work and producing a large new game with a relatively small team.

When *Pokemon Go* became a runaway hit they had problems keeping up with the massive player demand, issues they eventually corrected. That part of the story doesn't change the fact that Niantic and Google pulled off a near-perfect example of how to pivot.

DISCUSSING QUESTION 6.8

Have you ever "pitched" a big game to a publisher or boss in order to get budget approval and a formal signoff?

If not, have you pitched other kinds of projects in different settings?

If so, how well do you think you did?

This topic is most relevant for: Everyone, because the leader of any indie game has to make pitches in different settings to different audiences.

6.8.1 Becoming a Star Pitcher

You may be...

• Presenting your game to users or professionals at a conference or event

• Looking to recruit great people to work on your team

• Talking to journalists about your new game

• Networking to get people inside your current company excited about your great new game idea

These are all very different situations, but the one thing they all have in common is that you'll be making a "pitch" and hoping to get a positive response.

In some countries of the world the city, state or national governments offer financial support for promising new game studios. Many of the points below are relevant to pitching to judges for these kinds of programs, though there are very few such opportunities in the United States.

There are entire books written on how to create and present pitches. In the pages that follow I'll give you a top level crash-course, but there are many more resources on the Internet and in the library.

6.8.2 The Compelling One Sentence Summary

Many websites with advice for startups skip this first step, but in my experience it's vitally important.

You've already created a first draft of this summary, back when you answered the questions in Section 1 of this book!

6.8.3 The 30-Second Summary

In addition to your one-sentence pitch, you need to think about a version that lasts about 30 seconds.

This is sometimes called an "elevator pitch," based on the idea that if you bump into a potential partner, team member etc. in an elevator you can get her or him interested in your project before they reach their floor and get off.

If you were pitching the original Star Wars movie and had just 30 seconds to do so, you could say something like:

> It's a science fiction epic that stars Academy Award winner Sir Alec Guinness and a strong cast of young actors. The Director, George Lucas, has won a Golden Globe.

> It has amazing special effects, with wild looking aliens, cute robots and the biggest starship you've ever seen.

The heroes are people you'll want to cheer for, and the villain is imposing, ruthless and frightening.

And it has some of the best music and sound effects you've ever heard.

Compared to a single sentence, this description is richly detailed. Yet once you sit down to write your 30-second summary you'll discover how hard it is to fit within that tiny time limit.

6.8.4 The Two-Minute Summary

You know what you'd say if you met someone in an elevator. But what do you do if they get off the elevator with you and ask you to keep talking?

The two-minute summary is what you'll use when the 30-second pitch gets someone interested.

I've judged many indie game pitch competitions with time slots in the one minute to five minute range at events around the world. If you do try to win prizes at these events the two-minute version will often form the basis of what you do.

It gives you the chance to describe the highlights of your game, and it's good to go back to the basics:

- What category is the title, and on which platforms will it run?
- What makes this game unique and compelling in a crowded games market? Can anyone who sees the screen shots or the demo recognize how different and cool your game is? (If it's indistinguishable from other titles that's a problem you need to correct.)
- How will people learn about the game? Players can't buy a game they don't know exists, and partners won't be interested unless they think you can solve this problem.

- What kinds of players will want to buy or spend money on the game? Adults? Kids? RPG fans? Manga collectors?

- How big will the game's potential market be? Potential team members whom you're trying to recruit will care about this if they're considering working with you.

- How has the game been received thus far? That's the issue of "traction" we discussed above.

- How does your and/or your team's experience qualify you to build this game?

6.8.5 Crafting a Pitch Deck

A pitch deck is a slide show, one that's usually created with Microsoft Office PowerPoint (if you use a PC) or Apple Keynote (if you use a Mac).

There are many different books and articles about these presentations, and you can Google "how to build a pitch deck" to see multiple well-written examples.

Most will refer to raising money from investors, but having such a deck handy can help you gather support and interest in many other kinds of situations.

Here's a concise summary of key things to remember:

You should have no more than ten to twelve slides in your "initial presentation" deck. The objective is to get someone interested in your game, not to cover every detail and nuance.

You will probably have more slides "held in reserve" after your final official slide, but complete a base presentation that fits in that small footprint.

You should be able to present the full pitch deck in as little as

five minutes, or as much as 20 or 30 minutes. You'll decide the pacing and whether to add or omit details based on the audience.

In a formal one-hour meeting with a licensor, partner or investor much of that time will be consumed by questions you're asked and by discussions that follow. Allow time to listen to feedback and suggestions. That means planning a presentation that lasts 20 minutes (and can stretch to 30) for a 60-minute meeting slot.

Guy Kawasaki's famous font-size rule is, "Find the oldest person in the room, then divide their age in half. That number is the smallest font you should have in your presentation." (And his book, *The Art of the Start*, offers a lot more Silicon Valley wisdom.)

My personal not-so-famous font size rule: "Regardless of the audience, 30 is the smallest acceptable font size, because anything smaller means you have too many words on one screen."

You want the audience to listen to your voice, not read ahead on the slides. Include bold screen shots. Use headlines and short bullet points, not full sentences. If they want details you can follow up.

You can embed gameplay video if it is of high quality. Keep it short – 30 to 90 seconds is good. Just be aware that videos often fail to run when installed on different computers. If you're not using your usual laptop, leave time to test it before the meeting and have a back-up plan if it doesn't play or has no audio.

Apart from your video, don't use anything that will compete with the sound of your voice as you deliver your pitch. If possible, don't talk over the video: let it do its job.

In formal settings assume that some people will arrive late for your meeting, and don't let it throw you off. The meeting host will tell you when to start and whether you need to cover anything a second time.

Assume that some people will leave before you're done. They might have had another meeting and didn't want to walk out but had to. Don't beat yourself up about it and just keep going with your confident presentation.

6.8.6 Longer Presentations with Your Pitch Deck

We've covered several different kinds of short presentations. Once you're ready to deliver a concise pitch you've done much of the necessary work for longer presentations, prioritizing and polishing your message.

Many pitches that I see fail to describe the company's product or service in a clear and precise way. *Your one-sentence description solves that problem.*

Many pitches go on for several minutes without ever clearly describing why anyone would want to pay money for the game. *Your 30-second pitch will make this clear.*

Many pitches wander through various facts, features and claims, with some that are important and some that are close to irrelevant. *Your two-minute summary will hit just the most important high points and nothing else.*

Once you've been through those key highest-priority two minutes, I like to practice both a 5-minute and the 20-minute "complete pitch deck" version.

Be sure to apply the same discipline to these longer presentations that you used with the shorter formats. Include only the highest priority information and images. Cut ruthlessly any bullet, slide or image that does not directly support a key element of your game.

There's another critical skill we need to practice for these longer meetings, however. And it's one that many program never teach.

How would you feel if someone came over to your house to visit and then they did nothing but talk about themselves for an hour?

I'd start wondering how long it would be until they left.

Once you're outside the boundaries of "a brief pitch to see if you're interested," we don't just want to be doing a presentation.

We want to be having a conversation. We'll encourage questions and comments. We can ask our own questions of the group.

The objective here is not just being a polite visitor. If there's a good fit between your ideas and the opinions of your audience, an open and dynamic discussion will be the fastest and most compelling way to find it.

Not to mention the fact that it will make your presentation far more interesting to the people you're trying to impress.

6.8.7 How to Perfect Your Pitch

The key to perfecting any kind of pitch is simple, yet most entrepreneurs at pitch competitions don't follow it.

After you've prepared your short pitches and your pitch deck, here are the steps behind the "secret" of mastering your presentation:

Practice delivering each version of your pitch alone, ideally in front of the mirror. Use note cards or a written outline if you feel you need it. You'll feel self-conscious for a while, but this will pass.

Do this a few times a day, at whatever point you have the time. When you start to get tired, take a break or stop for the rest of the day.

Practice until:

• You don't need the note cards,

- You can talk about your game at a moment's notice, providing the right level of detail for any situation, and

- You hit all the right high points. You'll miss something small in one talk or another, and that's not a big deal.

Next, practice with a family member or friend who interrupts you periodically with questions. Answer the question, then work the conversation back to the content of your pitch. These interruptions happen all the time in real pitches, and it will keep you from getting flustered when it happens for you.

Stop practicing *before* **you memorize any presentation word-for-word (other than the one-sentence summary). If you find yourself reciting word-for-word from memory, deliberately work to change things up.**

Memorized presentations sound canned, rather than sincere and spontaneous. Your audience can feel like they're listening to an actor instead of a passionate presenter.

If you have a demo of your game, be sure to include it in your presentations whenever possible.

If you don't have a demo, prepare concept art or some other way to communicate the look and feel of your game. We know how many words each image is worth. Rehearse how you'll integrate these materials into your talk.

When you know in advance you'll be giving a pitch, take the time to research the people and company. LinkedIn profiles may identify companies you've both worked for, schools you both attended or shared interests that you can mention in your meeting. Establishing common ground with people can accelerate the process of building trust.

6.8.8 Don't Sabotage Your Pitch

After years of doing pitches and judging pitch competitions, I've developed a list of "things you shouldn't do." Some are gaffes, others are clichés, others are mistakes I've personally made and learned from.

Mistake: Not Arriving Early. Arriving right on time for a pitch meeting means you're late.

If you're showing slides or doing a demo, arrive a half hour early. Ask if you can have early access to the meeting room to set up and make sure everything works. Even if you have to wait to set up, it demonstrates that you prepared in advance, and many companies plan for visiting teams to have early access to conference rooms.

Even with no demos to set up, always arrive at least fifteen minutes early – add more of a safety margin if there's a long drive and traffic could be bad. It shows that you're prepared and reliable.

If you're flying to another city for a morning meeting, don't take an early flight that morning. If it's delayed or cancelled by weather, you miss your meeting time. Even if the bad weather was all over the news, you still look bad for not anticipating the problem and avoiding it.

In these cases it's better to fly into town the night before and either stay with friends or accept the extra cost of a hotel within a reasonable drive of the meeting site. If that expense is too great, it may mean that the meeting isn't worth scheduling at all.

Mistake: Running Long. There's always a time limit for a discussion, whether it's a spontaneous conversation (you can tell when people get bored or have to leave) or a scheduled meeting. Pace your presentation so you come in under that time limit.

A few years ago I was at a conference where ten of us each gave a three minute "flash presentation" on one idea. A very loud buzzer would sound when time was up. Only two of the ten speakers finished on time, so that the audience didn't have to hear the annoying buzzer. We were the two highest-rated speakers at the session.

I've judged pitch competitions where the time limit was one minute, two minutes or five minutes. At every event most presenters run long and have to be cut off. Even with these ridiculously short time slots it makes the presenter look unprepared.

In the super-short versions of your pitch you're not trying to tell your whole story. You're just trying to get people hooked so they want to learn more.

Mistake: Apologies, Self-Criticism etc. Modesty and humility are great personal qualities that I respect highly. But when you're standing in front of a room and pitching you want to demonstrate confidence.

"Please excuse me, I'm not very good at this."

"Sorry, I'm really nervous."

"Sorry, I forgot something important."

As natural and honest as it is to say these things, a pitch meeting is not the place to do it.

You'll make mistakes. I do it, everyone does it. But you have to remember what they teach actors in the theatre:

"No matter what happens, pretend it's all in the script and that everything is fine. Stay in character, and improvise until everything is going right again."

Even if you're convinced that people can tell you're nervous, don't apologize or acknowledge it. The longer you practice this, the less nervous you'll become.

If you recover graciously and confidently when people notice that things went wrong, you'll earn bonus points for being able to handle adversity under pressure.

Mistake: Reading Your Slides Out Loud. As I covered above, your slides should have very few words on them, with just the most important bullet points. If you read your slides aloud it bores the audience, since they can read the words all by themselves without your help.

Mistake: Typos. You want your audience to believe that you are committed to quality. You want to convince them that you'll pay attention to every detail.

If there are misspelled words, grammatical errors or mis-aligned images and text on any of your slides, it undermines those messages about quality. (And you can imagine how many times I've re-read this book looking for typo's!)

Mistake: The Infomercial Pitch. "Ladies and gentlemen, I am going to present to you a game that has such great sales potential that it won't just interest you, it will excite you! What would you say if I told you that we could make your smartphone screen play all of your favorite video games by *broadcasting* them from your console?"

My heart sinks. I am listening to an Infomercial Pitch, and I can't wait for it to be over.

At one pitch competition one of my fellow judges interrupted the presenting CEO to say, "But wait., there's more! Now what would you pay?" It was an embarrassing moment.

Mistake: "We Can Be Anything You Want Us to Be!" I went to college with a guy who would walk into the dining hall in the morning and ask, "Do you like my shirt? Yes? No? I can go back upstairs and change it if you want!" It was annoying.

Listen to suggestions openly and thoughtfully, write them down and consider them, but don't automatically agree if someone suggests a different path or feature unless it really does sound compelling.

Mistake: Arguing and Defending. You wouldn't imagine that people would go into meetings or pitch competitions and argue with the people they're trying to impress, but it happens all the time.

Usually – though not always — it's a mistake. The CEO feels like she's expressing confidence, but what she's really doing is sounding defensive.

The people in the room are thinking, "If the CEO is this argumentative now, what will she be like when they're facing a problem and we're trying to help fix it?"

Instead of arguing or defending your position, listen carefully, write down the comments and say something like, "Let me think about that," or "I'll do some research on that," or "That's not what we were thinking, but we should discuss it with the team."

A pitch meeting is not just where you present your game. You're also presenting yourself as a prospective partner, and everyone you pitch to will be evaluating you in this way.

Mistake: Contradicting or Interrupting Team Members. It's routine to have co-founders or key team members in the room for a pitch. They may take the lead in discussing topics like technology or marketing.

Potential partners value this approach because it gives them the chance to evaluate not just one person, but the leadership team as a whole. They can also get a feel for how well you work together.

Inevitably someone on your team will say something that's not quite right. Your natural instinct is to cut in and explain.

Don't do it. The people to whom you're presenting may start to wonder why you publicly disrespected your team member, or why you didn't prepare the team well for the meeting.

Whatever problem the misstatement created, you'll have a chance to fix it somewhere down the line.

Mistake: Not Taking Notes. We get so caught up in rehearsing and setting up that it's easy to forget something as important as having a way to take notes. Yet there is no easier way to communicate to people that you're there to listen and learn, not just to talk.

CHAPTER 50

Fundraising & Crowdfunding (6.9-6.10)

DISCUSSING QUESTION 6.9:

Is raising money from investors part of your plan for your indie game?

Have you ever pitched to investors to raise money for a game?

If not, have you pitched to investors for a different new company or project?

If so, how well do you think you did?

This topic is most relevant for: Everyone planning to raise money from investors (or from internal management) for their indie game.

6.9.1 About Games and Investment

How do you predict that a game will be a hit before it's introduced to the marketplace? If it's not a sequel or tied to a popular movie or TV franchise, such predictions are often wrong.

Some of my biggest hits were games I initially believed would have "good but not great" sales.

Some of the games I believed would be my most exciting sure-thing hits failed to find an audience and produced mediocre revenue.

Investors crave predictability, the ability to see clearly in advance how much revenue is going to be generated by a business.

VC's don't consider any startup that can't grow to be worth hundreds of millions of dollars at a minimum, and they don't consider investing less than a few million in those early stage companies.

Games are a very unpredictable business that rarely produces large new companies, which is why most investors and especially Venture Capitalists rarely consider risking money in our industry.

I was judging at a pitch competition in Silicon Valley a couple of years ago where a fellow judge (a prominent VC) asked me what kind of project I was working on.

"A new online game," I told him.

He shook his head and winced. "Good luck!" he told me. "I have no idea how to tell a hit game from a pile of #$%&, so I never invest in your sector."

"Wait, Don," you may say, "I've seen several articles about new game companies raising money from VC investors!"

Yes, there will always be exceptions, and don't hesitate to try to be one of them. But when you read about the newly-funded team one of three patterns will usually emerge:

- Their company already has a successful game that's making money, or...

- The founder or founding team started up a prior game company that made money and then was acquired for millions of dollars, or...

- The team led the creation of a major new hit for one of the big international publishers, earning a big pot of money for their employers

6.9.2 Angel Investors

Angel Investors are wealthy individuals who invest relatively small amounts of money in young companies in hope of a high rate of return. Typical angel investments may be in the $50,000-$250,000 range, and for that money they will get a percentage of the stock in a company. Although few game companies gain angel funding, it does happen.

In many jurisdictions (including California) individuals go through a process to be certified as "qualified investors," and laws restrict selling non-publicly traded stock to anyone who is not certified as qualified. To be "qualified" you have to a) have enough money that you can afford to lose what you're investing, and b) have business experience so you're qualified to judge the risks involved.

Many angel investors don't go it alone, but instead gather in groups to pool their knowledge and contacts. If you do a Google search on the term "angel investor groups" you'll see a variety of lists of such alliances, and can investigate which ones are based in your area.

Working with angel investors or groups does not place you in either a better or a worse situation than working with publishers or any other funding source. I've met some angels who are trustworthy "straight arrows." Via friends I know of angel investors who use the fine print in the contracts to cheat the game development teams whom they're supposedly helping.

The moral of the story is one you've seen before in these pages: always be cynical and investigate potential partners carefully. Always read every word of a contract and have an attorney help you on any deal that involves IP rights or more than a small number of dollars.

In the early days of Silicon Valley angels tended to be dentists, doctors and real estate professionals who had made a lot of money. They understood the risks of investing but liked the idea of betting money they could afford to lose on a company that could produce a big win.

In recent years the nature of angel investors has changed, and today many of them are veterans of the Valley and technology startups who made money as entrepreneurs. They now want to leverage that experience to bet money they can afford to lose on companies where their insider knowledge tells them that a real opportunity exists.

Angel investors who made their money working in the games industry are far more likely to take a chance on startups in our business than any other investor.

Their insider knowledge means they will ask you harder questions up front and give you better advice once they've invested and become advisors.

To pitch to any investor other than a games industry veteran and have a realistic chance of success you need to have already accomplished a lot with your indie game. You need to have:

- A game that you are already selling (directly or via free-to-play monetization) for real money to real customers
- A complete core team that is already working together
- Experience in leading similar game development teams or (ideally) successful startups

6.9.3 Other Funding Sources

There are other funding sources for indie games, and if you build a great game that's fun to play you may very well be able to earn, win or raise money from them.

The best known of these groups is Indie Fund, but if you do a Google search on "indie game funding sources" you'll see others as well. New options appear periodically. (Note: I have no professional affiliation with Indie Fund but several of its principals are professional friends and/or associates.)

Some indie game competitions also have cash prizes, or "in kind" donations from sponsors that can be valuable to indie teams. I've seen prizes like free web services hosting accounts with high bandwidth and concurrent connection allocations, which can save a team cash that they'd otherwise have needed to budget.

The best known of these events is the Independent Games Festival, but a Google search on "indie game competition prize" will bring up additional options.

Finally, there are game publishers who are trying to build new business models and experimenting with different ways to work with teams to build games. Kongregate, led by CEO Emily Greer, is the best-known such company, but every year or two I see someone come along and try a new publishing business model.

All of the options above are worth investigating. If your game is really fun and attracts loyal and lasting players it's realistic to believe you could earn financial support.

6.9.4 ROI and The Risk-Reward Ratio

Investors' results – like those of angel investors and many other businesses — are calculated on a formula called "Return on Investment" (ROI). If you take $100 and put it in the bank for a year and earn 1% interest, your ROI is 1% per year. If you buy a stock for $100 and one year later sell it (after commissions) for $110, your ROI is 10%.

ROI is one component of the equation that drives how you, your supporters, potential investors and even your competitors make business decisions. This is called the "Risk-Reward Ratio."

Formally, the Risk-Reward Ratio is a mathematical formula used by financial traders to evaluate the downside and upside of buying a stock or other asset at a given price.

The term has entered broader use in business, however, and can be applied to any deal. If you consider flying to New York for a meeting, you're risking the cost of the trip and at least two days of lost time you could have spent on your game. Against that risk you evaluate the potential reward if something good comes from the meeting.

Asking yourself, "Does the risk-reward ratio justify making the trip?" provides a framework for making a thoughtful, informed decision.

DISCUSSING QUESTION 6.10:

Have you ever tried using Kickstarter, Indiegogo or other crowdsourcing website to raise money for a project?

Is that part of your plan for your indie game?

This topic is most relevant for: Those considering crowdfunding for their indie game.

6.10.1 Crowdfunding Basics

Kickstarter, Indiegogo and similar websites offer creative people with great ideas the chance to earn pre-orders that will fund the creation of their indie game. Some teams have raised millions of dollars with promises of exciting new products and games.

In the early days of crowdfunding, however, some teams never delivered a finished product. The cold shower of skepticism that followed has made it harder — but not impossible — to use crowdsourcing to fund at least part of your indie game.

The two biggest fundraising services in the space are Kickstarter and Indiegogo. Kickstarter is significantly larger and has more traffic than Indiegogo.

Indiegogo is a worldwide service that covers any kind of fundraising. Kickstarter specializes in creative projects of all kinds and is focused primarily on North America and the U.K.

The typical Kickstarter game campaign allows buyers to pre-order special editions of the game in return for pledging their payments for those items several months (or even years) in advance. Then users get to follow the game's completion as "insiders," with frequent updates and exclusive previews.

Kickstarter screens the people who try to raise money on the platform. This is not a priority at Indiegogo.

If a campaign fails to reach its funding goal on Kickstarter, the effort is canceled and no money is collected from the people who pledged funds.

If an Indiegogo campaign fails to reach its goal it offers organizers the option to keep the partial funds, but charges a significantly higher commission.

As of this writing, Kickstarter charges a 5% commission plus a small funds processing fee. Indiegogo charges 5% to successful projects (and a credit card takes another 3% or so for processing), and 10% to those who keep a partial funding total.

Indiegogo uses credit cards, and has dropped the option to use PayPal. Kickstarter uses your Amazon account to accept the payment.

6.10.2 The Quicksand on the Beach

Every product has its own challenges on Kickstarter and Indiegogo.

Some game categories are unlikely to be funded via crowdsourcing, while others have especially good success rates.

If you look back at the most successful Kickstarters for games, you'll notice that most of them fit a simple pattern:

- They are updated versions of popular older games
- The marketing text (among other bullet points) appeals to people feeling nostalgic about the past

- The people who created the classic version are creating the update, so the game feels authentic
- The game's first platform is the PC, though it may also be ported to other systems
- The game is distributed on a DVD that's packed in a traditional game box, so the user can put the game on the shelf as part of their collection

If you look for what kinds of games have been unsuccessful in raising more than token sums of money, they fit a pattern as well:

- They are on smartphones or tablets, or are played online
- They are downloaded from an app store or website
- Having a "special boxed collector's edition" of the digital game doesn't seem to help

It's worth doing this research for yourself, and Kickstarter's website makes it easy to do so, with easy to find lists of current and past products.

6.10.3 How Crowdfunding Campaigns Work

Let's say that you're building a PC side-scrolling adventure called *Newton's Cave*, where gravity is pulling in a different direction each time you enter a new room. You're planning to sell the game on Steam for $14.95.

You have a small team and hope to build the initial version of the game quickly so a modest $25,000 budget will still cover everyone. You're paying yourself only a tiny salary.

You need to start preparing for your Kickstarter campaign several months before you plan to launch your fundraising effort. Your campaign page will be up for 30 days, and you'll be competing for attention with teams that spent thousands of dollars just on their Kickstarter page.

Here's what successful crowdfunded game developers do to set the stage for successful crowdfunding campaigns:

Write ad copy describing the wonderful game you're about to create.

Design illustrations (or, ideally, adapt completed game art) for the Kickstarter page.

Code at least a simple demo and create a video trailer that shows what the game will look like when it's played. The more impressive and complete they look, the more likely you are to generate excitement. If you can't produce a demo or trailer that shows the game in an impressive way you're probably not yet ready to pursue crowdfunding.

Cache posts, graphics and videos that you can drop onto your Kickstarter project page every day or two during the 30-day campaign, so there's always something new to see for visitors.

Design tiers of attractive rewards for people who pledge money to support your project. Actual campaigns may have ten to fifteen tiers of "rewards," and you can study the patterns from past successful games on the Kickstarter site.

A lot of work is required to follow through with your backers if you meet your goals, things like:

- Collecting hundreds of names and making sure they're spelled correctly for the credits
- Sending five different items to 172 different addresses after you pay for packing, stuffing and shipping.
- Designing, printing and sending out 50 T-Shirts after you find out what size each person needs, plus more for your team members and as contest prizes.

You may have to raise $30,000 this way in order to have $25,000 left to create your game. Some creators have misjudged costs and spent too much of the money they raised on rewards instead of on the product.

6.10.4 Stacking the Odds in Your Favor

About one third of Kickstarter projects succeed. The patterns I see are:

It's a lot easier to raise a small amount of money for a more basic project than to raise a bigger budget for something with lots of bells and whistles.

Treat the campaign like a 30-day full-time job. You'll spend lots of time looking for ways to publicize your game, and lots more interacting with people on social media, answering backers' questions and creating the steady stream of updates needed to build momentum.

Don't sell a product, tell a story. Instead of using just a headline like, "The world's greatest fly-swatter!" you can say:

"There I was, deep in the jungle, holed up in a rotting cottage at the abandoned plantation. The flies were everywhere, bloated with dengue fever and seeking exposed flesh. How could I fight them off? I looked down and saw the coil of galvanized wire on the pockmarked floor. In just minutes I had woven it into a tapered frame and wrapped it with the waterproof cover from my camera. It worked! Minutes later I crushed the last of the flies that lusted for my blood. Now you, too, can own the fly-swatter that saved my life..."

Use lots of images, lots of video, and have quality music on the video. Tell your story, and take the time (or hire a film student) to edit it well.

Use a nostalgia angle if you can. If your game isn't a remastered hit, try to evoke a now-lost time and place.

Unless your budget is huge, don't hire expensive crowdfunding experts. Use Google to find stories like "How Exploding Kittens Raised Millions" to guide you.

CHAPTER 51

Managing Risk (6.11-6.13)

DISCUSSING QUESTIONS 6.11 AND 6.12

6.11: What's the biggest risk your team faced on the largest project you've ever worked on?

6.12: What were the three biggest risks at the start of your most recent project?

What were the three biggest remaining risks when your team was nearing completion on its most recent project?

These topics are most appropriate for: Everyone

6.11.1 How the Best Teams Assess and Control Risk

I believe that a vital part of training every manager in companies large and small should be the continual and routine assessment of risk. Yet I see many management training programs that spend little or no time on the subject.

Why do I believe it pays off to routinely monitor risk, even when no major issues are brewing?

Because that's the best way to keep major issues from brewing. The small amount of time that routine risk reviews take is more than made up if you avoid just one significant problem a year.

It took me far too long in my career to drum this wisdom through my thick skull, but I see continual reminders of its importance.

6.11.2 A Weekly Routine

You can buy entire books on this topic, but here's a top level summary of a popular risk management process that takes just a few minutes a week.

Each week the team's leaders review a list of the three to five greatest risks currently facing the company (or project, etc.). For each risk they list:

• The likelihood that the problem will occur

• The scope of the potential impact, and

• Actions we can take *now* to prevent or reduce the potential problem

For example:

Risk: Bad weather causes flights to be canceled so some team members miss most of our all-hands meeting.

• Likelihood: Low, except for team members flying from Miami

• Impact: We miss the chance to plan together as a team or have to pay for a second offsite

• Steps We're Taking Now: If the weather forecast looks threatening Jen will evaluate if we can fly anyone in a day early and pay for hotel

Once managers have learned the system and written the initial risks, most weekly reviews are quick check-ins that take very little time.

(Question 6.12 is also covered by the text above.)

DISCUSSING QUESTION 6.13

Does your game have any elements that require import or export controls, etc.?

Is there anything potentially controversial about your game that could create problems if you release it in other cultures?

This topic is most relevant for: Everyone

6.13.1 Problems Aren't Always Obvious

If your game does not have cutting-edge encryption or AI there is little likelihood you'll encounter export controls, but it's always good to check if you have advanced technology.

The second question is far harder to research, but it's worth talking to friends and allies from different cultures to try to anticipate problems.

We once shipped a successful role-playing game where our artists decorated a building with some routine-looking geometric shapes. A few days after the game shipped we started getting angry messages from followers of a major religion, with supporters both in the U.S. and in other parts of the world. More and more messages came in.

It turns out that one of the geometric shapes an artist had drawn was, by coincidence, offensive under the beliefs of that religion.

We had to scramble. We changed the art in the game and worked with our publisher to release a patch so the offending image would vanish from players' systems. We sent messages to apologize to the people who complained, explained that we had meant no offense and had removed the image from the game.

In this case we were fortunate. The organizers of the protests realized that the incident was an accident and that we had meant no disrespect. They sent us thank you messages and, best of all, replaced the complaints on their website with praise for our correction and our company.

Not all such innocent mistakes are resolved quickly like this one, and we spent a lot of team members' time rushing to implement the changes.

Some problems are impossible to anticipate for small teams with limited budgets. But if there's even a tiny chance that anything in your game that could raise these issues, it's best to do the research to identify it before your game ships.

Avoiding problems costs far less time and money than suffering the financial and reputation costs of correcting a problem later.

PART VII

NEXT STEPS

CHAPTER 52

Next Steps: The Question

QUESTION 7.1

For my last question in this book I'm going to ask you to use your imagination.

A magical genie has decided to reward you for all the good deeds you have done.

You are transported back to your old home, the place where you lived when you were twelve years old. It is late at night and everyone else is asleep.

You are not alone in the room. Sitting across from you is your 12-year-old self. Even though you are both the same person, the adult you and the 12-year-old you can talk to each other in the same way that any two people can talk.

The genie will allow you to tell your 12-year-old self three things about your grown-up life, and see how "the younger you" reacts at age 12.

Tomorrow morning the 12-year-old version of you will have no memory of this conversation. But for tonight you can share the three things that you would have most wanted to know back then about your future life.

And you'll get to see how you as a child would react to knowing those three facts.

What three details about your life do you share?

How does the 12-year-old you respond?

Please take your time, write down your responses, and answer fully from your deepest thoughts. Think only about your own opinions, not about what others may want you to think or do. Do not look ahead to other questions until you have finished this one.

CHAPTER 53

My Story: Thanking a Man Named Ethan Allen

We're used to thinking of certain kinds of "serious games" as "doing good in the world."

Teaching sick kids about why it's important to take their medications. Giving inner city classrooms access to interactive learning activities. Allowing hospital teams to practice evacuation drills without having to move their seriously ill and injured patients.

Those are all wonderful and noble missions, and I have great respect and admiration for the people who create these serious games.

But they aren't the only kinds of games that can make big positive impacts on peoples' lives.

In Section 1's "My Story" chapter I wrote about how I re-designed a board game called *All Star Baseball* back when I was 15, but as a teen-ager never thought of submitting my work to the big game company in Chicago.

As an adult I've always remembered that experience, and reminded myself to never give up on pitching my ideas and giving them a chance.

I had no way of knowing it back then, but that work I did as a teenage hobby laid the foundation for my career. As an adult I led the design on several major baseball video games.

The old *All Star Baseball* board game was invented by a former Major League player named Ethan Allen (no relation to the furniture stores or American patriot of the same name). The game had already been on the market for over twenty years before I discovered it as a young boy.

Allen died in 1993, and I deeply regret never tracking down his address and writing to him after I became an adult. If I had done so, part of the letter might have read like this:

Dear Mr. Allen:

I wanted to write to thank you for inventing the All Star Baseball board game, which I played constantly when I was in junior high and high school.

First of all, I'm a big baseball fan and I loved playing your game because I felt like I really was managing my favorite players.

But your game was much more important to me than just the fun I had while playing.

I grew up in an alcoholic family, and most evenings things got loud and difficult around our house. I would retreat into my room and play All Star Baseball and try to block out everything that was going on around me. Your game was my escape.

I know you created the game so that kids and families could enjoy managing baseball teams. But for me your game did far more than just provide fun. It provided me with a haven, a safe zone where I could study baseball in a far kinder fictional world than the real world around me.

You helped me get through some very tough years, and I'll always be grateful to you.

— Don Daglow

I now hear similar stories from people about how they got through tough times by playing one of my games while they were growing up. A couple who met in an online game I designed fell in love "in the real world," got married and had a child.

It's a great feeling. Any one of us can build games that have a positive impact on other people's lives, in ways we can never fully anticipate.

Bringing families together, making lonely people feel more connected, or just giving a kid in a tough situation a positive experience to drown out a hostile world. Any of these results could inspire someone to send you a letter that says, *"Your game was much more important to me than just the fun I had while playing"*

If you're weighing whether or not you want to pursue your indie game, keep this phenomenon in mind.

What kind of letter of thanks would you like someone to send to you?

CHAPTER 54

What to Do With Your Answer (7.1)

"THE WORLD IS IN PERPETUAL MOTION, AND WE MUST
INVENT THE THINGS OF TOMORROW.
ACT WITH AUDACITY."

— Madame Clicquot

DISCUSSING QUESTION 7.1

For my last question in this book I'm going to ask you to use your imagination.

A magical genie has decided to reward you for all the good deeds you have done.

You are transported back to your old home, the place where you lived when you were twelve years old. It is late at night and everyone else is asleep.

You are not alone in the room. Sitting across from you is your 12-year-old self. Even though you are both the same person, the adult you and the 12-year-old you can talk to each other in the same way that any two people can talk.

The genie will allow you to tell your 12-year-old self three things about your grown-up life, and see how "the younger you" reacts at age 12.

Tomorrow morning the 12-year-old version of you will have no memory of this conversation. But for tonight you can share the three things that you would have most wanted to know back then about your future life.

And you'll get to see how you as a child would react to knowing those three facts.

What three details about your life do you share?

How does the 12-year-old you respond?

This topic is most relevant for: Everyone

7.1.1 Returning to The Beginning

The Passion-Process-Product method I describe in this book isn't a road map leading from one place to another.

It's a pyramid, with your passions as the foundation. The process we evolve and the product we launch are supported by that foundation, without which they're just a set of inanimate building blocks.

That's why we always have to come back to our passions. And why I chose to end this book with a unique question.

A quote (which I've seen attributed to both Peter Graham and Thomas M. Disch) states, "The Golden Age of science fiction is 12." That's when your mind is still open to the exciting what-if of science fiction, but has become sophisticated enough to consider adult challenges.

To me, 12 is that crossroads age when you have real dreams for your life, but you have no idea what's really going to happen.

If I could go back and tell that 12-year-old me three facts about my life now, I'd probably say things like:

1. "Everything turned out OK, despite all the rough times I went through as a kid."
2. "I married a wonderful girl and we have two great sons and three grandchildren whom we adore."
3. "I've spent most of my career designing and producing video games and doing work I love, teamed with people whom I care about and respect."

Considering how badly I felt about myself back then, I think I'd have been overjoyed to hear those things.

How would the 12-year-old version of you react to your career choices and your game idea?

How do you feel after thinking about the discussion with the 12-year-old you?

If all of these thoughts and feelings align reasonably well with your plans, it's all good. If you've developed new dreams as an adult, that's great as well: lasting passions discovered at age 25 or age 50 are just as valid as those discovered in childhood.

If something about this dialogue between the young you and the adult you doesn't connect to the dream you're chasing, however, don't just push the feelings under the rug.

Look back at the answers you've written — just for yourself — to the questions in this book. What could you change about your plan that would make you feel better?

Don't worry if every detail doesn't feel exactly right. I've had times in my life when it took me a year or more to fill in important blanks in my plans.

Figuring out what we *really* want to do, what we *deeply* want to do, can take time.

But it's worth it.

CHAPTER 55

Epilogue

"STEVE JOBS COULD BE HELL TO WORK WITH, AND HE
COULD BE GREAT TO WORK WITH.
WHAT THE STEVE JOBS MOVIE MISSES, WHAT ALL THE
BOOKS ARE MISSING, IS WHAT I REMEMBER MOST
ABOUT HIM. HE HAD THIS INCREDIBLE ZEST, THIS
INCREDIBLE DRIVE TO GO OUT AND CREATE
SOMETHING.
I THINK OF HIM AND I THINK, 'LET'S GO BUILD
SOMETHING GREAT!'"

— David Grady
March 18, 2016

EPILOGUE

I close this book with the quote above because it connects the legend of one of our most respected entrepreneurs with the heart of everyone who has ever wanted to build a new game.

David Grady has spent over 20 years at Apple and before that worked at Next, another Steve Jobs startup. David and I worked together at Electronic Arts from 1983-87, and this quote comes from our conversation at an EA reunion.

It really made me think about why it is that we want to create indie games.

I've worked in creative startups for over 30 years. You know there's a financial upside, the potential for a big win. You also know that it could all go nowhere and end badly.

The mood in all of the successful new companies I've seen, however, is not the quest for riches. It's not the hunger for respect and fame. It's not the fear of failure.

The emotion that fuels winning startups is the desire to build something great. The game may be different for every one of us, but the passion that drives it is the same.

If you've felt it, you know what I mean.

I hope this book helps you act on those feelings and to create your indie game. I hope that the questions I've asked have inspired answers that are all your own.

I wish you much success and even more happiness.

Acknowledgements

Special thanks to Meggan Scavio and the GDC Advisory Board, Frank Sliwka, Stephan Reichart, Tobias Kopka, Steve Hoffman, Naomi Kokubo, Thomas Dlugaiczyk, Dr. Jörg Müller-Litzkow, Francesca Fanini and Giovanni Barbieri for giving me the chance to hone these ideas with great audiences and teams in the U.S., Canada and Europe.

I'm also grateful to Raj Lai, Cynthia Lee and the Stanford Business School Igniters program and to Dr. Vijay Sathe of The Drucker School of Management at Claremont Graduate University for their feedback, guidance and support on this book.

Rami Ismail wrote the thoughtful Introduction at the opening of this book, and I am deeply grateful for his contributions and ideas. Jeff Braun also gave me valuable feedback.

The list of mentors and teammates who taught me the lessons in these pages is very, very long. In partial payment of my debts of gratitude, the list below includes one major influence from each job in my career.

Gabe Damico, Principal of Claremont High School, gave me my first entrepreneurial job after my friend Terry Morrison and I went into the community to market our Adult School Spanish classes. He taught me that with a small budget you can still make a difference.

Claire Gray, a fellow teacher at Rancho Cucamonga Middle School, taught me how planning and process could make a complicated job feel simple. Her advice freed me to work both creatively and efficiently, and transferred readily when I moved from classroom to business,

Dr. Chris Arce, Superintendent at Cucamonga School District, gave me my first full-time management job. He role-modeled an intense, unselfish commitment to quality that didn't change with every political micro-climate.

Gabriel Baum, VP of Applications Software at Mattel Electronics, gave me my first executive position as Director of Intellivision Game Development. He taught me how companies were different than schools, and channeled my occasional "over-enthusiasm" in productive ways.

Trip Hawkins recruited me into a startup that grew into a major international company, and taught me how Silicon Valley entrepreneurship was different from traditional corporations. Many other people on the EA team also taught me lessons that have benefited me ever since.

Doug, Gary and Cathy Carlston at Broderbund Software taught me how to put a family twist on the hard-edged business lessons I'd learned, and reminded me about the power of believing in my natural management style.

I learned from too many great teammates over 20 years at Stormfront Studios to boil it down to just one person. Early team members Mark Buchignani, David Bunnett, Katie Kelly and Hudson Piehl were pivotal to our success. Board Chairman Bob Wallace and members Tony La Russa, Tim Larkin, Stan Roach, Mark Stevens and Seth Willenson were my teachers and mentors, each for many years.

At The Strong National Museum of Play, now-retired CEO Dr. G. Rollie Adams and his successor Steve Dubnik both demonstrated that a non-profit could have as effective an operation as any other kind of company.

Finally, my wife Marta and our sons Michael and Christopher and their families have shared every step of this journey with me. It is the lessons of life that we've all learned together that are the most important, and without their constant connection and support I would never have learned much of anything at all.

About the Author

3-time Inc. 500™ CEO Don Daglow has served as a game designer, programmer, producer and executive in a games industry career that covers much of the lifespan of Silicon Valley. Teams under his leadership have shipped games with an aggregate of over $1 billion in retail sales.

His work has been honored with a Technical Emmy®, multiple Game of the Year awards, and the CGE Award in 2003 for "groundbreaking achievements that shaped the video game industry." In 2018 he was inducted as a member of the Wall of Fame at the Computerspielemuseum in Berlin. His credits include over 100 different games as a designer, programmer, producer, executive or advisor.

Don advises game companies and software startups, coaching both new and experienced CEO's, executives and groups facing the challenges of team-building, studio management, software development, industry growth and competition.

His clients range from small startups to large international publishers, and he regularly presents keynotes and conference sessions at events around the world.

He also serves as Senior Director for Strategic Partnerships at The Strong National Museum of Play in Rochester, NY; as an advisor and mentor at the Founders Space accelerator in San Francisco; and as the volunteer President of the Academy of Interactive Arts & Sciences Foundation.

Originally trained as a playwright, Don began his career as a teacher and writer. Starting in 1971, he wrote mainframe computer games as a hobby before the introduction of Pong and home computers, and entered the games industry early in the first cycle of home video games.

Starting as one of the original five Intellivision engineers at Mattel Electronics in 1980, he became Director of Applications Software for what grew to be a billion-dollar business. In 1983 he joined a small Silicon Valley startup called Electronic Arts, which went public and became a large international corporation. After working as an executive for Broderbund, which was sold to The Learning Company for $416 million, he founded Stormfront Studios, which he led for 20 years.

In 2008 Don accepted a Technical and Engineering Emmy® Award from the National Academy of Television Arts and Sciences for his creation of *Neverwinter Nights*, the first graphical MMORPG, which paved the way for the multi-billion-dollar *World of Warcraft*.

He lives in Marin County, California with his wife Marta.

His professional website is www.daglowslaws.com.

Index